THE ANGLO-SAXON POETIC RECORDS

A COLLECTIVE EDITION

———————

II
THE VERCELLI BOOK

THE
VERCELLI BOOK

EDITED BY

GEORGE PHILIP KRAPP

LATE PROFESSOR OF ENGLISH IN COLUMBIA UNIVERSITY

NEW YORK

COLUMBIA UNIVERSITY PRESS

PREFACE

In accordance with the plan of this collective edition of Anglo-Saxon poetry, as announced in the Preface to the first volume, containing the texts of the Junius Manuscript, the poetical parts of the Vercelli Book are here grouped together in a second volume. Although the original compilers of the Vercelli Book, as of the other extant Anglo-Saxon miscellanies, apparently had no very strict principles of similarity in mind in determining what should be included in their collection, nevertheless the Vercelli Book, like the Junius Manuscript, exhibits a certain degree of uniformity. For the poems of the Junius Manuscript are examples of versified Biblical narrative, whereas the poems of the Vercelli Book are legendary and homiletic in character. The two longest poems of the Vercelli Book are ANDREAS and ELENE, saints' lives of less authenticity than the Scripture itself, and like the prose homilies and the other poetical pieces in the Vercelli Book, probably designed for occasional use to supplement and lighten the formal offices of the service. The grouping of these poems in a volume of their own, therefore, reflects something more than a mere accident of preservation within the limits of a single manuscript.

Two excellent photographic reproductions of the poems of the Vercelli Book are available, that of Wülker, in a volume published in 1894, which contains reproductions only of the poetical parts of the manuscript, and that of Foerster, published in 1913 and containing both the prose and poetical texts of the manuscript. The present edition has been based upon these reproductions, and as the manuscript is in the main in an excellent state of preservation, the construction of the text has presented comparatively few difficulties. On those rare occasions when it was necessary to support the reading of the reproductions by other authority, especially in those passages in which stains or blots have obscured the readings of the manuscript, definite acknowledgement of this obligation has been made.

In accordance with the general principles of this collective edition, the text of the poems of the Vercelli Book has been conservatively treated. Emendations for metrical reasons have been introduced very sparingly, and then not to make the text correspond to any particular set of metrical convictions, but only when metrical considerations seem to support other evidence that some accidental disturbance has taken place in the transmission of the text. The same remarks apply to orthography. Accidents in writing befall every scribe, and obvious accidents have been corrected. But it is scarcely necessary for a modern editor to be a greater purist in spelling than an eleventh century professional scribe, especially one so conscientious and capable as the scribe of the Vercelli Book appears to have been. It is to be regretted that the present state of Anglo-Saxon scholarship does not permit more positive convictions with respect to the authorship and date of composition of the Anglo-Saxon poetical monuments, with respect also to the methods of composition and construction employed by Anglo-Saxon poets, or to the metrical principles according to which they wrote, or to the mixture of linguistic forms, dialectal or otherwise, which appear in the recorded texts. If a sceptical attitude towards all these questions still seems necessary after so many years of study, the hope nevertheless remains that further examination, and from new angles, will bring more certain results.

In the Introduction to this volume will be found a full list of the accent marks in the poetical parts of the Vercelli Book. No such complete statement was made of the accents of the Junius Manuscript in the first volume of this collective edition, and when the materials for that volume were being assembled, the editor doubted whether the usefulness of such a list would compensate for the amount of space required by it. These doubts have now been resolved, partly on further reflection, partly in deference to the opinions of others. It has therefore seemed advisable to add to the list of accented words in the Vercelli Book, a full list of the accented words in the Junius Manuscript as providing at least materials for study. It is obvious, however, that the whole question of the accents in

Anglo-Saxon manuscripts cannot be disposed of on the basis of poetical texts only, and that for a complete account of the matter, prose texts must also be drawn into consideration.

The editor wishes to take this opportunity to acknowledge gratefully the aid of Mr. Elliott Van Kirk Dobbie in assembling and seeing through the press the materials of this volume, as also of the volume previously published, containing the poems of the Junius Manuscript.

CONTENTS

INTRODUCTION

I

THE MANUSCRIPT

The Vercelli Book, also known as the Vercelli Codex or Codex Vercellensis, is preserved in the chapter library of the cathedral at Vercelli in northern Italy. The library at Vercelli contains another famous manuscript, a text of the gospels perhaps written by Eusebius, which is also referred to at times by the name Codex Vercellensis.[1] The Anglo-Saxon manuscript is designated in the collections of the library as Cod. CXVII. It is a parchment manuscript of one hundred and thirty-six folios, of uniform size and character. Like the Junius Manuscript, the Vercelli Book was apparently conceived and executed as a single volume into which a variety of matters, prose as well as verse, and in this latter respect, differing from the Junius Manuscript, was to be placed.

The size of the folios in the Vercelli Book is on the average 31 by 20 centimeters, that is, approximately 12.2 inches by 7.8 inches. The space covered by writing on the folios is approximately 24 by 15 centimeters, that is 9.4 inches by 5.8 inches. The pages of the manuscript were prepared for a varying number of lines to be written on the several pages, but never for less than twenty-three or more than thirty-three. Sometimes a blank space for one or more lines takes the place of writing where sectional divisions occur, thus reducing the number of lines actually written but not the number of lines provided for writing. The grouping of the folios according to the number of lines arranged for on them is as follows:

2a–11a	24 lines		19a–24b	24 lines
11b	25 "		25a–32b	29 "
12a, 12b	24 "		33a–47b	24 "
13a–18b	25 "		48a–55b	25 "

[1] See Foerster, *Il Codice Vercellese*, p. 7.

56a, 56b	23 lines		111b–120b	31 lines
57a–104b	24 "		121a–134b	32 "
105a–109b	32 "		135a	31 "
110a–111a	33 "		135b	28 " (incomplete)

The last written page of the manuscript, fol. 135b, contains only twenty-eight lines, which means that the text the scribe was copying came to an end before the bottom of the page was reached. A number of other folios are only partly filled with writing, for example fol. 16a, 24b, 29a, 54a, 71a, 101a and 120b. On fol. 24b there are only fourteen lines of writing. But these blank spaces all occur on pages on which the work the scribe was copying came to an end before the bottom of the page was reached. There are no illustrations in the manuscript, except for one small animal figure at the foot of fol. 49b, and no indication that any of the blank spaces were left for illustrations to be supplied after the text was copied.

One may infer from this list that the manuscript was not prepared for writing all at one time, but at various times as the work of transcribing proceeded, and to a certain extent with the gatherings of the manuscript as the units of work. Thus the third gathering of the manuscript, fol. 19–24, is written throughout with twenty-four lines on a page, the fourth gathering, fol. 25–32, with twenty-nine lines on a page, the fifth and sixth, fol. 33–47, again with twenty-four lines, the seventh, fol. 48–55, with twenty-five lines, the greater part of the eighth to the fourteenth gatherings, fol. 56–104, with twenty-four lines, and the rest of the gatherings with lines varying from thirty-one to thirty-three. It will be seen therefore that from the fifteenth gathering to the end, the manuscript is written somewhat more closely than in the earlier parts. With respect to fol. 111b, which has only thirty-one lines, although the rest of the gathering to which it belongs has thirty-three or thirty-two lines, it should be noted that the bottom margin on this page is rather large and that the last line on this page is written more amply than the rest of the page, with long tails to the letters. From this we may infer that this page was intended to have one or two lines more than actually appear in the writing, thus bringing it into harmony with the other folios of its gathering.

On fol. 56a–56b there are written only twenty-three lines, the smallest number on any pages of the manuscript, but the reason for this was that there is a hole in the parchment at the bottom of the page which would have made it difficult to get in another line without crowding. This folio therefore really goes with the rest of its gathering and several that follow, all of the folios in gatherings eight to fourteen, fol. 56–104, having been planned for twenty-four lines. The last two pages of the manuscript, fol. 136a–136b, are blank.

The contents of the several folios in terms of the line numberings of this edition of the poetical parts of the manuscript are given in Table I at the end of this Introduction.

The manuscript as a whole is well preserved and the writing is clear and legible, except that certain places in it have suffered from the application of some discoloring material, possibly an acid, which has made it difficult, and in some instances impossible to read the writing in these passages. Thus fol. 1a-1b has been rendered quite illegible, except for traces of a large capital H on fol. 1a, and so also part of fol. 54a. The blotting out of some of these passages appears to have been accidental, but in other instances, as on fol. 75b, the blotting out was done line by line in a way which shows that it was intentional. No obvious reason appears, however, why the manuscript should have been treated in this way. The pages on which evidences of blotting are present in the manuscript, according to Foerster's reproductions, are as follows: fol. 1a, 1b, 2a, 25a, 26a, 36b, 37b, 38a, 38b, 42b, 54a, 54b, 55b, 57a, 65a, 75b, 77a, 84a, 85b, 86a, 86b, 106b, 119a, 121a, 134a, 135a, 135b. Several of these are smaller blots which may have been the result of scribal mishaps with ink, but most of them were caused by a stain of some kind, intentionally or unintentionally applied.

The folios of the manuscript were assembled in gatherings which contain a number of folios varying from two to nine. The last folio of the manuscript, fol. 136, was attached as a single folio to the last gathering of the manuscript. The gatherings of the manuscript were numbered from I to XIX, and lettered from A to T. The numbers and letters were added, according to Foerster, p. 9, by another scribe at a later date than that at which the texts in the manuscript were transcribed, a number at the top of the first page of each gathering, and a letter at the bottom of the last page of each gathering. Some of these have been cut off, or are illegible in the facsimile, but those which remain are given in the first and third columns of the following list of the gatherings.

Number	Folios	Letter	Number	Folios	Letter
	1–9	A	XI	80–85	
II	10–18	B	XII	86–91	M
III	19–24		XIII	92–98	N
IIII	25–32	D	XIIII	99–104	O
V	33–40	E	XV	105–111	P
VI	41–47	F		112–118	
VII	48–55	G	XVII	119–120	
	56–63		XVIII	121–128	S
IX	64–71	I	XIX	129–135	
X	72–79	K			

But the gatherings of the manuscript as they now appear are not all complete in their original forms, certain folios having disappeared from the manuscript. These losses occur between folios as here indicated:

42–43	1 folio	85–86	1 folio, perhaps more
55–56	1 or possibly 2 folios	100–101	1 folio
63–64	1 folio	103–104	1 folio at least
75–76	possibly 1 or 2 folios	111–112	1 folio
83–84	1 folio	118–119	1 folio

The folios as they now stand in the manuscript are numbered consecutively from 1 to 135 in Arabic numerals on the upper right-hand corner of the recto of each folio by a modern hand, but no original folio numbering for the separate folios is present in the manuscript.

It was the opinion of Wülker that at least two and possibly three different hands appear in the Anglo-Saxon writing in the manuscript.[1] But there can be little doubt that the manuscript as a whole was the work of one scribal hand. Napier saw only one handwriting in the manuscript,[2] and this is also the

---

[1] *Codex Vercellensis*, p. vii, *Grundriss der Geschichte der angelsächsischen Litteratur*, p. 239.

[2] *Zeitschrift für deutsches Altertum* XXXIII, 67.

opinion of Foerster,[1] who infers from the writing that the scribe was a man of mature years with a firmly established style of writing. Foerster considers it possible, however, that a few of the corrections in the manuscript may come from a different hand than that of the scribe, though the greater number of them, not large in any case, were unquestionably made by the scribe. Foerster also doubts that the signatures on the gatherings, both the numerals at the beginnings and the letters at the ends, were the work of the scribe who wrote the body of the manuscript. On these questions, however, the evidence is not conclusive, and it is quite possible that both the body of the manuscript as it stands and the minor additions, except for the Arabic folio numberings and a few other additions to be noted, was the work of a single scribe. The exceptions that must be considered consist of several short sentences in Latin which have nothing to do with the main content of the manuscript, written on blank spaces in the manuscript, and a few other minor additions. For the sake of completeness of record, all of these casual additions, both of words and designs, are given in the following list of folios on which they occur:

24*b*, bottom: *Adiutor meus esto domine ne derelinquas deus salutaris meus.*

49*b*, bottom: A drawing of a dog, running and barking.

65*b*, right margin, five lines from bottom: A small capital *A*, similar to an *A* in the adjoining text; possibly a specimen or trial by the scribe.

112*a*, lower left corner: A trial sketch for the head of a large zoömorphic capital *M* on the same page.

119*a*, upper left corner: *xb* (probably *xƀ*, with upper part of ƀ cut off).[2]

121*a*, top, near right margin: *xƀ*.

123*a*, top, near left margin: *xƀ* (tip of ƀ cut off).

123*a*, bottom, right side: Two small and crudely drawn figures, apparently intended to be human profiles.

126*a*, upper left corner: *xb* (probably *xƀ*, with upper part of ƀ cut off).

---

[1] *Il Codice Vercellese*, p. 15.

[2] See *Records I, The Junius Manuscript*, p. xvii.

Last (unnumbered) page in MS., reverse side at bottom: The words *Cum peruenisse*, in small capitals, upside down.

The date of the handwriting of the manuscript has been given variously. Grimm thought the writing belonged to the end of the ninth or beginning of the tenth century,[1] but it is now generally agreed that this date is too early. Wülker gave the date as the beginning of the eleventh century,[2] Holthausen as the second half of the tenth century.[3] Keller is more precise and endeavors to establish the date of the writing as between 960 and 980,[4] or still more definitely, between 970 and 980.[5] Foerster hesitates to express himself quite so precisely and gives the date as the second half or towards the end of the tenth century.[6]

II

ORIGIN OF THE MANUSCRIPT

The presence of this manuscript in so unexpected a place as Vercelli in northern Italy has naturally been the occasion of much surmise. There can be no question that the manuscript was written and produced in England. Its presence in Italy is therefore no evidence of an interest in the copying and preserving of Anglo-Saxon records in Italian libraries. On the contrary the manuscript probably owes its existence to the collecting zeal of some one of those patrons of letters in England in the tenth century whose efforts account for the Junius Manuscript, the Exeter Book, and other West-Saxon transcriptions, these being perhaps only occasional survivals from an originally much larger representation of the body of Anglo-Saxon literature.

No direct evidence is available to explain the presence of the Vercelli Manuscript in Italy, and the indirect evidence is far from conclusive. The view that the manuscript was brought

[1] *Andreas und Elene*, p. xlv.
[2] *Codex Vercellensis*, p. viii.
[3] *Cynewulfs Elene*, p. ix.
[4] Keller, *Angelsächsische Palaeographie*, p. 40.
[5] *Reallexicon der germanischen Altertumskunde* (1911), Vol. I, p. 102.
[6] *Il Codice Vercellese*, p. 14.

to Italy by Cardinal Guala, papal legate in England in the time of King John and of Henry III, has much to recommend it,[1] but Foerster has pointed out some reasonable objections to this explanation.[2] Foerster is inclined to think that the manuscript was brought to Italy in the eleventh or twelfth century, when the reading of an Anglo-Saxon manuscript was still possible to one interested in such studies, or if not at this early date, then in the sixteenth century as a more or less accidental result of the humanistic interest in the collecting of books and manuscripts at that time. But it seems scarcely credible that interest in the content of the manuscript should have led anyone to transport so bulky an object all the hard way from England to Italy in the eleventh or twelfth century. If it cannot be assumed that the manuscript owes its presence in Italy, directly or indirectly, to Cardinal Guala and his interest in English affairs, the most plausible supposition is that it reached its present resting place at a comparatively late date and as a chance addition to the collections of the library at Vercelli. It is possible that the wanderings of the manuscript after it left England and before it reached Vercelli were extensive, but if so, the course of its travels cannot now be followed.

III

THE CONTENTS OF THE MANUSCRIPT

The first folio of the manuscript apparently once contained the beginning of the first homily, but now only the remains of a large capital *H* are visible at the top left-hand corner of fol. 1*a*. The initial word of this homily may have been *Her*, as of the homily beginning on fol. 25*a*, of the one beginning on fol. 65*a*, and of several others in the manuscript. Foerster notes that the first two pages of the manuscript (i.e., fol. 1*a*–1*b*) are illegible, and that therefore the beginning of the first text in the manuscript is lacking. In the following list of contents, the titles of the poems as supplied by modern commentators and

---

[1] See Cook, *Cardinal Guala and the Vercelli Book* (1888), Krapp, *Andreas and the Fates of the Apostles* (1906), pp. x–xiv.

[2] *Il Codice Vercellese*, pp. 27–40.

a brief description of the subject of each homily are given, and, except for the first, the opening sentence of the homily. A good many, though not all of the homilies have titles in the manuscript, but none of the poetical texts is provided with a special heading of any kind. The titles of the poems as they are used in this edition are supplied by the editor.

fol. 1a–9a. A Homily on the Passion.

fol. 9b–12a. A Homily on the Last Judgment: Men ða leofestan, þæs myclan domdæges worc bið swiðe egeslic 7 andryslic eallum gesceaftum.

fol. 12b–16a. A Homily on Christian Virtues: Broðor þa leofestan, ic cyðe þæt þreo þing synt ærest on foreweardum æghwylcum men nydbehefe to habbanne.

fol. 16b–24b. A Homily on Penance in prospect of the Last Judgment, with a dialogue of the Soul and the Body: Men þa leofestan, ic eow bidde 7 eaðmodlice lære, þ ge wepen 7 forhtien on þysse medmiclan tide for eowrum synnum.

fol. 25a–29a. A Homily on the Birth of Christ, entitled, "To middan wintra. Ostende nobis domine": Her segð þis halige godspel be þære hean medomnesse þisse halgan tide þe nu onweard is 7 us læreð þætte we þas halgan tiid gedefelice 7 clænlice weorðien godes naman to lofe 7 to wuldre, 7 ussum sawlum to ecre hælo 7 to frofre.

fol. 29b–52b. ANDREAS.

fol. 52b–54a. THE FATES OF THE APOSTLES.

fol. 54b–56a. A Homily entitled, "Incipit narrare miracula que facta fuerant ante aduentum saluatoris, domini nostri Iesu Cristi": Her sagað ymb ðas mæran gewyrd þe to þyssum dæge gewearð, þætte ælmihtig dryhten sylfa þas world gesohte 7 þurh unwemme fæmnan on þas world acenned wæs.

fol. 56b–59a. Homily II.[1] Against extravagance and gluttony: Butan tweon lar is haligdomes dæl 7 ealles swiðost.

---

[1] Apparently only six homilies are numbered, beginning after the first two poems. No trace of a number I appears on fol. 54b, but a II is written at the bottom of fol. 56a, and evidently belongs to the following homily.

fol. 59*a*–61*a*. Homily III. On the Last Judgment and the torments of hell: Men ða leofestan, manað us 7 myndgað on þyssum bocum scs gregorius se halega writere se ðis gewrit sette 7 wrat.

fol. 61*a*–65*a*. Homily IIII. On Death, its terrors and suddenness: Men ða leofestan, manað us 7 myngaþ þeos halige boc þæt we sien gemyndige ymb ure sawle þearfe.

fol. 65*a*–71*a*. Homily V. On the Transitoriness of the World and its joys: Her sagað on þyssum halegum bocum be ælmihtiges dryhtnes godspelle, þe he him sylfum þurh his ða halegan mihte geworhte mannum to bysene 7 to lare.

fol. 71*b*–73*b*. Homily VI entitled, "Spel to forman gangdæge": Men ða leofestan, þis syndon halige dagas 7 halwendlice 7 ussum sawlum læcedomlice.

fol. 73*b*–75*b*. Homily entitled, "Spel to ðam oðrum gangdæge": Girsandæg we wæron manode, men þa leofestan, þissa haliga daga bigangnes.

fol. 75*b*–76*b*. Homily entitled, "Spel to þriddan gangdæge": Dis is se þridda dæg, men þa leofestan, þysse halgan tide þe us on swiðe wel gelimpeð þæt we ealle eaðmodlice sculon dryhtne þeowian 7 wel forð gelæstan Ꝥ we nu ær on þyssum dagum lærde wæron.

fol. 76*b*–80*b*. Homily entitled, "Larspel to swylcere tide swa man wile": Men ða leofestan, þis synt halige dagas 7 gastlice 7 ussum sawlum læcedomlice.

fol. 80*b*–85*b*. Homily entitled, "Alia omelia de die iudicii": Men, sægð us on þyssum bocum hu se halga thomas godes apsł acsode urne dryhten hwænne antecristes cyme wære.

fol. 85*b*–90*b*. Homily entitled, "Omelia epyffania domini": Men, sceolon we nu hwylcumhwegu[1] wordum secgan be ðære arweorðnesse þysse halgan tide 7 þysses halgan dæges.

fol. 90*b*–94*b*. Homily entitled, "De purificatione sancta Maria": Men, sægeð us 7 myngaþ þis halige godspel be þysse arwyrðan tide þe we nu to dæge gode ælmihtigum to lofe 7 to are wyrðiaþ.

---

[1] With *m* erased following *hwylcumhwegu*.

fol. 94*b*–101*a*. Homily entitled, "De sancto Martino confessore": Men, magon we nu hwylcumhwego wordum asecgan be þære arwyrðnesse þysse halgan tide.

fol. 101*b*–103*b*. Soul and Body I.[1]

fol. 104*a*–104*b*. Homiletic Fragment I.[1]

fol. 104*b*–106*a*. Dream of the Rood.

fol. 106*b*–109*b*. Homily: "Men ða leofestan, us gedafenaþ ærest þæt we gemunen 7 gereccen be gode ælmihtigum þe geworhte heofonas 7 eorðan 7 ealle gesceafta.

fol. 109*b*–112*a*. Homily on the deadly sins: "Men ða leofestan, þis syndon halige dagas 7 halwendlice 7 urum sawlum læcedomlice.

fol. 112*a*–116*b*. Homily: "Men ða leofestan, us ys mycel þearf þæt we god lufien of eallre heortan 7 of eallre sawle 7 of eallum mægene.

fol. 116*b*–120*b*. Homily on the Christian virtues: "Her sægð hu scs isodorus spræc be ðære sawle gedale 7 be þæs lichoman.

fol. 121*a*–133*b*. Elene.

fol. 133*b*–135*b*. Prose life of St. Guthlac: Wæs þær in þam sprecenan iglande sum mycel hlæw of eorþan geworht.

IV

LARGE CAPITALS IN THE MANUSCRIPT

In general, a large capital is used at the beginning of each of the homilies in the manuscript, and at the beginning of the first and all succeeding sections in the poems. A list of the sectional divisions in the poems in terms of the line numberings of this edition is given in Table II at the end of this Introduction.

In two places, at the beginning of Section [XII] of Andreas, fol. 46*a*, and at the beginning of the Fates of the Apostles, fol. 52*b*, a space was left for a large capital, which was not filled in, though apparently a wrong capital was first written in the passage in Andreas, see l. 1253 and footnote, which was later erased and nothing supplied to take its place.

---

[1] Both of these poems are fragments. One or more pages are missing between folios 103 and 104, so that the end of one poem and the beginning of the other have been lost.

Counting the nearly effaced *H* at the top of fol. 1*a*, there are
in all fifty-five of these large capitals. Nearly all of them are of
the plain, unornamented type. On fol. 49*a*, however, at the
beginning of Section [XIV] of ANDREAS, there is a large zoömorphic *H*, in a good style very similar to the large capitals of the
early pages of the Junius Manuscript. It should be noted that
on the verso of the folio, i.e., fol. 49*b*, occurs the animal drawing
previously mentioned. On fol. 106*b* and on fol. 112*a* are large
capital *M*'s of a curious and somewhat awkward type—an
animal head with an arm or branch projecting out of the top
of the head to each side. Although these are quite similar,
the second is obviously the more crudely drawn of the two, and
is perhaps a copy of the first, made by a less experienced artist.
These *M*'s were apparently drawn before the rest of the text
was written in, the text being made to fit the convolutions of
the capitals. After a large capital, the rest of the word in which
the capital occurs is usually written in small capitals, of the
same general style as the large one, but about half the size.
Sometimes the entire first line is capitalized, as on fol. 9*b*, 109*b*,
112*a*. On fol. 109*b*, two large *M*'s and a smaller *E* have been
erased before the *M* which actually begins the homily. From
these descriptions it will be seen that very little attention was
paid to the decoration of the manuscript. An ornamental, red
colored ink was used three times in the manuscript, in capitals
and titles at the beginning of homilies, on fol. 71*b*, fol. 73*b* and
fol. 75*b*.[1] These tinted openings are not reproduced in color
in Wülker's or Förster's reproductions of the manuscript, but
the one on fol. 75*b* is reproduced in color in *Mr. Cooper's Report
on Rymer's Foedera*, at the end of Appendix B, Plate I.

V

SMALL CAPITALS IN THE MANUSCRIPT

In the use of small capitals ANDREAS differs in some respects
from ELENE. In ELENE personal names are very frequently

[1] Förster, *Der Vercelli-Codex*, in *Studien zur englischen Philologie*, Vol.
L (1913), p. 24.

capitalized, e.g. *Constantinus*, ll. 8, 79, 103, *etc.; Elene*, ll. 219, 266, 332, etc., but *elene*, ll. 1051, 1198; *Iudas*, ll. 609, 627, 655, but *iudas*, ll. 418, 586; *Cyriacus*, ll. 1058, 1068, 1097, but *ciriacus*, l. 1129, *cyriacus*, l. 1211. In ANDREAS and in the FATES OF THE APOSTLES personal names as such are not capitalized. In ANDREAS, only four proper names are capitalized, two with initial *I, Iudea*, l. 560, *Iosephes*, l. 691, *Moyse*, l. 1513, and *Platan*, l. 1651. In the FATES OF THE APOSTLES, capital *I* appears in *Iohanne*, l. 23, *Iacob*, l. 35, *Indeum*, l. 43, capital *P* in *Petrus*, l. 14, *Philippus*, l. 37, the only other capitalized name being *Simon*, l. 77.

Throughout the manuscript, *in* is very frequently capitalized, as in AN. 41, 52, 78, *etc.*, EL. 6, 9, 127, *etc.* Very frequently *ic* is written with a capital *I*, as in AN. 72, 81, 97, 99, 110, EL. 288, 345, 353, 419, 574, *etc.* These capital *I*'s were undoubtedly written in these words, as occasionally in proper names, in order to give the letter a readily distinguishable form, for the same reason, therefore, that the dot over *i* was supplied at a later time, and that the acute accent appears over *i* even in Anglo-Saxon manuscripts.

In both ANDREAS and ELENE a small capital frequently marks the beginning of a sentence, but more frequently the sentence-beginning is unmarked by a capital. In ELENE, for example, a small capital begins a sentence in *Wæs*, l. 11, *Foron*, l. 21, *For*, l. 35, *Woldon*, l. 40, *þa*, l. 69, *etc.*, in ANDREAS in *þam*, l. 14, *Oft*, l. 17, *þa*, l. 40, *etc.* In ANDREAS a small capital within a sentence most frequently marks the beginning of an important syntactical division of the sentence, as in AN. 281: Ne magon þær gewunian · wid ferende ne þær elþeodige eardes brucað · Ah in þære ceastre cwealm þrowiað *etc.* Or in AN. 327: (he is. . .) án ece god · eallra gesceafta · Swa he ealle befehð ánes cræfte · *etc.*, or AN. 403: þafigan ne woldon · Ðæt hie forleton *etc.* Or in AN. 558: Saga þances gleaw þegn gif ðu cunne · Hu ðæt gewurde · *etc.* Only rarely does the text of ANDREAS depart from the rule of capitalizing only the beginnings of important syntactical units. An interesting case where a word is apparently capitalized for emphasis is AN. 569: ah he þara wundra · A dóm ágende · *etc.*, where *a*, although it

belongs metrically to the preceding half-line, is capitalized
(and preceded by a point) because it is a very important word
and its full force might be missed by the reader.

In ELENE the use of small capitals is less carefully regulated.
Sometimes capitals are used at the beginning of short phrases,
as in EL. 109: (Heht þa. . .) þæt halige treo him beforan ferian
on feonda ge mang · Beran beacen godes *etc.* Or in EL. 124: þa
wæs þuf hafen · Segn for sweotolum *etc.* Or in EL. 88: swa
him se ár ábead · Fæle friðo webba. Or in EL. 992: næs þa
fricgendra under gold homan gád in burgū, Feorran geferede.
This use of the capitals in ELENE is so frequent as to be characteristic of the poem. It is also frequent in the DREAM OF THE
ROOD, as in 1. 23: hwilum hit wæs mid wætan be stemed · besyled mid swates gange · Hwilum mid since gegyrwed · *etc.*
In general SOUL AND BODY I and HOMILETIC FRAGMENT I re-
strict the small capitals to the beginning of the sentence, but
þonne, SOUL AND BODY 86, is capitalized, being the resumption
of the main clause after the enumeration of the various lesser
evils. A survey of the small capitals as they are listed for the
poetical parts of the Vercelli Book at the end of this Introduction will show how frequently the capitals occur in small con-
nective words, like *ac, swa, ða, nu, hu*, how largely they were
therefore structural and syntactical in the intent of the scribe.

Throughout the poetical parts of the manuscript, and especially in ANDRÉAS, there is a gradation in size of the small
capitals, but whether this is a reasoned effort to indicate degrees
of capitalization, is open to question. It is especially hard to
separate the small capitals of larger size from the smaller ones,
because of the varying styles which are employed. There
seems, for instance, to be only one small capital F, and one N.
On the other hand, we have D and $ð$ as capitals, which vary in
size, one sometimes being the larger, sometimes the other. Frequently, however, attempts to distinguish these capitals in
function can be recognized, as in SOUL AND BODY I, 1–37, where
Sceal, l. 9, and *Cleopað*, l. 15, have the larger small capitals,
but *Hwæt*, l. 22, and *Eardode*, l. 33, have the smaller ones. On
the other hand *hwæt*, l. 17, is not capitalized at all, perhaps because it is obvious from the context that the quotation begins

there. In AN. 254–295 is found the same situation. The *H*
of *Hie*, l. 254, is not as tall a letter as the *H* of *Hwanon*, l. 258,
but it is heavier and fatter, and from the way it is finished off
it is obvious that it is a more important capital than the other.
Then *hwanon*, l. 256, is not capitalized, but *Hwanon*, l. 258,
has the small capital of smaller size just mentioned.

It is only in cases like these that any deliberate distinction
between small capitals of larger and smaller size can be traced.
In ELENE the small capitals are much more consistent in size
and shape, with no apparent gradation. The same is true of
the DREAM OF THE ROOD, and it is probably more than a coin-
cidence that these two poems come close together near the end
of the book, where the 31- or 32-line page, beginning with the
fifteenth gathering of the manuscript, is standard.

As a part of the record of the poetical portions of the manuscript, the small capitals in these texts are given in a list in
Table III at the end of this Introduction.

In the prose texts the use of small capitals varies quite as
much as in the poems. Latin quotations, which are plentiful
toward the beginning of the manuscript, but less so toward
the end, generally begin with a capital letter, e.g. *Ego*, *Numquid*,
fol. 2*b*, *Reus*, fol. 3*b*, *Ergo*, fol. 5*a*, *Qui*, fol. 27*b*, *Nolite*, fol. 28*a*,
etc., but not *beati*, fol. 26*b*. Personal names vary. In the first
homily we have *iohannes*, *petrus*, fol. 2*b*, *crist*, fol. 3*a*, *pilatus*,
fol. 4*a*, and this is uniformly the custom in this homily. In the
third homily we have *iohannes*, fol. 12*b*, 13*b*, *esaiam*, fol. 13*b*,
esaias, fol. 14*a*, but whenever a personal name begins a sentence
it is capitalized, e.g., *Agustinus*, fol. 14*b*, *Moyses*, *Crist*, *Paulus*,
fol. 15*a*. In general, non-capitalization of personal names is the
rule in the homilies.

The small capitals in the homilies are also of various sizes,
as in this passage on fol. 64*a*:

Ac [*very small capital* A] utan þydan us to þam uplican rice ·
forðan þær is þæt wuldor þæt nænig man ne mæg mid his wordum asecgan · Ða [*small capital* ð] wynsumnesse þæs heofon
cundan lifes · Ðær [*small capital* ð] bið lif butan deaþe · 7 god
butan ende · 7 yld butan sare · 7 dæg butan nihte · And [*much
larger capital* A] þær bið gefea butan unrotnesse · 7 rice butan
awendednesse· 7 ne þearf man *etc.*

Here there is obviously an attempt to distinguish the capitals according to syntax, but no simple generalizations can be made for the manuscript as a whole, or indeed for the separate homilies. Thus on fol. 17*a* the manuscript reads:

Her ne mæg nan yfel ece beon · Forþan þeos woruld nis ece · Her is lytelu unrotnes · Ac þær is singalo nearones · her syndon lytle wynlustas ác þær syndon þa ecan tin trego þon for worhton · her bið unglædlic hleahter · Ac [*a very small capital* A] þær is se *etc.*

In this passage the first two sentences, with their contrasts, are capitalized, whereas the rest are not. This suggests that it was considered sufficient to indicate the structure at the beginning, to prepare the reader for what is to come, any further capitalization being thus unnecessary. In the prose, as in the poems, the beginnings of sentences and of important clauses are frequently but not always capitalized.

The best generalization that can be made is that capitalization in the manuscript, in the verse as well as in the prose, is purely pragmatic in origin and intention, that it was intended more as a rhythmical guide to the reader, to tell him when to pause, when to lift his voice, when to emphasize a word, than as a systematic logical or syntactical accompaniment of the text.

VI

ABBREVIATIONS IN THE MANUSCRIPT

The common abbreviations in the poetical portions of the manuscript, which have all been resolved in the text without comment, except in cases of special interest, are (1) a line, or macron, somewhat resembling the tilde, over a vowel, sometimes over a consonant, to indicate the omission of one or more letters following; (2) ꝥ for *þæt;* (3) 7 for *ond, and.*

The tilde or macron occurs most commonly in dative plural endings, but not consistently. Thus on fol. 29*b*, the manuscript reads *fyrn dagū,* AN. 1, but *tunglum,* AN. 2. On fol. 30*a* occurs *scyld hetū,* AN. 85, and *werigū,* AN. 86, but *wroht smiðum,* AN. 86. The manuscript shows similar irregularity throughout.

The tilde is also frequently used in the particle *þoñ* for *þonne*, *þā* for *þam*, and in *hī* for *him*, *frā* for *fram*, *ḡhwā* for *gehwam*, and less frequently in nouns, adjectives or verbs, as in *hear locan* for *hearmlocan*, An. 95, *grāra* for *gramra*, *id*. 217, *grā hydiges* for *gramhydiges*, *id*. 1694, *ȳrþa* for *yrmþa*, *id*. 970, *frū bearn* for *frumbearn*, *id*. 1294, *frēme* for *fremme*, *id*. 1354, *wælgrī* for *wælgrim*, *id*. 1415. Several times in Andreas, the tilde occurs over *g*, as in *ḡhwā* for *gehwam*, An. 121, and *bletsunḡ* for *bletsunge*, *id*. 223. The manuscript reading *gwyrhtum*, An. 1180, may be an error for *gewyrhtum* or for *ḡwyrhtum*.

In the other poetical texts of the manuscript, besides the common *-ū* for *-um*, *-ñ* for *-ne*, and other frequently occurring abbreviations, the following abbreviations may be noted: *frȳðe* for *frymðe*, Soul and Body I, 79, *dōdæge* for *domdæge*, *id*. 96; *dreā* for *dream*, Homiletic Fragment I, 2; *gebrinḡ* for *gebringe*, Dream of the Rood 139; *hā* for *ham*, El. 143, *frā* for *fram*, *id*. 190, 701, *þrȳ* for *þrym*, *id*. 483, 815, *þrȳma* for *þrymma*, *id*. 483, 519, *þrȳme* for *þrymme*, *id*. 329, 754, *þrȳmes* for *þrymmes*, *id*. 348, *frēme* for *fremme*, *id*. 524, *wōma* for *womma*, *id*. 1310, *clōmum* for *clommum*, *id*. 696, *gelāþ* for *gelamþ*, *id*. 962, and several exceptional abbreviations, *ḡ* for *geseh*, *id*. 841, which the scribe seems to have written first merely as *ḡ* and then to have supplemented this by writing *seh* above the line, *middan ḡ* for *middangeard*, *id*. 16, 774, and *7swer̄* for *andsweredon*. A noteworthy use of the runic symbol *p*, the symbol regularly used by the scribe for *w*, occurs twice in the manuscript, on fol. 128*b* and fol. 131*b*, in El. 788, 1089. The symbol is written with a dot before and after, and it stands for the word *wyn*, according to Cook, or *waldend*, according to Wülker. This use of a runic symbol to stand for a word is similar to that in the signatures of the name of Cynewulf on fol. 54*a* and fol. 133*a* of the manuscript, but the use is restricted to these four places in the manuscript.

The abbreviation *þ̄* for *þæt* occurs approximately four times as many times as the unabbreviated *þæt* in Andreas, but only four times altogether in Elene, three times in Soul and Body I, and not at all in the text of the other poems. The abbreviation *oþþ̄* occurs once in An. 1574, but not elsewhere in the poems. The spelling *ðæt*, with initial *ð*, is not abbreviated in the poems.

In only seven instances in ANDREAS does *ond* occur written out, ll. 945, 1001, 1203, 1307, 1395, 1400, 1719; to these should perhaps be added *on*, l. 1039, apparently an error for *ond*. Elsewhere in ANDREAS the customary abbreviation 7 occurs. In ELENE, *ond* occurs written out four times, ll. 930, 976, 983, 1209; elsewhere the abbreviation is used. In each of the four instances where *ond* is written out, the *o* is a small capital in ELENE, whereas it never is in ANDREAS. In the other four poems, only the abbreviation occurs.

Where *ond-* occurs in compound words, the usage of the scribe varies. In ANDREAS the verb *ondswarian* and its forms occur with 7 five times, with *ond-* five times; *ondswerian* occurs once unabbreviated. The noun *ondsware* occurs three times written out, and *andsware* occurs twice written out. The form *7sware* occurs seven times. The form *7wist* occurs in AN. 1540, the only instance of the word; *7langne* occurs in AN. 1274, but *ond-langne*, l. 818, and *ondlange*, l. 1254. The form *7sware* occurs once in SOUL AND BODY I, 106. In ELENE, *andsware* occurs in ll. 567, 1002, but *7sware* nine times. The verb form *7swer* occurs once, l. 396, and also *7wlitan*, l. 298, *7weardlice*, l. 1140, *7sæc*, l. 472, *7wyrde*, ll. 545, 619, *7wearde*, l. 630, none of these words occurring unabbreviated. Since the spelling *ond* is the more frequent in this manuscript when the word is written out, the abbreviation has been regularly so resolved in the texts of the present volume.

In the prose parts of the manuscript, abbreviations are some-what more fully used than in the poetical parts, but in the same ways, except that no runic symbols stand for words in the prose parts. A few of the more notable abbreviations of the prose are as follows: *c̄* for *cwæð*, fol. 12*b*, 13*a*, 13*b*, etc., *cw̃* for *cwæð*, fol. 15*b*, 120*b*, *m̃ þa l̃* for *men þa leofestan*, fol. 9*a*, 117*b*, and also *men þa l̃*, fol. 23*b*, 24*b*, *men ð l̃*, fol. 80*a*, and occasionally merely *m̃*, fol. 19*a*, 19*b*, etc.; *dryhne* for *dryhtne*, fol. 9*a*, and also *drih* for *drihten*, fol. 9*a*; *herig̃* for *herigode*, fol. 19*a*; *aплas* for *apostolas*, fol. 71*b*; *sc̄s* for *sanctus*, fol. 71*b*, etc.; *ðð* for *Dauid*, fol. 14*a*, etc.; *ioh̃* for *Iohannem*, fol. 85*b*. Latin passages in the prose text contain many abbreviations of the customary and easily recognizable types, e.g., *dŝ* for *deus*, *dño* for *domino*, *scdm̃* for *secundum*, *ūr* for *uester*, etc.

VII

PUNCTUATION AND ACCENT MARKS

The metrical punctuation in the poems of the Vercelli Book is very irregular, and contrasts sharply with the careful system of metrical points in the Junius Manuscript. A large part of the pointing in the Vercelli Book seems to be syntactical, rather than metrical in purpose. Usage varies from poem to poem, and therefore the six poems must be taken up separately. The metrical points in the later poems of the manuscript are much less frequent than in ANDREAS.

An examination of the points in AN. 1–276 shows that the pointing is metrical, but by no means as consistently so, as in the Junius Manuscript. In AN. 1–100 there are 89 points, and this ratio, 89 to 200 half-lines, does not change materially in the rest of the poem.

A good example of the pointing is to be found in AN. 25–39: swelc wæs þeaw hira· þæt hie æghwylcne ellðeodigra· dydan him to mose mete þearfendū· þara þe þæt ealand utan sohte· Swylc wæs þæs folces freoðo leas tacen unlædra eafoð· þæt hie eagena gesihð· hetted heoro grimme· heafod gimme· Ágeton gealgmode gara ordum· syððan him geblondan bitere to somne · dryas þurh dwolcræft· drync unheorne· se on wende gewit wera ingeþanc heortan hreðre· hyge wæs on cyrred· þæt hie ne murndan æfter man dreame· hæleþ heoro grædige· ac hie híg 7 gærs· for mete leaste· meðe gedrehte·

The pointing here seems to be partly syntactical, partly metrical, though mainly syntactical. If the metrical intention had been uppermost in the mind of the scribe, one would at least expect points after *mose* and *tacen* in this passage. But that the metrical intention of the points was not entirely absent is evidenced by the fact that once in a while the scribe breaks out into a flurry of them, e.g., ll. 190–201:

Hu mæg ic dryhten min ofer deop ge lad· fore gefremman on feorne weg· swa hrædlice· heofona scyppend· wuldres wal-dend· swa ðu worde becwist· Ðæt mæg engel þin· eaðge feran· of heofenum con him holma begang· sealte sæstreamas· 7 swan rade· waroð faruða gewinn· 7 wæter brogan· wegas ofer wid land· nesynt me winas cuðe· eorlas ellþeodige· ne þær æniges wát hæleða gehygdo· ne me here stræta ofer cald wæter cuðe sindon·

A case might also be made for syntactical pointing here, but what syntactical value the points have may be explained as due to the peculiar structure of Anglo-Saxon verse.

In AN. 1–276 there are only three points which do not come at the end of a half-line. They are after *lungre,* l. 77, *him,* l. 189, and *scealtu,* l. 220. Similar pointing occurs elsewhere, as in l. 601, where section [VI] begins: Ða gen weges· weard· word hord onleac· The pointing in these passages seems to be without rime or reason,.unless it may have been intended to indicate some kind of rhetorical emphasis in reading. It is possible that in l. 77 the scribe regarded the line as ending with *lungre,* and *scyle* as belonging to the next line.

The only generalization which seems possible for ANDREAS is that the pointing, as a whole, is highly unsystematic and regularly conditioned neither by meter, syntax, nor sentence-rhythm, though any of these may have been the reason for individual points. The person—scribe or author—who inserted these points probably had a reason for each one, or most of them, but present knowledge of the technique of Anglo-Saxon poetry is not much furthered by his use of them.

In the FATES OF THE APOSTLES, the points are on the same system, or lack of system, as in ANDREAS, ranging from infrequent pointing in ll. 6*b*–22 to regular pointing in ll. 58–65*a,* except that no point follows *gesohte,* l. 62*a.* But this word comes at the end of a line and perhaps no point was felt to be necessary there.

In SOUL AND BODY I it is possible to make some generalizations. One notices first the recurring point-pattern in such phrases as the following:

Wære þu þe wiste wlanc· 7 wines sæd· l. 39.

strange gestryned· 7 gestaðolod þurh me· l. 45.

men to ge mæccan· ne meder ne fæder· ne nænigum gesybban
    ll. 53–54.

secan þa hamas þe ðu me her scrife· 7 þa arleasan eardungstowe·
    ll. 70–71.

Þonne ðu æfre on moldan man gewurde· oððe æfre fulwihte
onfon sceolde· ll. 86–87.

It will be observed that these coördinate constructions are very
consistent in the pointing, which may be rhythmical or syntactical. On the other hand, in ll. 57–60, the manuscript reads:

Ne mæg þe nu heonon adon hyrsta þy readan· ne gold ne seolfor
ne þinra goda nán ne þinre bryde beag· ne þin gold wela· ne nan
þara goda þe ðu iu ahtest·

One would expect more pointing here than the manuscript
gives. In general, the points, which are rather infrequent in
this poem, less than 60 in 166 lines, seem to have been inserted
for syntactical or rhythmical, rather than for metrical, purposes.

In HOMILECTIC FRAGMENT I the points are also infrequent,
about 12 in 47 lines, and of these the following may be noted
especially:

manig· 7 mislic· in manna dreā· l. 2.
in wita for wyrd· weoruda dryhten· l. 10.
sare mid· þonne se sæl cymeð· l. 23.

Concerning these and the remaining points, no generalization
is possible.

In the DREAM OF THE ROOD, the metrical points vary
strangely. On fol. 104b (ll. 1–21), where there are 24 lines on a
page, the points are rare, and seem to mark syntactical pauses
within sentences, or else sentence-closes, as in: fægere æt foldan
sceatum· swylce þær fife wæron *etc.*; ne wæs ðær huru fracodes
gealga· Ac hine þær *etc.* On the next three pages (fol. 105a–
106a) the number of lines on a page jumps to 32, and coincidently
with this change the pointing also changes. From *wendan*,
l. 22, the first word on fol. 105a, to *bestemed*, l. 22, there is no
pointing; but there is a point after *bestemed*, and then a point
after each half-line, except after *licgende*, l. 24, to the end of l.
25. This is obviously metrical pointing, but it stops as suddenly
as it began. In ll. 32–51a, the pointing becomes more abun-
dant, but it appears to be syntactical, marking off the short
sentences in this part of the poem. After l. 52 the points again
become very infrequent, with apparently no consistency in
their use.

In ELENE the first thing one observes is that of the 14 points which occur in EL. 1–100, all but three are followed by small capitals, as follows: after *hereteman*, l. 10, *Hreð gotan*, l. 20, *geador*, l. 26, *burg wigendra*, l. 34, *breahtme*, l. 39, *sceawedon*, l. 58, *gesægon*, l. 68, *woma*, l. 71, *toglad*, l. 78, *ðe*, l. 81, *abead*, l. 87. This indicates unmistakeably their syntactical character. In general, the points mark the ends of sentences or parts of sentences. The three exceptions are after *foron*, l. 21, where the *n* has apparently been added later, and the point inserted to separate the words; after *cyning*, l. 32, where the function of the point is not at all obvious; and after *gearu*, l. 85, where separation of words written closely together is perhaps again the intention. This syntactical function of the points continues throughout the poem, and in most, nearly all, cases a small capital follows. Frequently the point is shaped like a comma.

The other marks of punctuation used in the poetical parts of the manuscript are :7 and :~, which regularly mark the ends of sections, and frequently occur within sections, at times not differing in function from a plain point, as after *drynces*, SOUL BODY I, 41, *wolde*, *id.* 83, *treow*, DREAM OF THE ROOD 17, *fornam*, EL. 131, *þanon*, *id.* 143. Sometimes a semicolon (: or ˙/) occurs, but very rarely, as after *wære*, SOUL AND BODY 21, *cure*, *id.* 155.

The only certain thing about all this punctuation is its extreme irregularity and frequent aimlessness. It seems quite probable, however, that much of this inconsistency is due to the heedlessness of scribes in transmitting what may have been originally a more systematic style of punctuation, or perhaps to the editorial policy of the scribe of the Vercelli manuscript. His principle seems to have been not to punctuate the poetical texts metrically, though occasionally he may have introduced metrical points unreflectingly, and perhaps under the influence of copy which contained a greater abundance of metrical pointings.

A dot over the letter *y* which appears frequently in the Vercelli Book, but not in the Junius Manuscript, is scarcely to be regarded as a form of punctuation, but as a part of the letter itself. The purpose of this dot seems to have been to give the letter a distinctive mark of recognition. Several different styles of *y* appear in the manuscript, especially one in which the two upper arms and the lower stroke of the letter are straight lines, and a second in which both of the upper arms and also the lower stroke are markedly curved. The first may be called the straight and the second the curly *y*. The curly *y* was frequent, according to Keller, *Angelsächsische Palaeographie*, pp. 40–42, in the first half of the tenth century. The straight *y* was in origin an earlier style of writing, and it is above the straight *y* that the dot usually occurs in the Vercelli Book. But all straight *y*'s are not uniformly provided with a dot, and on the other hand, occasionally the later curly *y* has a dot. After its early use the dot above the straight *y* was discontinued for a time in the practice of Anglo-Saxon scribes, according to Keller, but with the scribal reform at the beginning of the tenth century, the dot came in again, and by the eleventh century, the undotted *y* had practically disappeared. So far as the Vercelli Book is concerned, the writing of *y* is notable mainly for its unsystematic and eclectic character.

Accents in the Poems

Scattered throughout the manuscript, both in prose and verse texts, occur numerous acute accent marks placed above letters. These accents occur regularly only above vowel symbols, although *edniwinga*, An. 783, has the mark over the *g*, probably through inadvertence, instead of over the second *i* of the word. The marks are of varying degrees of heaviness, depending on the strength of the strokes of the pen with which they were made, but there is no indication that the scribe intended any difference of kind in the accent marks. The purpose or purposes for which these accent marks were made is not always clear, nor is it altogether certain whether they were made by the scribe as he wrote or were inserted afterward, though there seems no good reason for assuming anything other than that they were made by the scribe as he wrote.

In Andreas, Fates of the Apostles and Elene accent marks occur with about the same degree of frequency, the percentages of accents in proportion to the lines being respectively .182, .172 and .164. In the shorter poems the accent marks are a good deal less frequent, .06 per cent in SOUL AND BODY I, .085 in HOMILETIC FRAGMENT I, and .038 in the DREAM OF THE ROOD.

That these accent marks were not consistently used to indicate vowel length is obvious from an examination of the list of them given at the end of this Introduction. It is indeed questionable whether they were intended to indicate vowel length at all. Naturally vowel length frequently coincides with metrical stress and in such instances the accent may as well have been intended to indicate stress as vowel length. In any case poets and scribes of the Anglo-Saxon period could scarcely have had etymological length of vowels in mind in the placing of these accent marks, and if they were intended to indicate anything with respect to the character of the vowel sounds, it was more probably some shade of quality than a degree of quantity. Not infrequently accents appear over vowels historically short, especially *gód*, as in AN. 758, 760, 925, 999, 1030, *etc.* to distinguish the word for "god" from *gōd*, "good." This use occurs only in the text of ANDREAS. Other examples of accents over short vowels are *wég*, AN. 223, *hýge*, *id.* 578, *gewít*, *id.* 645, *ongín*, *id.* 741, *gehýgd*, *id.* 772, *héonan*, *id.* 791, *inwít*, *id.* 946, *gewínn*, *id.* 958, *hlíndura*, *id.* 993, *hríne*, *id.* 1000, *lóf*, *id.* 1006, *hófe*, *id.* 1008, *hínca*, *id.* 1171, *círm*, *id.* 1237, *wíne*, *id.* 1464, *éngan*, EL. 712. Accent marks over short vowels are less frequent in ELENE than in ANDREAS. The frequency of accents over the letter *i*, long and short, suggests that the accent here was merely a distinguishing part of the letter, like the later conventional dot. The letter most frequently provided with an accent is *a*. In some instances the accent seems to be merely a syllabic indication, as in those many compounds in which the prefix *a-* is given an accent, or in writings like *bán hús*, AN. 1240, *brím rade*, *id.* 1262, or compounds with *or-*, *un-*, as in *órlege*, AN. 1146, *únhwilen*, *id.* 1154, *órmǽte*, *id.* 1166, *únfyrn*, *id.* 1371. Stress accent seems to be indicated in the writing of proper names, as in *merme donía*, AN. 42, *ísrahelum*, *id.* 165, *hábráháme*, *id.* 779, *isáác*, *id.* 793, *achágia*, AP. 16, *ir tácus*, *id.* 68, and certainly *hwǽt*, AN. 676. Accent on an inflectional ending, as in *hǽfdón*, AN. 785, or *fárá*, *id.* 1023, 1060, may also have been rhetorical, though accents of this kind occur very infrequently.

Sometimes, though rarely, a vowel letter is doubled, presumably as a variant of the accent mark, and sometimes both double spelling and accent occur, as in *óor*, AN. 649, *táan*, *id.* 1099, *fáá*, *id.* 1593, *fáa*, *id.* 1599.

Although the accent marks in the poetical texts are certainly not applied in accord with any single system, they are by no means haphazard and accidental or ornamental additions to the text. As a part of the record of the manuscript, accented words in the poetical texts of the Vercelli Book are listed in Table IV at the end of this Introduction. For the purpose of comparative study, the accent marks in the Junius Manuscript are also given in this table. A bar separating the parts of a word has been inserted in certain words in these lists, as in *á* | *hwurfon*, Page 1, GEN. 25, the purpose of the bar being to indicate that the part of the word before the bar stands at the end of the line in the manuscript, the scribe's intent in these accents apparently being to call attention to the syllabic division of the word. Syllabic division as it appears in the manuscript in all other words is also indicated, since there seems to be no doubt that the scribes frequently used the accent merely to mark the syllabic character of a word. A bibliography of studies of the accents in Anglo-Saxon manuscripts will be found in Kennedy, *A Bibliography of Writings on the English Language from the Beginning of Printing to the End of 1922*, p. 134.

PUNCTUATION AND ACCENT-MARKS IN THE PROSE TEXTS

The point occurs in the prose texts as in the poems, although obviously its use here is syntactical only. The following passage, taken from the first homily, fol. 2*b*, is representative:

Hwæt ic openlice 7 undearnunga middan geard lærde· 7 symle þær eower gesomnung wæs In eowrum templū þyder ealle iudas comon· þonne ic his ealle lærde · ne ic owiht dearnunga spræc· nemin lar ówiht diogol wæs·

The tendency is to separate the various syntactical or rhythmical units of a sentence, but not to carry out this separation rigorously or completely.

In the fifth homily, and in those which immediately follow ANDREAS and the FATES OF THE APOSTLES, the punctuation is

appreciably less frequent than in the preceding prose texts.   In
the latter part of the book, beginning with fol. 106b, where the
writing is smaller and with more lines on a page, the punctuation becomes again more frequent.   The use of punctuation
varies so much from homily to homily, and even within a
homily, that, as in the verse, no single guiding principle can be
discovered.

   The semicolon (;) occurs in the prose also, e.g. fol. 11a, l. 11;
fol. 15a, l. 22, etc.   In the fourth homily, and particularly from
fol. 16b to fol. 18b, this sign is quite frequent, in contrast to its
infrequency in the other parts of the manuscript.   But the use
of the semicolon is also quite inconsistent, for instance, in a
passage on fol. 18b:

[. . .] þ hie ne magon ongytan nan þing butan þa myrhðe þæs
dryhtnes wuldres; He us gelifæst hæfð on þyssum middan gearde;
7 we hī under þydde bion sculon· gif we hit earnian willað:
Nu we sindon m̄ on þysne middan geard etc.

The colon, as after willað, rarely occurs in the prose texts.

   The accent-marks in the prose texts, like those in the verse,
usually occur over vowels historically long.   In frequency they
vary considerably; in five lines on fol. 10b the words rên, dôm,
blácan, and wóp have accents, but this is unusual, and on fol.
11b the only word accented is gedóó.   Sometimes a long vowel
is distinguished by doubling the letter, with or without an accent, as in aa, fol. 12a, tiid, fol. 25a, tíid, fol. 25b, and gedóó
above.

   In general, it may be said that accents do not occur as often
or as consistently in the prose as in the poems, and that they
are much less frequent in the later than in the earlier part of
the book.   The habits of punctuation as they appear in the
prose texts are nevertheless quite in harmony with those that
are present in the verse texts of the manuscript.

VIII

THE POEMS IN THE MANUSCRIPT

   The poems in the Vercelli manuscript are not provided with
titles, nor are they distinguished by any formal marks peculiar
to them from the prose parts of the manuscript.   Each poem

begins with a large capital, except the FATES OF THE APOSTLES, in which space for the capital was left but the letter itself was never supplied, and HOMILETIC FRAGMENT I, the beginning of which is lacking through a loss of one or more folios in the manuscript. After the initial large capital, the remaining letters of the first word of each poem is written in smaller large capitals, except in the DREAM OF THE ROOD, where only the first two letters of the first word are capitalized. The beginnings of the poems indeed are not more definitely marked than the sections in the poems. This informal treatment of the openings of the poems contrasts sharply with the treatment of the openings of the homilies. Many of the homilies not only have titles, but the openings are also more elaborately capitalized, a number of times through the whole of the first line of a homily, and most of the few attempts at decorative capitals also appear at the beginning of homilies. From this one may perhaps infer that the homilies were more highly esteemed for the purpose for which the volume was made than the poems.

The first poem in the manuscript, on fol. 29b–52b, is ANDREAS, a narrative account of the life of St. Andrew derived ultimately from the Greek Πράξεις Ἀνδρέου καὶ Ματθεία εἰς τὴν πόλιν τῶν ἀνθρωποφάγων, edited by Bonnet, Acta Apostolorum Apocrypha, Vol. I, Part 2, pp. 65–116 (1898). The poem was made from a Latin version of the Greek text not now extant, so far as is known, in a complete form.[1] An Anglo-Saxon prose life of St. Andrew is preserved in two manuscripts, the manuscript of the Blickling Homilies and MS. 198, Corpus Christi College, Cambridge, accessible in Bright's Anglo-Saxon Reader, pp. 113–128. This prose version is ultimately of the same origin as ANDREAS, but the two are independently derived from their source.

The narrative in ANDREAS follows the source very closely and no serious question of omission or interpolation occurs in the consideration of the poem. But because ANDREAS is followed in the manuscript by the FATES OF THE APOSTLES, and because this latter is such a short poem and nevertheless

[1] See Krapp, Andreas, pp. xxi ff.

contains one of the four well-known runic signatures of Cynewulf, an attempt has been made to attach it to ANDREAS as a
part and conclusion of that poem. Nothing in the manuscript
justifies such a disposition of the FATES OF THE APOSTLES. The
poem begins with a large capital, or rather space for one, the
capital never having been supplied, and it is separated from
what precedes by the usual spacing. It is true that the method
used by the scribe in separating the different sections of a poem
is exactly the same as that used in separating quite different
poems. But since this is so, the arrangement of the poem in the
manuscript provides no argument either one way or the other
concerning the theory of the FATES OF THE APOSTLES as an
integral part of ANDREAS. Internal evidence, however, speaks
more decisively. ANDREAS has its single source, as has already
been pointed out, and there is no evidence that the author of
ANDREAS endeavored to manipulate or to enlarge the structure
of the narrative as his source gave it. The FATES OF THE
APOSTLES has a different but quite as definite a source, although
the exact text which the Anglo-Saxon poet used has not been
discovered. But it must have been some Latin list of the
Apostles, their missions and passions, of a type commonly
current at the time the Anglo-Saxon poem was written, and
possibly of Irish origin.[1] The general agreement in subject
matter of ANDREAS as the story of the life of an apostle and of
the FATES OF THE APOSTLES as a brief martyrology of the
apostles is an evidence of the selective choice of the person who
brought together the materials of the Vercelli Book, but not of
any constructive intent on the part of the author of ANDREAS.

It should be noted, however, that the passage on fol. 54a,
comprising AP. 96–122 and containing the runes which combine
to form the name Cynwulf, stands on this folio by itself, and
it has been argued from this that the FATES OF THE APOSTLES
really ends with l. 95b, and that the runic passage, ll. 96–122,
happens to have been misplaced, its proper position being at
the end of ANDREAS, as an epilogue to that poem. But again
nothing in the manuscript record justifies such an assumption,

---

[1] See Krapp, *Andreas*, pp. xxix–xxxii, Hamilton, *Modern Language Notes*
XXXV, 385–95 (1920).

except the very slight evidence that the runic passage does begin on a new page. But there is no mark of punctuation at the conclusion of the preceding page, and the first word of the runic passage on fol. 54a does not begin with a large capital or any other indication that it is a new poem or even a sectional division of a larger poem. The text on the page preceding fol. 54a fills the page completely, the number of lines on the page being twenty-five, and the scribe was consequently compelled to begin on a new page with the words that follow. If it were certain that ANDREAS was written by Cynewulf, one might be inclined to stretch the point a little and to assume that the runic passage at least formed the conclusion of ANDREAS. Or of course it may be argued, as it was by Sievers,[1] that the passage on fol. 54a belongs neither to the FATES OF THE APOSTLES nor to ANDREAS, but to some unknown poem. But it is very far from certain that ANDREAS was the work of Cynewulf, and one hesitates to attach any part of the FATES OF THE APOSTLES to that poem. On the strength of the runic signature, the FATES OF THE APOSTLES has been generally assigned to Cynewulf. It may seem strange that Cynewulf should have taken the trouble to add his name to so slight a poem as the FATES OF THE APOSTLES, but on the other hand, it is not improbable that Cynewulf attached a higher value to the poem than the modern reader is inclined to do.[2]

The third poem in the manuscript, on fol. 101b–103b, follows a homily which ends on fol. 101a, on a page containing only seventeen lines of writing, the rest of the page being left blank. The poem begins at the top of fol. 101b with the usual capitals that mark the beginnings of new texts. In content the poem is an address of the soul to the body after death. Another version of the poem which loosely parallels the text in the Vercelli Book is contained in the Exeter Book. To distinguish the two versions, the one in the Vercelli Book is called SOUL AND BODY I, and the version in the Exeter Book is called SOUL AND BODY II. The poem ends abruptly in the middle of a sentence

[1] *Anglia* XIII, 21–25.
[2] For discussions of these questions of structure, see the titles in the Bibliography.

at the foot of fol. 103*b*. The concluding parts of the poem were undoubtedly contained on the one or more folios now missing from the manuscript between fol. 103–104. But probably not much of this poem has been lost, for the text that follows in the manuscript as it now exists is HOMILETIC FRAGMENT I, which occupies only fol. 104*a* and five lines at the top of fol. 104*b*, in all forty-seven lines of text. A good share of the missing page or pages was not improbably occupied by the beginning of this poem.

The poem following SOUL AND BODY I is designated as HOMILETIC FRAGMENT I to distinguish it from another similar fragment contained in the Exeter Book and designated HOMILETIC FRAGMENT II. The beginning of this poem is missing for the same reason that the conclusion of SOUL AND BODY I is missing, but short as the surviving fragment is, probably not much has been lost. For the fragment is a loose amplification of Psalm XXVIII, and the beginning of the fragment corresponds to the third verse of the Psalm, which as a whole contains only nine verses. So far as this evidence goes, it seems to indicate therefore that not more than one or two folios may have been lost between fol. 103–104.

After HOMILETIC FRAGMENT I comes the DREAM OF THE ROOD in the manuscript, extending from the sixth line on fol. 104*b* to the bottom of fol. 106*a*. The poem begins in the usual way with capitals and with spacing separating it from the text that precedes, and it ends with no indication of incompleteness or loss on fol. 106*a*. The text is rather closely written on fol. 105*a*–106*a*, these pages each containing thirty-two lines; but this can scarcely be taken as evidence that the scribe wanted to crowd the text of the DREAM OF THE ROOD within a certain space, for the pages that follow fol. 106*a* contain a homily and these also are written with thirty-two lines on a page.

The earlier editors assigned the DREAM OF THE ROOD to Cynewulf, but no direct evidence and very little indirect evidence is available to justify such an ascription. Certain similarities of phrasing, sometimes helpful in determining the text, connect the runic inscription on the Ruthwell Cross with this poem, and also the very brief inscription on the Brussels Cross, the plausible assumption being that these inscriptions were extracted from the text of the poem. It is not improbable that the DREAM OF THE ROOD was written by Cynewulf, but the lack of evidence, except that of a general and circumstantial character, forbids any positive statement.

The sixth and last poem in the manuscript is ELENE, contained on fol. 121a–133b. It begins at the top of fol. 121a, following a prose text which ends on fol. 120b at the middle of the page, the rest of the page being left blank. The narrative proper of ELENE ends on the twenty-first line of fol. 132b with the word *finit* and the usual punctuation indicating the close of a section, and it is followed on the same page by the opening of the passage containing the runic signature of Cynewulf. This passage extends through the sixth line on fol. 133b and is numbered XV, as a section of ELENE. It is followed in turn on the seventh line of fol. 133b by a part of the prose life of St. Guthlac, without section numbering. The poem is undoubtedly complete, but the prose life of St. Guthlac, although it begins as a new division, opens in the middle of a narrative with allusions to preceding matter not contained in this text. By virtue of the runic symbols on fol. 133a, in the passage following the end of the narrative of ELENE, this is one of the few Anglo-Saxon poems the authorship of which is unquestioned, for all agree that the poem was written by Cynewulf. This runic passage, it should be noted, is an appendage or epilogue to ELENE. The text of ELENE ends with the twenty-first line of fol. 132b of the manuscript and it ends with the word *finit*. This is the conclusion of a section numbered fourteen, and following it comes the number fifteen and the opening of the runic passage in the usual way as a new section. The runic passage therefore fills the remainder of fol. 132b, that is, ten lines, the whole of fol. 133a, and six lines of fol. 133b, where it ends with *Amen*. Nothing in the content of this runic passage connects it inescapably with ELENE, and indeed it is so different in general style that it would seem to have been composed as an entirely independent effort. The connection of the runic passage with the rest of the poem is therefore not structural but casual, though this fact scarcely justifies any doubts of it as a genuine addition to ELENE.

The actual text which Cynewulf had before him as his source in the composition of ELENE has not been discovered. It is almost certain, however, that Cynewulf followed his source closely and there are no questions of interpolation or structural misplacement to be considered. In its relation to its source, ELENE therefore resembles ANDREAS. The source of the poem was a Latin legend of the invention of the Cross, differing from but similar to that given in the Acta Sanctorum.[1] Other very similar forms of the Cross legend are to be found in a Latin *Acta Cyriaci* from Codex Paris. 2769, and in the Greek Λόγος τῆς εὑρέσεως τοῦ τιμίου καὶ ζωοποιοῦ σταυροῦ, from Codex Graecus Monacensis 271.[2] In the *Heilagra manna sögur* there is a Norse version of the Cross legend which in many places shows a striking resemblance to *Elene*.[3] An even closer similarity with *Elene* is shown by the Irish version in the Leabhar Breac[4] and by an Anglo-Saxon prose homily entitled *þære halgan rode gemetnes* in MS. Auct. F. 4. 32 in the Bodleian Library.[5] It is quite probable[6] that the Irish version and the two Anglo-Saxon versions were from a common Latin source, made in Ireland, perhaps from a still earlier Greek text.

IX

TABLE I

CONTENTS OF THE FOLIOS OF THE MANUSCRIPT

The contents of the folios of the Vercelli manuscript containing poetical texts are given in terms of the line numbers of this edition in the following table.

---

[1] Acta Sanctorum, Maii I, 445–448. See Glöde, *Anglia* IX, 271–318.

[2] These two texts are printed in Holder, *Inventio Sanctæ Crucis*, pp. 1–13, 30–39.

[3] *Heilagra manna sögur*, ed. Unger, Christiania, 1877, Vol. I, pp. 303–308. See Golther, *Literaturblatt* VIII, 261–263, and Brenner, *Englische Studien* XIII, 480–482.

[4] Schirmer, *Die Kreuzeslegenden im Leabhar Breac*, St. Gallen, 1886, pp. 8–19, with a German translation, pp. 31–44.

[5] Morris, *Legends of the Holy Rood* (E. E. T. S., O. S. 46), pp. 3–17.

[6] See Brown, *Englische Studien* XL. 1–29.

[1] Here the poem ends in the middle of a sentence. One or more sheets of the MS. are missing, containing the ending of this poem and the beginning of the next.

HOMILETIC FRAGMENT I

Page	Line	to	Line	Page	Line	to	Line
104a	1 sorh		41 wyn-	104b	41 -sume		

DREAM OF THE ROOD

104b			21 beacen	105b	61 hefian		105 on
105a	22 wendan		61 ðam	106a	105 domdæge		156 wæs

ELENE

121a	1 þa		49 hæfdon	128a	703 Is		756 legene
121b	49 to		97 sorgleasra	128b	756 sweorde		807 gecnawen
122a	97 secga		145 Constan-tino	129a	808 on		857 engla
				129b	858 geþro-wode		913 wæs
122b	145 cyning		193 willan				
123a	194 Ða		240 ic	130a	913 Syððan		966 breostum
123b	240 sið		290 geardagum	130b	967 Ða		1023 golde
124a	291 wyrðe		341 geeacnod	131a	1023 beweor-cean		1074 cininges (MS. cining)
124b	341 þurh		388 þonne				
125a	388 nu		443 frignan				
125b	443 ond		497 larum	131b	1074 ryhte		1138 gnyrna
126a	498 feore		551 caseres	132a	1138 to		1196 ge-
126b	551 bodan		600 georne	132b	1196 -læste		1253 wundor
127a	600 bæd		650 man-	133a	1253 onwrigen		1312 gemylted
127b	650 -rime		703 hungre	133b	1312 Swa		1321 Amen[1]

X

TABLE II

SECTIONAL DIVISIONS IN THE POEMS

The division of the longer poems of the manuscript is indicated by a mark of punctuation at the end of the several sections, followed by spacing and by a capital letter at the beginning of the succeeding section, and by numbering. But all of these indications are not uniformly present, and only in ELENE do section numberings appear. The sectional divisions of the poems in terms of the line numbers of this edition are as follows, the numbers bracketed being those which do not appear in the manuscript:

ANDREAS

[I] AN. 1–121	[III] AN. 230–351
[II] AN. 122–229	[IV] AN. 352–468

---

[1] The poem ends six lines from the top of the page, and is followed by the prose life of Guthlac which concludes the manuscript.

XI

Tᴀʙʟᴇ III

SMALL CAPITALS

Aɴᴅʀᴇᴀs

5 Syððan	97 Ic	194 Ðæt	270 Him
14 Þam	98 Ne	202 Him	277 Eft
17 Oft	99 Ic	205 Nis	278 Of
26 Þæt	110 Ic	207 Ðæt	279 Ne
29 Swylc	111 In	212 Ne	281 Ah
32 Ageton	113 Is	214 Beo	285 Him
40 Þa	117 In	216 Ðu	290 Him
41 In	121 In	217 In	292 We
51 Abreoton	147 Ða	220 Scealtu	299 Him
52 In	157 Swa	231 In	301 Næbbe
72 Ic	163 In	239 Se	304 In
78 In	169 In	240 Syðþan	305 Him
81 Ic	174 Ðu	245 Þrymlice	307 Hu
85 Ðæt	175 Siðe	247 Sittan	315 Ða
88 Æfter	177 Swa	254 Hie	317 Ne
92 Ða	183 Ðær	258 Hwanon	319 Ðæt
93 Wrætlic	185 Nu	260 Him	322 Swa
94 Mæres	190 Hu	261 Swa	327 Swa

1252 Halig	1358 Habbað	1443 No	1563 Is
1261 Ofer	1362 Aclæc-	1450 Ða	1581 Symble
1264 In	1363 Hwæt	1451 Sie	1582 Swa
1266 Acol	1364 Nu	1455 Swa	1591 Nalas
1269 Ða	1377 In	1461 Mago-	1598 Ðrage
1272 Heton	1380 In	1463 In	1601 Hie
1273 In	1383 Ðu	1471 Næs	1602 Nu
1274 Ða	1385 Of	Ne	1604 Se
1284 Ic	1386 Ða	1472 Ne	1609 Ne
1293 Ne	1394 Ða	1473a Ne	1613 Sende
1299 In	1401 Næfre	1473b Ne	1619 In
1300 Sleað	1404 Sint	1476 Ac	1621 Haliges
1307 Ond	1406 Hwæt	1481 Mycel	1649 In
1308 In	1413 Hwæt	1482 In	1651 Platan
1309 In	1414 Ic	1487 Hwæðre	1661 þa
1316 Hwæt	1418 Ðu	1492 He	1669 Ne
1317 Hwær	1419 þa	1504 Inflede	1672 In
1328 Swa	1422 Ne	1512 On	1674 Syððan
1331 In	1423 Ne	1513 Moyse	1685 In
1332 In	1425 Nu	1517 Nu	1686 In
1334 Hie	Is	1522 Næs	1687 Swylce
1337 Syððan	1429 Him	1543 Ne	1703 In
1345 Hearm-	1431 Ne	1547 Ðær	1706 Ða
1347 Ne	1432 Ic	Innan	1710 Hie
1356 Vton	1436 On	1558 Nu	

FATES OF THE APOSTLES

11 Sume	In	70 Hyrde	88 Nu
14 Petrus	33 Næs	In	96 Her[2]
16 In	35 Iacob	72 Ðurg	98 Hwa
18 Ne	37 Philipus	75 Næron	105 NV[1]
23 Hwæt	42 Huru	77 Sohton	107 Sie
Iohanne	43 Indeum	Simon	109 Ic
25 Se	45 In	84 Idle	111 Nat
27 Syððan	50 Swylce	85 ÐVs[1]	118 In
30 He	63 Hwæt		

SOUL AND BODY I

9 Sceal	17 Hwæt	33 Eardode	42 Forðan
15 Cleopað	22 Hwæt	39 Wære	46 Ic

[1] These words were written with capitals of varying size, the first one larger, the second smaller, but both to be regarded as small capitals.

[2] From this point on in the poem some small capitals may be hidden by the blot or stain in the MS.

61 Ac	92 Ðonne	117 Se	159 Wolde
76 Forðan	95 Ac	155 Forþan	168 Wat
86 Þonne	108 Bið		

HOMILETIC FRAGMENT I

2 In	8 Forðan	13 In	35 Inwit
6 In	10 In	15 In	

DREAM OF THE ROOD

11 Ac	24 Hwæðre	47 Inwid-	95 Nu
13 Syllic	28 Ic	Ic	115 Ac
Ic	30 Genaman	59 Sare	117 Ne
18 Hwæðre	39 Ongyrede	63 Aledon	119 Ac
21 Forht	43 Ac	65 Ongunnon	131 Nah
23 Hwilum	44 Rod	78 Nu	132 Ac

ELENE

6 In	153 Heht	320 Eodan	499 To
8 Constan-tines	157 Ða	326 Hio	511 Nu
9 In	163 þe	329 þrungon	517 Forðan
11 Wæs	166 Hio	330 In	522 Forðan
21 Foron	169 þa	332 Elene	527 In
27 For	175 Ðæt	336 In	528 Ðus
35 For	177 In	339 Eow	551 Caseres
40 Woldon	181 Alysde	345 Ic	565 Heo
59 Ðæt	189 Ðus	353 Ic	573 Elene
69 þa	198 Ongan	377 Eodan	574 Ic
72 þuhte	209 Iudea	389 Ða	575 In
79 Constan-tinus	210 In	391 In	578 In
82 Ðeah	212 þa	396 Hie	584 Ða
88 Fæle	219 Elene	404 Elene	595 In
91 Wæs	225 Ongan	411 Eodon	598 Hio
103 Constan-tinus	229 Ða	412 In	602 In
105 Heht	237 Leton	417 þa	604 Elene
109 Beran	243 þær	419 Ic	609 Iudas
124 Segn	256 Ðær	426 Nu	611 Hu
127 Instæpes	266 Elene	436 Swa	620 Elene
132 Sume	274 In	441 Gif	621 Gif
138 Ða	282 Ða	448 Ne	In
144 þa	288 Ic	462 Ða	623 In
148 Gewat	293 Hwæt	468 Næfre	627 Iudas
150 Com	305 In	469 Ac	632 Hu
	306 Swa	484 In	638 Ic
	308 Inwit-	487 Ðeoden	642 Elene
	313 Gangaþ	492 Stephanus	655 Iudas

662 Him	812 Inwrige	967 In	1104 Leort
667 Iudas	813 Nu	972 In	1109 Ða
669 Him	821 In	976 Ond	1118 In
680 Ingeþanc	822 In	979 Ða	1120 Nu
683 Ic	823 Stephanus	983 Ond	1122 Nu
685 Elene	825 In	986 In	In
691 Heht	827 Ongan	991 In	1125 Ða
693 In	832 In	992 Feorran	1152 In
694 In	He	993 In	1155 Ðinga
699 Ic	833 In	1007 Constan-	1160 Heht
708 Soð	839 þa	tinus	1181 He
713 Hie	841 Inbryrded	1017 Ða	1191 Cuþ
725 Dryhten	845 In	1025 Besetton	1201 Heht
736 In	852 Hwæt	1032 Godcunde	1204 In
740 In	859 Ne	1037 In	1209 Ond
746 In	867 Gesæton	1045 Inbryrded	1217 Ða
750 Halig	876 Heht	1048 In	1223 In
764 In	895 Ingemynde	1050 Siððan	1228 On
765 In	900 Ongan	1054 þæt	1252 Ingemynd
767 In	906 In	1055 In	1258 In
770 In	911 Feala	1058 Cyriacus	1280 Ðonne
772 Gif	920 In	1061 In	1290 In
774 In	921 Ic	1062 þa	1296 In
775 In	930 Ond	1068 Cyriacus	1297 In
778 In	934 Iudas	1073 þu	1299 In
781 In	942 In	1086 Nu	1304 Wuldor-
783 Gedo	943 In	1088 In	1305 In
806 Iudas	952 Elene	1097 Cyriacus	1315 Moton
In	966 In		

XII

TABLE IV

A

ACCENTS IN THE VERCELLI BOOK

*fol. 29*b	*fol. 30*a	131 wíc
An. 2 tír eadige	*An.* 50 hell fúse	*fol. 31*a
15 ígland	51 Á breoton	*An.* 140 mód
32 ágeton	64 á	140 on wód
38 híg	73 á dreogan-	150 bán hring-
42 merme do-	ne	as
nía	*fol. 30*b	165 ísrahelum[1]
42 mán | fulra	*An.* 123 to glád	171 þá

---

[1] There is a distinct stroke over *i*, probably intended as an accent.

*fol. 31*b	*fol. 35*b	721 écan
An. 180 mán fulle	*An.* 485 tír	*fol. 39*a
183 wát	492 áne	*An.* 724 ámearcod
190 mín	492 má	724 ís
199 wát	510 éce	725 híw
202 éce	*fol. 36*a	726 áwriten
203 á	*An.* 532 ár yða	731 séce
212 wác	535 ðé	736 áhleop
214 tíd	*fol. 36*b	741 ongín
*fol. 32*a	*An.* 552 wís	747 éce
An. 222 ge | stígan	561 Áhof	749 sǽ strea-
223 bæð wég	569 wis dóm	mas
232 an rǽd	569 Á	751 gód
233 hige róf	570 dóm ágen-	758 gód
247 sǽ	de	760 gód
249 éce	570 ǽnigne	*fol. 39*b
254 stód	578 Hýge	*An.* 767 mán
258 áne	*fol. 37*a	768 brand
*fol. 32*b	*An.* 587 wín	hata ?[2]
An. 296 á | gifen	589 áfedde	769 fág
298 áras	597 spéon	770 æl fǽle
*fol. 33*a	*fol. 37*b	770 ór cnawe
An. 326 án	*An.* 624 wís	771 mód
327 ánes	628 ágef	772 ge hýgd
339 dóm	634 hran ráde	775 gán
339 áhwette	645 ge wít	778 tó
*fol. 33*b	649 óor	779 hábráháme
An. 355 dóm weor-	*fol. 38*a	782 on fón
ðunga	*An.* 661 sige déma	783 edniwinga
371 glád	663 sínra	785 hæfdón
*fol. 34*a	674 ahóf	786 gewát
An. 381 sǽ flotan	675 wóðe	791 hrá
383 ár geblond	676 Hwǽt	793 isáác
400 árás	678 nú	797 Hwá
*fol. 34*b	680 ór hlytte	*fol. 40*a
An. 416 áhóf	*fol. 38*b	*An.* 805 ge áclód
423 lád	*An.* 694 mán	829 áras
430 fára	703 án	*fol. 40*b
443 ástod	703 éce	*An.* 838 hádor
*fol. 35*a	703 gód	841 stán
An. 445 yð líd	708 ástag	851 ór gete
450 áras	712 ágræfene[1]	853 ár welan
476 lýt	719 ís	865 ábrug | don

[1] With *g* inserted above the line.
[2] Wülker, Bibliothek II, 205, records an accent over *t*, but it is doubtful if there is any accent.

---

[1] The accent over *m*, but meant for *o*?

[1] For *sár*.
[2] There are no accents on fol. 101*b*.
[3] Only part of the accent visible in the MS. (Wülker).
[4] There are no accents on fol. 105*b*.

743 á
753 tú
*fol. 128*b
El. 758 brogden
    mǽl
766 wið sóc
768 fúl
768 fáh
769 þín
770 áweorpan
783 þín
786 tíd
787 bán
788 þín
792 nú
793 úp
799 éce
801 á
802 úp
803 réc
805 ǽ gleaw
*fol. 129*a
Bl. 811 mán weor-
    cum
821 mín
828 ánhydíg
837 á hofun
843 á | hóf
846 ásetton
856 tíd
*fol. 129*b
El. 861 á hafen
867 áhofon
869 tíd
878 áhof
880 hús

884 áhafen
884 hrá
886 ród
886 áræred
888 bú
901 ǽclæca
904 íceð
906 mán frem-
    mende
*fol. 130*a
El. 923 góda
924 fáh
925 þúrh
940 sár
941 mán frea
946 án for lete
954 tír eadig
*fol. 130*b
El. 970 ǽ
975 hálig
981 róm ware-
    na
989 mód
991 gád
1002 hǽl
1011 ród
*fol. 131*a
El. 1037 wíc
1039 wið sóc
1041 ǽ
1054 sacerd hád
1062 ǽ
1063 mód
1065 fét
1071 ácwæð

1074 róde
*fol. 131*b
El. 1075 á hangen
1077 gén
1079 gén
1081 á
1091 gén
1095 glæd mód
1117 án mode
1121 ǽr
1128 ge áclod
1136 lác
*fol. 132*a
El. 1152 wite dóm
1174 dón
1185 gár þræce
1187 ǽ glæce
1189 ge wód
*fol. 132*b
El. 1208 tíd
1217 gén
1223 ród
1225 á weoxe
1236 fród
1236 fús
1242 wis dóm
1242 fáh
1247 á mæt
1249 bán cofan
*fol. 133*a
El. 1268 líf wynne
1311 fýr
*fol. 133*b
El. 1314 fýr
1317 mána

B

ACCENTS IN THE JUNIUS MANUSCRIPT

The total number of accents in the Junius Manuscript is something over three thousand, or in terms of percentage, .622 in proportion to the number of verse lines in the manuscript. This contrasts with only .161 percent in the poetical parts of the Vercelli Book. The accents are relatively most numerous in Genesis B, the percentage being .932 for that section of Genesis, but only .1596 for Genesis A. After Genesis B, the most heavily accented text is Exodus, with .753 percent. The percentage for Daniel is .528, for Christ and Satan it is .438. In Christ and Satan, the percentage of accents in the portion written by the first scribe is 1.081, in that by the second scribe, it is .301, and .450 for the small part written by the third scribe. This uneven distribution of the accents probably bears some relation to the texts which the scribes used for copying. The letter over which accents most commonly appear is *a*, and after this letter, *i*, *o*, *e* and *æ* in order, with relatively few accents over the remaining symbols.

Gollancz suggests[1] that the accent marks of the Junius Manuscript are possibly by several hands. They are certainly very different in form, but these differences scarcely prove that they were made by different persons. In Liber I two forms of accents may be distinguished, a long slanting accent which is found throughout Liber I and not at all in Liber II, and a shorter and less slanting accent, which in Liber I is found only in the first thousand lines of Genesis but which occurs regularly throughout Liber II. The first occurrence of the second, or shorter and more vertical, type of accent is on page 6 of the manuscript, in *hólm* (Gen. 120), and the last occurrence on page 46 of the manuscript, in *éðyl* (Gen. 962). Within these limits accents of this type are very frequent, especially on pages 18 to 23 of the manuscript, where they far outnumber the other accents. For instance, on page 23 of the manuscript, the accents in *fús* (Gen. 443), *lap wende mód* (l. 448), *gódes* (l. 458), *bí* (l. 460), *útan* (l. 461), *ýldo* (l. 464), *gódes* (l. 465), *liðe* (l. 468), *béam* (l. 468), *écnisse* (l. 469), *onbát* (l. 470), *swáre* (l. 472) are of the long, slanting type, while all the other accents on this page are of the shorter and more vertical type. On page 23 of the manuscript there are a number of accents in red ink, as in *dǽdum* (l. 451), *mểnn* (l. 451), where not only the double accent but also the added final *n* is in red, *ófætes* (l. 461), and *wáldend* (l. 462). Only on page 23 are these red accents to be found. These accents in red are all of the shorter type.

It is sometimes impossible to be sure to which of the two types an accent belongs, and consequently no attempt has been made to distinguish the two types in the following list. In the collotype reproduction of the Junius Manuscript by Gollancz, the accents do not always clearly show, and for this reason the following list of accents has been completely based upon the original manuscript.

Page 1	Page 2	75 sár
Gen. 1 V́s	Gen. 44 réce	78 ǽr
ís	Page 4	Page 5
6 ór	Gen. 53 ác	Gen. 84 órleg nið
7 á	mód	93 hú
16 líf frean	58 hís	99 úp roder
19 ác	62 fáum	100 síd
25 á | hwurfon	67 wǽr leas	104 ác

---

[1] *The Cædmon Manuscript*, p. xxiv.

[1] With second d added above the line.
[2] With y written above first e.

awénde¹
hít
hím
259b ón gán
hím
úp
260 síteð
ón
261 hé
né
262 hís
ófermod
263 áhóf
hís
héte spræ |
ce
264 ongéan
265 hís
líc
266 né
hé
hís
267 géonger-
dome
268 þéodne
þúhte
269 máran
270 sé
gód
Page 15
Gen. 272 sé
273 hú
hé
hím
274 híge
276 trýmede
277 góde
278 íc
281 tó
282 íc
283 hím
íc
gód

hé
284 bíg stan-
dað
stríðe
286 ráed
287 fón
289 þís
290 íc
áwiht
291 góde
íc
292 sé
294 áheb | ban
Page 16
Gen. 299 þá
301 hís
302 grám
304 ácwæð
305 ón
306 þá
Page 17
Gen. 313 æfyn
úngemet
314 fýr
éd | neowe
316 fýr
gár
318 hím
321 þé
ǽr
hýldo
322 þá
ǽr
Page 18
Gen. 325 bráde
lígas
éac
récas
326 þégnsci | pe
327 gál
beswác
328 ofer hýgd
329 wíte

330 þá
fýre
bótme
331 hátan
héll
333 líges
fúll
334 fǽr
ongéaton
335 wíta
únrím
338 ofer móda
ǽr
339 héarran
léof
340 dýre
dóle
341 gálscipe
342 mó | de
ýrre
mórðer
ínnan
343 níobedd
345 sátan
hét
swéartan
346 grúndes
347 Sátán
máðelode
349 ǽr
350 hís
forspéon
351 ofer métto
éalra
353 hím
ínnan
354 hís
héortan
hát
hím
356 ís
þés²
úngelic

¹ a added above the line.
² With e altered from æ.

357 ǽr
héan
Page 19
Gen. 358 heofon ríce
mín
360 rómigan
gedón
361 fýre
362 hélle
hátan
heofon ríce
benúmen
363 háfað
geméarcod
364 mé
367 wésan
wýnne
wé
368 wá
lá
hán | da
gewéald
369 áne
tíd
úte
371 ác
íc
ríc | es
374 hér
fýr
375 úfan
áne
377 hát
378 slíð hearda
379 mín
fét
380 hánda
gehǽfte
héldora
381 forwórhte
wíhte
mǽg
382 líoðo ben-
dum

383 héardes
385 íc
387 adáme
Page 21
Gen. 389 Ác
wé
nú
394 bescýrede
395 geméarcod
món
396 hís
ónlicnesse
397 wé
398 ádáme
399 sóme
ándan
400 sínes
401 íc
níotan[1]
402 éades
403 nú
404 wé
405 bebéad
hím
ón
406 á hwet
Page 22
Gen. 409 íc
þǽgne
þéoden
madmas
410 géara
wé
gódan
411 gewéald
415 úp
416 hím
417 feðer hó-
man
419 ádam
éue
422 móton
wélan
ágan

423 wé
heofon rí |
ce
424 ríce
ís
425 ís
mínum
426 heofon
ríce
429 sóna
híe
hím
430 hís
gebódscipe
431a hím
432 súm
433 hú
íc
434 hím
438 lǽte
íc
440 ún wurð
lice
Page 23
Gen. 442 ándsaca
443 fús
frǽtwum
fǽcne
444 þóne
fúll
héarde
gebánd
445 spángum
sprǽca
féla
446 þánon
448 léolc
laþ wende
mód
449 swáng
fýr
twá
féondes
crǽfte

[1] With *i* altered to *e*.

---

[1] The accent is over *r*, but apparently belongs to *ea*.
[2] Second *n* added above the line.
[3] Second *a* altered from *o*.
[4] *e* added above the line.
[5] The accent is over the *h*, and may belong to either *æ* or *i*.

973 ǽr boren
982 ún rǽden
984 agéat
987 arǽred
992 tánas
Page 48
Gen. 994 brád
996 wópe
997 ác
1005 ǽdre
1006 íc
    ór
    fóre
1009 géan
1011 wǽr fæsne
    rínc
1016 ác
1017 hróðra
1019 ár leas
1023 ǽnigre
    áre
1024 woruld
    ríce
    íc
1026 íc
Page 49
Gen. 1027 wéan
    wénum
1028 mán scyld-
    igne
1030 hís
1032 ádemest
    ádrifest
Page 50
Gen. 1037 on drǽdan
    brógan
1039 freo mág-
    um
    fáh
1040 sínum
1043 ón
1044 tírfæst
1045 fréa
1046 grétan
1048 mán scyld-
    igne

1049 sínum
1050 geomor-
    mód
1051 wíc
1055 énos
1060 sweord
    bérende
    héton
1061 wócan
Page 52
Gen. 1068 gewát
1071 aldor gedál
1072 fród
1077 áda
    wǽs
1081 swég
1083 tubál
1085 ǽrest
1089 wíde
1092 un árlic
1097 órd banan
Page 55
Gen. 1106 séth
1107 ðáh
1110 woruldríce
1111 éce
1113 lífes
1115 ásceaf
1118 stríenan
1119 ellenróf
Page 56
Gen. 1132 geícean
1134 énos
1135 sé
1137 gréne
    grǽs
1139 hér
1142 frið | gedál
Page 57
Gen. 1143 hím
1144 énos
1145 sǽd | ber-
    endes
    líce
1146 hé
    hér

1147 ǽr
    hér
1149 ǽrest
1150 éð | le
1156 énose
Page 58
Gen. 1160 malale |
    hél
1161 rím
1162 geícte
1165 éac
    tíd dæge
1166 rúm
    rím
1167 lánd
1168 ma | lale-
    hél
1169 frum |
    gára
1172 tó
    wǽs
1173 hís
1174 íared
1176 malalehél
Page 59
Gen. 1176 hér
1178 gewát
1182 ǽfæst
1183 frum gár
    freo mágū
1185 woruld
    ríce
1186 éac
    sǽl
1188 wǽs
    énoc
1189 hér
    gýt
1192 gewát
1193 niht
    gerímes
Page 60
Gen. 1196 rínce
1199 dóm
1200 wǽs
1206 dóþ

1383 réðe
1385 ár leasra
1387 héa
1388 á hóf
1389 míd
1392 wíde
     rád
1394 fór
     fǽre
1396 hrínon
1400 gedále
1401 áhafen
1402 égor here
Page 70
Gen. 1405 éce
     éd monne
Page 71
Gen. 1409 wócre
1412 wíd land
     ongán
1415 égstream
1417 fór
1419 á hof
1420 rím getæl
1422 héah
1428 rúme
1430 wíde
     bǽron
1435 út
     þá
1438 wǽre
     lét
1440 éac
1442 húse
     út
1443 Nóe
Page 72
Gen. 1444 láde
1445 síd
1446 wǽg þele
1447 ác
     hréaw
1459 ác
1460 Gewát
1461 sécan

1462 wǽg
     sígan
1463 rínce
1464 Ðá
     éft
1465 wíde
1466 rum gál
1471 gewát
     éft
1473 án
1476 þá
1478 áne
1479 ác
1481 ætýwan
Page 73
Gen. 1484 heofon
     ríces
1485 eðel stól
     éft
1488 út
1489 óf
     héan
1490 wǽg þrea
Page 74
Gen. 1497 lác
1498 rǽd fæst
1499 dǽl
     sínum
1507 gódum
     dǽ | dum
1509 ára
1511 tó
     nóe
1512 nú
     tíres
1513 geféan
1514 ge | íceað
1517 ælgréne
1519 un ár | lice
Page 75
Gen. 1523 geféon
1524 ác
1533 ára
1535 íc
1537 égor here
1538 wíd land

1540 scúrj
     bogan
1544 fére
1551 nóes
1555 Nóe
1559 sǽda
Page 76
Gen. 1561 géar torhte
1563 wíne
1565 líce
1577 þá
     cám
1578 nóes
1580 áre
1582 ác
1584 réste
Page 77
Gen. 1587 géoce
     góde
1588 sém
Page 78
Gen. 1588 slǽpe
1589 lámehes
     sóna
1590 chám
1591 áre
1593 sár
1596 chám
1597 fréc | ne
     scódon
1598 þá
     nóe
1599 sínū
     sídan
     ríces
1600 lífes
1603 strýndon
     béorht
1607 á
Page 79
Gen. 1610 tó
     dóme
1614 ún lytel
1617 chús
     chám

¹ First *n* added above the line.

Page 107
Gen. 2341 mód ge-
ðance
2347 fród
2354 éce
2356 gán
2358 Íc
2359 nú
2361 wor | uld
ríce
gebíde
2363 íc
2364 nís
2367 stépan
2368 wǽre
gelǽtan
2371 hǽse
2375 móde
Page 108
Gen. 2377 á
tír
2378 dóm | fæst
2379 woruld
ríce
2380 fǽre
Page 109
Gen. 2383 ác
fród
2385 ón
gelýfde
2386 spéd
2388 ahóf
2389 þá
gód
2391 wórdum
mín | um
2392 fórð
2393 íc
tíd
2396 wíc
worn gehát
2397 mín
2399 ǽdre
ellor fúse
2400 spédum
2401 gástas

2407 ár fæst
hím
ún | lýtel
2408 Íc
gehýre
2410 sprǽce
2412 íc
nú
2413 ebréa
dón
2416 ínwit
Page 110
Gen. 2417 líg
Page 111
Gen. 2419 wíte loccas
2422 gód
2424 ác
tó
2425 stið mód
2426 áras
síne
ǽfen tíd
2429 árones
2431 éagum
arás
2432 togéanes
grétan
2437 árna
únc
2439 bídan
2440 tó
úp
Page 112
Gen. 2444 ón
2445 ést
2446 wísade
ín
2449 gewát
2450 ǽfen scíma
2451 lást
2452 þýstro
2453 sǽs
síd land
2454 únleofe
2455 ácsian

2457 lóth
út
2458 áras
2461 ún scom-
lice
ár | na
gýmden
Page 113
Gen. 2462 árás
rǽd
2463 út
2465 árones
2466 Hér
ún wemme
2467 míne
2470 íc
2471 ǽr
2472 ún gifre
2473 Ón foð
ágon
2474 mí | ne
2475 íc
mót
Page 114
Gen. 2476 gemǽne
2477 ár lease
2479 á | ferige
2483 hér
aldor déma
2485 hándum
2487 síne
þá
2488 ár fæste
2489 ín
2491 for sǽton
Page 115
Gen. 2494 reðe móde
2495 ác
fróme
wǽron
2498 wíte
2499 tó
lóthe
Page 116
Gen. 2502 éac
2503 alǽde

Page 207
Dan. 633 wǽda
639 ríce
cóm
Page 207
Dan. 644 wíte
646 ác
650 becwóm
654 dóm
662 cwóm
664 wíde
670 ríce
Page 209
Dan. 675 awóc
677 ríces
679 caldéas
680 médum
682 lét
blǽd
684 ún rihtum
685 ríce
686 hám sit-
tende
687 ǽr
695 sǽton
698 gerǽdum
703 hét
705 ǽr
Page 210
Dan. 706 genámon
708 blǽd
for brǽcon
717 tó
722 wáge
723 bóc stafas
726 wíte
Page 212
Dan. 733 arǽdan
735 cóm
741 ǽ cræftig
745 ór læg

750 ǽr
ǽ
758 sín
760 wǽre
ána
761 dóm
762 ríces
Page 213
Sat. 1 eorð búen-
dum
2 míht
stréngðo
3 ðá
fóldan
4 gesétte
mónan
5 út
sǽ
6 wólcen¹
7 ybmlyt²
9 sǽ
géond |
wlítan
10 ágen
11 aríman
rǽgnas
scúran
12 énde rím
13 sóðan
míht
14 swá
gást
15 síx
17 Hwá
ís
18 éce
19 dréamas
dúguðe
20 Ádam
cýn
21 órd fru-
man

22 hím³
móde
míhte
swá
25 héo
hélle
hám
26 án
óðrū
átole
scréf
27 héo
bídan
28 Sáran
náles
30 ác
31 níðær
néssas
32 ána
34 út
39 fýrclom-
mum
40 nú
42 wéan
43 héh sélda
44 iú
Page 214
Sat. 45 sóng
47 héh seld
48 wíte
49 bídan
béndum
51 átole
56 héofnes
59 wéndes
ðú
60 wé
61 þín
swá
63 ꝥ
ðín
64 máre

---

¹ *e* added above the line.
² Accent on *b*; intended for *y*?
³ *eo* above *i*.

65 fácnum
71 bláce
73 ǽglecan
74 ánmedlan[1]
76 ágen
77 wítes
  wórn
  ge félde
79 fýre
  dréam
80 índraf
81 iú
82 dréam
83 ðéos
84 hógade
Page 215
Sat. 86 ágan
87 éall
88 hám
89 wéne
90 ðó ne
91 hám
92 tír
94 úpp heo-
  fon[2]
95 ágan
  átola
  hám
97 ǽce
99 wálica
  hám
  wítes
100 Nágan
  ús
101 genípe
  Hǽr[3]
  swǽg[3]

102 gewúnade
  wítes
103 réðe
106 áhte
107 átolan
  éðele
  gebídan
108 déman
109 fágum
  féran
110 hám
113 órd
114 wénan
115 ǽfre
  wílle
  aléfan[4]
117 écne[5]
118 wíta
  wealdén-
  des[6]
119 héan
120 wúldre
  benémed
121 dréam
  ágan
122 úppe
Page 216
Sat. 126 éarfoðo
127 fýr leoma
  stód
128 géond
131 hát
135 þés
136 ínne weard
139 má
141 úppe
144 mót

146 tó
147 þá
149 úngelíce
150 iú
155 fáh
156 wítes
159 fírna
160 út
161 wítū
  wérig
162 gelícost
  út
  þorh dráf[7]
165 dǽg
  dréam
166 þréat
  úp heofen
167 éam
  léas
  écan
  dréames
168 gerǽcan
170 éarum
  scéal
Page 217
Sat. 173 ágan
175 ágan
176 ascéaden
  scíran
177 aléded
178 becwóm
179 fáh
181 écan
184 wéan
  wítu
185 góda
  iú dǽdū

---

[1] *an* added above the line.
[2] Second *þ* added above the line.
[3] *æ* altered to *e* by erasure of *a*.
[4] *y* written above *e*.
[5] *n* added above the line.
[6] First *e* added above the line.
[7] With *u* above *o*.

---

[1] *n* added above the line.
[2] *h* added above the line.

656 heofen |	691 þé	713 wéan
déman	692 géara[2]	lég[3]
662 écan	698 éac	714 láþan
663 ús	wíd	715 hréam[4]
667 ǽr	síd	717 ánd sacan
668 gedéaf	708 ǽr	718 stód
673 éce	*Page 229*	729 lá
683 búende[1]	*Sat.* 712 ǽglęce	nú
689 éce		

---

[1] *ú* added above an erasure.

[2] With *o* above *a*.

[3] *e* altered from *æ*.

[4] *h* added above the line.

BIBLIOGRAPHY

I. Manuscript and Reproductions

1845 QUARTERLY REVIEW. [Review of Owen Jones, The Ecclesiastical Architecture of Italy, etc.] *Quarterly Review* LXXV, 334–403. Note on Vercelli and Cardinal Guala, pp. 398–399.

1877 KNÖLL, P. Collation of Elene. *In* Zupitza, Cynewulfs Elene, 1st ed., pp. ix-xi. See under III (d).

1882 WÜLKER, RICHARD P. Ueber das Vercellibuch. *Anglia* V, 451–465.

1888 COOK, ALBERT S. Cardinal Guala and the Vercelli Book. University of California, Library Bulletin, No. 10. Sacramento, 1888.

1889 COOK, ALBERT S. Supplementary Note to "Cardinal Guala and the Vercelli Book." *Modern Language Notes* IV, 424–425.

1889 NAPIER, ARTHUR S. Collation der altenglischen Gedichte im Vercellibuch. *Zeitschrift für deutsches Altertum* XXXIII, 66–73.

1894 WÜLKER, RICHARD P. Codex Vercellensis. Die angelsæchsische Handschrift zu Vercelli in getreuer Nachbildung. Leipzig, 1894.

1902 KRAPP, GEORGE P. The First Transcript of the Vercelli Book. *Modern Language Notes* XVII, 342–344.

1913 FÖRSTER, MAX. Der Vercelli-Codex CXVII nebst Abdruck einiger altenglischen Homilien der Handschrift. *In* Festschrift für Lorenz Morsbach, Halle, 1913, pp. 20–179.

1913 FOERSTER, MASSIMILIANO. Il Codice Vercellese con Omelie e Poesie in Lingua Anglosassone. Roma, 1913.

II. Complete Texts

1836 [THORPE, BENJAMIN.] Appendix B to Mr. Cooper's Report on Rymer's Foedera, pp. 47–138. Printed, London, 1836; published, London, 1869. Based on a copy made by Dr. Maier.

1843, KEMBLE, JOHN M. The Poetry of the Codex Vercellensis,
1846 with an English Translation. Part I, London, 1843; Part II, London, 1846.

1857, GREIN, CHRISTIAN W. M. Bibliothek der angelsächsischen
1858 Poesie. 1. Band, Göttingen, 1857; 2. Band, Göttingen, 1858. The Vercelli poems, vol. 1, pp. 198–204; vol. 2, pp. 7–52, 105–137, 142–147.

1894 WÜLKER, RICHARD P. Bibliothek der angelsächsischen Poesie. 2. Band. Leipzig, 1894. The Vercelli poems, pp. 1–201.

III. EDITIONS OF SEPARATE TEXTS

1. Andreas

1840 GRIMM, JACOB. Andreas und Elene. Cassel, 1840.

1885 BASKERVILL, W. M. Andreas, a Legend of St. Andrew. Boston, 1885 (2d ed., 1891).

1906 KRAPP, GEORGE P. Andreas and the Fates of the Apostles. Two Anglo-Saxon Narrative Poems. Boston, 1906.

2. Fates of the Apostles

1906 KRAPP, GEORGE P. See under 1.

3. Dream of the Rood

1854 BOUTERWEK, KARL W. Cædmon's des Angelsachsen biblische Dichtungen. 1. Theil. Gütersloh, 1854. Text of Dream of the Rood, with a German translation, pp. clxviii-clxxvi.

1866, STEPHENS, GEORGE. The Old-Northern Runic Monuments
1867 of Scandinavia and England. Vol. I. London and Köbenhavn, 1866–67. Text of Dream of the Rood, with an English translation, pp. 423–429.

1873 PACIUS, A. Das heilige Kreuz, angelsächsisches Lied, stabreimend übersetzt und erklärt. Gera, 1873.

1888 KLUGE, FRIEDRICH. Angelsächsisches Lesebuch. Halle, 1883 (3d ed., 1902).

1905 COOK, ALBERT S. The Dream of the Rood. An Old English Poem Attributed to Cynewulf. Oxford, 1905.

1926 CRAIGIE, W. A. See under IV.

4. Elene

1840 GRIMM, JACOB. See under 1.

1877 ZUPITZA, JULIUS. Cynewulfs Elene. Berlin, 1877 (2d ed.,

1883; 3d ed., 1888; 4th ed., by A. Herrmann, 1899). The
text of the fourth edition repeats that of the third.

1889 KENT, CHARLES W. Elene, an Old English Poem. Boston,
1889 (2d ed., 1903). Based on Zupitza's text.

1905 HOLTHAUSEN, FERDINAND. Cynewulfs Elene (Kreuzauf-
findung) mit Einleitung, Glossar, Anmerkungen und der
lateinischen Quelle. Heidelberg, 1905 (2d ed., 1910; 3d ed.,
1914).

1919 COOK, ALBERT S. The Old English Elene, Phoenix, and
Physiologus. New Haven, 1919.

IV. PARTIAL TEXTS

1840 KEMBLE, JOHN M. See under VI.

1847 EBELING, FRIEDRICH W. Angelsæchsisches Lesebuch. Leipzig, 1847. Andreas 1155–1252, Elene 1–98.

1849 KLIPSTEIN, LOUIS F. Analecta Anglo-Saxonica. Vol. II.
New York, 1849. Soul and Body I, 127–166.

1850 ETTMÜLLER, LUDWIG. Engla and Seaxna Scôpas and Bôceras.
Quedlinburg and Leipzig, 1850. Andreas 1067–1606, Elene
1–193, 1236–1621.

1855? MÜLLER, THEODOR. Angelsächsisches Lesebuch. Not published; written about 1855. See Krapp, Andreas and the
Fates of the Apostles, p. lxxiii.

1857 LEO, HEINRICH. See under VI.

1874 HAMMERICH, FREDERIK. See under VI.

1876 SWEET, HENRY. An Anglo-Saxon Reader. Oxford, 1876
(9th ed., revised by C. T. Onions, 1922). Dream of the
Rood 1–94, 131–148 (1st ed., only ll. 1–89).

1880 KÖRNER, KARL. Einleitung in das Studium des Angelsächsischen. 2. Teil. Heilbronn, 1880. Elene 1–275.

1900 COOK, ALBERT S. A First Book in Old English. Boston,
1900. Andreas 235–874a.

1909 WILLIAMS, O. T. Short Extracts from Old English Poetry.
Bangor, 1909. Andreas 122–160, 981–1023a, 1026–1036,
1093–1134, 1219–1278a; Soul and Body I, 15–64, 127–164;
Homiletic Fragment I; Elene 105–147, 219–275, 662–706,
827–892a.

1919 WYATT, ALFRED J. An Anglo-Saxon Reader. Cambridge,
1919. Dream of the Rood 28–89.

1922 SEDGEFIELD, W. J. An Anglo-Saxon Verse Book. Man-
chester, 1922. Elene 1236–1276a.

1926 CRAIGIE, W. A. Specimens of Anglo-Saxon Poetry. Vol. II.
      Edinburgh, 1926. Andreas 1–58, 123*b*–156, 235–314, 359–
      381, 433*b*–457, 573–594, 706–760, 773–810, 818–856, 859–
      891, 981–1019*a*, 1067–1183, 1219–1273, 1296–1310, 1478–
      1546, 1569–1595*a*; Fates of the Apostles 1–87; Dream of the
      Rood entire; Elene 1–147, 212–275, 417–535, 598–684, 716–
      801, 827–893, 967–1042.
1927 TURK, MILTON H. An Anglo-Saxon Reader. New York,
      1927. Elene 56*b*–147, 219*b*–275, 839–893, 967–1032*a*, 1236–
      1321.

V. TRANSLATIONS

1843, KEMBLE, JOHN M. See under II.
1846
1854 BOUTERWEK, KARL W. See under III, 3.
1857 LEO, HEINRICH. See under VI.
1859 GREIN, CHRISTIAN W. M. Dichtungen der Angelsachsen
      stabreimend übersetzt. 2. Band. Göttingen, 1859. The
      Vercelli poems, pp. 1–46, 104–149.
1866, STEPHENS, GEORGE. See under III, 3.
1867
1873 PACIUS, A. See under III, 3.
1874 HAMMERICH, FREDERIK. See under VI.
1882 HICKEY, EMILY H. The Dream of the Rood. *Academy* XXI,
      248–249.
1888 WEYMOUTH, RICHARD F. A Literal Translation of Cyne-
      wulf's Elene. London, 1888.
1889 GARNETT, JAMES M. Elene; Judith; Athelstan, or the Fight
      at Brunanburh; and Byrhtnoth, or the Fight at Maldon.
      Anglo-Saxon Poems. Boston, 1889 (2d ed., 1900, with
      Dream of the Rood added).
1890 BROWN, ANNA R. The Dream of the Holy Rood. *Poet-lore*
      II, 371–374. Dream of the Rood 1–89.
1895 MENZIES, JANE. Cynewulf's Elene, a Metrical Translation
      from Zupitza's Edition. Edinburgh and London, 1895.
1898 STEINECK, H. Altenglische Dichtungen in wortgetreuer
      Übersetzung. Leipzig, 1898. Elene, pp. 103–143.
1899 ROOT, ROBERT K. Andreas: the Legend of St. Andrew,
      translated from the Old English. New York, 1899.
1902 COOK, ALBERT S., AND C. B. TINKER. Select Translations
      from Old English Poetry. Boston, 1902 (2d ed., 1926).

Andreas 235–253, 369–381, 433–457, 857–891, 1522–1546; Dream of the Rood entire; Elene 109*b*–142*a*, 237–255, 1236–1276.

1902 HALL, JOHN LESSLIE. Judith, Phoenix and other Anglo-Saxon Poems. New York, 1902. Andreas, pp. 60–119.

1904 HOLT, LUCIUS H. The Elene of Cynewulf. New York, 1904.

1910 KENNEDY, CHARLES W. The Poems of Cynewulf. London and New York, 1910. Of the Vercelli poems, contains Andreas, Fates of the Apostles, Dream of the Rood, Elene.

1915 OLIVERO, FEDERICO. Traduzioni dalla poesia Anglo-sassone, con introduzione e note. Bari, 1915. Dream of the Rood; Elene 99–147, 219*b*–260, 725–801.

1922 SPAETH, J. DUNCAN. Old English Poetry. Princeton, 1922. Dream of the Rood 1–70, 73*b*–91, 122–156; Elene 1–147, 212–275, 802–812, 827–893, 967–1032*a*.

1927 OLIVERO, FEDERICO. Andreas e i Fati degli Apostoli. Traduzione dall' anglosassone con introduzione e note. Torino, 1927.

1927 GORDON, ROBERT K. Anglo-Saxon Poetry. London and Toronto, 1927. Contains all the Vercelli poems except Homiletic Fragment I.

VI. CRITICAL DISCUSSIONS

1840 KEMBLE, JOHN M. On Anglo-Saxon Runes. *Archaeologia* XXVIII, 327–372. Text of Elene 1256*b*–1271*a*.

1844 KEMBLE, JOHN M. Additional Observations on the Runic Obelisk at Ruthwell; the Poem of the Dream of the Holy Rood, [etc.]. (Letter to Sir Henry Ellis, read November 24, 1842.) *Archaeologia* XXX, 31–46.

1857 LEO, HEINRICH. Quæ de se ipso Cynevulfus (sive Cenevulfus sive Coenevulfus) poeta Anglosaxonicus tradiderit. Halle, 1857. Text of Elene 1237–1321, with German translation.

1860 DIETRICH, FRANZ. Kynewulfi Poetae Aetas, aenigmatum fragmento e codice Lugdunensi edito illustrata. Marburg, 1860.

1865 DIETRICH, FRANZ. Disputatio de cruce Ruthwellensi. Marburg, 1865.

1865 GREIN, CHRISTIAN W. M. Zur Textkritik der angelsächsischen Dichter. *Germania* X, 416–429. The Vercelli poems, pp. 421, 423–425.

1869 RIEGER, MAX. Über Cynevulf. *Zeitschrift für deutsche Philologie* I, 215–226, 313–334. Discussion of the rune passages, pp. 219–226.

1874 HAMMERICH, FREDERIK. Aelteste christliche Epik der Angelsachsen, Deutschen und Nordländer. Ein Beitrag zur Kirchengeschichte. Aus dem Dänischen von Al. Michelsen. Gütersloh, 1874. Text of Dream of the Rood 1–69, with German translation.

1877 KERN, H. Angelsaksische Kleinigheden. *Taalkundige Bijdragen* I, 193–209. Notes on An. 770, El. 531.

1878 WÜLKER, RICHARD P. Ueber den Dichter Cynewulf. *Anglia* I, 483–507.

1878 SIEVERS, EDUARD. [Review of Zupitza, Cynewulfs Elene.] *Anglia* I, 573–581.

1879 FRITZSCHE, ARTHUR. Das angelsächsische Gedicht Andreas und Cynewulf. *Anglia* II, 441–496. Also separately, Halle, 1879.

1879 KÖRNER, KARL. [Review of Zupitza, Cynewulfs Elene.] *Englische Studien* II, 252–262.

1879 TEN BRINK, BERNHARD. [Review of Zupitza, Cynewulfs Elene.] *Anzeiger für deutsches Altertum* V, 53–70.

1880 ZUPITZA, JULIUS. Kleine Bemerkungen. *Anglia* III, 369–372. Textual notes on Andreas 145, 483.

1881 COSIJN, P. J. Anglosaxonica. *Tijdschrift voor Nederlandsche Taal- en Letterkunde* I, 143–150. Textual notes on Elene.

1881 NAPIER, ARTHUR S. Zu Andreas 1182. *Anglia* IV, 411.

1882 SIEVERS, EDUARD. [Review of Körner, Einleitung.] *Göttingische gelehrte Anzeigen*, August 9, 1882, pp. 993–1001.

1881 KLUGE, FRIEDRICH. Anglosaxonica. *Anglia* IV, 105–106. Note on Andreas 1661.

1883 JANSEN, GOTTFRIED. Beiträge zur Synonymik und Poetik der allgemein als ächt anerkannten Dichtungen Cynewulfs. Münster, 1883.

1884 SCHÜRMANN, JOSEPH. Darstellung der Syntax in Cynewulfs Elene. Körting's *Neuphilologische Studien*, No. 4, pp. 287–395. Also separately, Paderborn, 1884.

1884 EBERT, ADOLF. Über das angelsächsische Gedicht: Der Traum vom heiligen Kreuze. Berichte über die Verhandlungen der königlich sächsischen Gesellschaft der Wissenschaften, Philologisch-Historische Classe, XXXVI, 81–93.

1884 HOLTBUER, FRITZ. Der syntaktische Gebrauch des Genitives in Andreas, Guðlac, Phönix, dem heiligen Kreuz und der Höllenfahrt. Halle, 1884.

1884　KLUGE, FRIEDRICH. [Review of Zupitza, Cynewulfs Elene, 2d ed.] *Literaturblatt* V, 138–139.

1884　VARNHAGEN, HERMANN. [Review of Zupitza, Cynewulfs Elene, 2d ed.] *Deutsche Litteraturzeitung* V, 426–427.

1885　SIEVERS, EDUARD. Zur Rhythmik des germanischen Alliterationsverses. II. *Beiträge* X, 451–545. Textual notes on the Vercelli poems, pp. 516–518.

1885　RAMHORST, FRIEDRICH. Das altenglische Gedicht vom heiligen Andreas und der Dichter Cynewulf. Berlin, 1885.

1885　RÖSSGER, RICHARD. Über den syntaktischen Gebrauch des Genitivs in Cynewulfs Crist, Elene und Juliana. *Anglia* VIII, 338–370. Also separately, Halle, 1885.

1886　ZUPITZA, JULIUS. Zur Frage nach der Quelle von Cynewulfs Andreas. *Zeitschrift für deutsches Altertum* XXX, 175–185.

1886　GLÖDE, OTTO. Untersuchungen über die Quelle von Cynewulf's Elene. *Anglia* IX, 271–318. Also separately, Rostock, 1885, in briefer form but with introduction on the history of the Cross.

1886　SARRAZIN, GREGOR. Beowulf und Kynewulf. *Anglia* IX, 515–550.

1887　SIEVERS, EDUARD. Zur Rhythmik des germanischen Alliterationsverses. III. *Beiträge* XII, 454–482. Textual notes on the Vercelli poems, p. 478.

1887　BASKERVILL, W. M. [Review of Wülker, Bibliothek, 2. Band.] *American Journal of Philology* VIII, 95–97.

1887　FRUCHT, PHILIPP. Metrisches und Sprachliches zu Cynewulfs Elene, Juliana und Crist auf Grund der von Sievers Beitr. X 209–314. 451–545 und von Luick Beitr. XI 470–492 veröffentlichten Aufsätze. Greifswald, 1887.

1887　KENT, CHARLES W. Teutonic Antiquities in Andreas and Elene. Halle, 1887.

1887　BRIGHT, JAMES W. Notes on the Andreas. *Modern Language Notes* II, 160–164.

1887　BASKERVILL, W. M. Other Notes on the Andreas. *Modern Language Notes* II, 302–304.

1887　BRIGHT, JAMES W. Prof. Baskervill's Notes. *Modern Language Notes* II, 304–306.

1888　NAPIER, ARTHUR S. The Old English Poem The Fates of the Apostles. *Academy* XXXIV, 153.

1888 WÜLKER, RICHARD P. Die Bedeutung einer neuen Entdeck-
      ung für die angelsächsische Literaturgeschichte. Berichte
      über die Verhandlungen der königlich sächsischen Gesell-
      schaft der Wissenschaften, Philologisch-Historische Classe,
      XL, 209–218. With a facsimile of fol. 54a.

1888 CREMER, MATTHIAS. Metrische und sprachliche Unter-
      suchung der altenglischen Gedichte Andreas, Guðlac,
      Phoenix (Elene, Juliana, Crist). Ein Beitrag zur Cyne-
      wulffrage. Bonn, 1888.

1888 PROLLIUS, MAX. Ueber den syntactischen Gebrauch des
      Conjunctivs in den Cynewulfschen Dichtungen Elene,
      Juliana und Crist. Marburg, 1888.

1888 LEIDING, HERMANN. Die Sprache der Cynewulfschen Dich-
      tungen Crist, Juliana und Elene. Marburg, 1888.

1889 BRENNER, OSCAR. [Review of Zupitza, Cynewulfs Elene,
      3d ed.] Englische Studien XIII, 480–482.

1889 REUSSNER, H. ADOLF. Untersuchungen über die Syntax in
      dem angelsächsischen Gedichte vom heiligen Andreas.
      Halle, 1889.

1889 COOK, ALBERT S. The Affinities of the Fata Apostolorum.
      Modern Language Notes IV, 7–15.

1889 NAPIER, ARTHUR S. Odds and Ends. Modern Language
      Notes IV, 274–280. Note on An. 254–255.

1889 SARRAZIN, GREGOR. Die Fata Apostolorum und der Dichter
      Kynewulf. Anglia XII, 375–387.

1889 WÜLKER, RICHARD P. Zu Anglia XII, 375ff. Anglia XII,
      464.

1890 HINZE, WILHELM. Zum altenglischen Gedicht Andreas.
      Erster Teil. Berlin, 1890.

1890 BAUER, HERMANN. Ueber die Sprache und Mundart der
      altenglischen Dichtungen Andreas, Guðlac, Phönix, hl.
      Kreuz und Höllenfahrt Christi. Marburg, 1890.

1890 COSIJN, P. J. Cynewulf's Runenverzen. Verslagen en
      Mededeelingen der koninklijke Akademie van Wetenschap-
      pen. Afdeeling Letterkunde. 3. Reeks, 7. Deel, pp. 54–
      64. Interpretation of the rune passages.

1891 SIEVERS, EDUARD. Zu Cynewulf. Anglia XIII, 1–25. Dis-
      cussion of the rune passages.

1891 HOLTHAUSEN, FERDINAND. Zu alt- und mittelenglischen
      Dichtungen. Anglia XIII, 357–362. Textual notes on
      Andreas 489, 1090, Elene 1277.

1891 HOLTHAUSEN, FERDINAND. Zur Textkritik altenglischer Dichtungen. *Beiträge* XVI, 549–552. Textual notes on Andreas.

1892 MATHER, FRANK J. The Cynewulf Question from a Metrical Point of View. *Modern Language Notes* VII, 193–213.

1892 COSIJN, P. J. Aanteekeningen op den Beowulf. Leiden, 1892. Textual notes on Elene, p. 32.

1892 GOLLANCZ, ISRAEL. Cynewulf's Christ. An Eighth Century English Epic. London, 1892. Excursus on the rune passages, pp. 173–184.

1892 TWEEDIE, W. M. Kent's Cynewulf's Elene. *Modern Language Notes* VII, 123–124. Note on Elene 348–349.

1893 COOK, ALBERT S. The Date of the Old English Elene. *Anglia* XV, 9–20.

1893 WACK, G. Artikel und Demonstrativpronomen in Andreas und Elene. *Anglia* XV, 209–220.

1894 TAUBERT, EUGEN M. Der Syntactische Gebrauch der Präpositionen in dem angelsächsischen Gedichte vom heiligen Andreas. (Ein Beitrag zur angelsächsischen Grammatik.) Leipzig, 1894.

1895 TRAUTMANN, MORITZ. Der Andreas doch von Cynewulf. *Anglia*, Beiblatt VI, 17–22.

1895 TRAUTMANN, MORITZ. Zu Cynewulfs Andreas. *Anglia*, Beiblatt VI, 22–23. Addenda to the preceding.

1895 SARRAZIN, GREGOR. Noch einmal Kynewulfs Andreas. *Anglia*, Beiblatt VI, 205–209.

1895 SWAEN, A. E. H. Notes on Cynewulf's Elene. *Anglia* XVII, 123–124.

1896 PRICE, M. B. Teutonic Antiquities in the Generally Acknowledged Cynewulfian Poetry. Leipzig, 1896.

1896 COSIJN, P. J. Anglosaxonica. III. *Beiträge* XXI, 8–26. Textual notes on Andreas, pp. 8–21.

1896 COSIJN, P. J. Zu Andreas 575. *Beiträge* XXI, 252.

1896 BLOUNT, ALMA. The Phonetic and Grammatical Peculiarities of the Old English Poem Andreas. Presented to the Faculty of the Cornell University for the degree of Doctor of Philosophy. June, 1896. (In Manuscript.)

1897 TRAUTMANN, MORITZ. Wer hat die Schicksale der Apostel zuerst für den Schluss des Andreas erklärt? *Anglia*, Beiblatt VII, 372–373.

1898 BRANDL, ALOIS. Zu Cynewulfs Fata Apostolorum. *Archiv* C, 330–334.

1898 TRAUTMANN, MORITZ. Kynewulf der Bischof und Dichter. (Bonner Beiträge zur Anglistik, Heft I.) Bonn, 1898. Discussion of the rune passages, pp. 43–70.

1898 WÜLKER, RICHARD P. [Review of Trautmann, Kynewulf der Bischof und Dichter.] *Anglia*, Beiblatt IX, 161–166.

1899 BUTTENWIESER, ELLEN C. Studien über die Verfasserschaft des Andreas. Heidelberg, 1899.

1899 EMERSON, OLIVER F. The Legend of Joseph's Bones in Old and Middle English. *Modern Language Notes* XIV, 331–334. Note on Elene 787.

1899 TRAUTMANN, MORITZ. Zu Cynewulfs Runenstellen. *Bonner Beiträge* II, 118–120. Addenda to the discussion of the rune passages in his Kynewulf der Bischof und Dichter.

1899 SIMONS, RICHARD. Cynewulfs Wortschatz. (Bonner Beiträge, Heft III.) Bonn, 1899.

1899 BINZ, G. [Review of Trautmann, Kynewulf der Bischof und Dichter.] *Englische Studien* XXVI, 388–393.

1900 SARRAZIN, GREGOR. [Review of Trautmann, Kynewulf der Bischof und Dichter.] *Zeitschrift für deutsche Philologie* XXXII, 547–549.

1901 BOURAUEL, JOHANNES. Zur Quellen- und Verfasserfrage von Andreas Crist und Fata. *Bonner Beiträge* XI, 65–132.

1901 HOLTHAUSEN, FERDINAND. Zu alt- u. mittelenglischen Dichtungen. XIV. *Anglia* XXIII, 516. Notes on Elene 377–378, 533–535.

1901 HOLTHAUSEN, FERDINAND. Zur Quelle der altenglischen Fata Apostolorum. *Archiv* CVI, 343–345.

1901 SKEAT, W. W. Andreas and Fata Apostolorum. *In* An English Miscellany, pp. 408–420. Oxford, 1901.

1902 HOLTHAUSEN, FERDINAND. Zu alt- u. mittelenglischen Denkmälern. XVI. *Anglia* XXV, 386–392. Note on Elene 30f.

1902 STRUNK, W. Notes on Cynewulf. *Modern Language Notes* XVII, 371–373. Note on Elene 581.

1902 BARNOUW, A. J. Die Schicksale der Apostel doch ein unabhängiges Gedicht. *Archiv* CVIII, 371–375.

1903 BROWN, CARLETON F. Cynewulf and Alcuin. *Publications of the Modern Language Association* XVIII, 308–334. Note on Elene 1277–1321.

1904 KRAPP, GEORGE P. Scurheard, Beowulf 1033, Andreas 1133. *Modern Language Notes* XIX, 234.

1904 KLAEBER, FR. Emendations in Old English Poems. *Modern Philology* II, 141–146. Note on Fates of the Apostles 47.

1904 HOLTHAUSEN, FERDINAND. Zu Cynewulfs Elene v. 140. *Anglia*, Beiblatt XV, 73–74.

1904 KLAEBER, FR. Zu altenglischen Dichtungen. *Archiv* CXIII 146–149. Notes on Soul and Body 5, Elene 140–141, 918–919.

1905 HOLTHAUSEN, FERDINAND. Die Quelle von Cynewulfs Elene. *Zeitschrift für deutsche Philologie* XXXVII, 1–19.

1905 SCHWARZ, FRANZ. Cynewulfs Anteil am Christ. Eine metrische Untersuchung. Königsberg, 1905.

1905 KRAPP, GEORGE P. Notes on the Andreas. *Modern Philology* II, 403–410.

1905 BRANDL, ALOIS. Zum ags. Gedichte Traumgesicht vom Kreuze Christi. Sitzungsberichte der königlich preussischen Akademie der Wissenschaften, 1905, pp. 716–723.

1906 KLAEBER, FR. [Review of Cook, Dream of the Rood.] *Anglia*, Beiblatt XVII, 97–102.

1906 HOLTHAUSEN, FERDINAND. Zur altenglischen Literatur. II. *Anglia*, Beiblatt XVII, 176–178.

1906 IMELMANN, RUDOLF. [Review of Holthausen, Cynewulfs Elene.] *Anglia*, Beiblatt XVII, 225–226.

1906 KLAEBER, FR. Notizen zu Cynewulfs Elene. *Anglia* XXIX, 271–272.

1906 HERZFELD, GEORG. [Review of Cook, Dream of the Rood.] *Archiv* CXVII, 187–189.

1907 HOLTHAUSEN, FERDINAND. Zur Textkritik altenglischer Dichtungen. *Englische Studien* XXXVII, 198–211.

1907 GRATTAN, J. H. G. [Review of Krapp, Andreas and the Fates of the Apostles.] *Modern Language Review* II, 175–176.

1907 COOK, ALBERT S. Dream of the Rood 54. *Modern Language Notes* XXII, 207.

1907 HOLTHAUSEN, FERDINAND. Zur altenglischen Literatur. III. *Anglia*, Beiblatt XVIII, 77–78. Note on Elene 531–535.

1907 HOLTHAUSEN, FERDINAND. Zur altenglischen Literatur. IV. *Anglia*, Beiblatt XVIII, 201–208. Notes on Elene 532, 1164, 1277.

1907 KLAEBER, FR. Cynewulf's Elene 1262f. *Journal of English and Germanic Philology* VI, 197.

1907 TRAUTMANN, MORITZ. Berichtigungen, Erklärungen und Vermutungen zu Cynewulfs Werken. *Bonner Beiträge* XXIII, 85–146. Notes on the rune passages, pp. 137–139, 143–146.

1907 SARRAZIN, GREGOR. Zur Chronologie und Verfasserfrage angelsächsischer Dichtungen. *Englische Studien* XXXVIII, 145–195. "Kynewulf," pp. 145–158; "Andreas," pp. 158–170.

1907 BROWN, CARLETON F. The Autobiographical Element in the Cynewulfian Rune Passages. *Englische Studien* XXXVIII, 196–233. Interpretation of the Elene rune passage, pp. 203–219.

1908 BROWN, CARLETON F. Irish-Latin Influence in Cynewulfian Texts. *Englische Studien* XL, 1–29.

1908 VON DER WARTH, JOHANN J. Metrisch-sprachliches und Textkritisches zu Cynewulfs Werken. Halle, 1908.

1908 JANSEN, KARL. Die Cynewulf-Forschung von ihren Anfängen bis zur Gegenwart. (Bonner Beiträge, Heft XXIV.) Bonn, 1908.

1908 KLAEBER, FR. Jottings on the Andreas. *Archiv* CXX, 153–156.

1910 KOPAS, WILHELM. Die Grundzüge der Satzverknüpfung in Cynewulfs Schriften. Breslau, 1910.

1910 HOLTHAUSEN, FERDINAND. Zur altenglischen Literatur. XI. *Anglia*, Beiblatt XXI, 174–176. Textual notes on Fates of the Apostles and Elene.

1910 HOLTHAUSEN, FERDINAND. Zur Quelle von Cynewulfs Elene. *Archiv* CXXV, 83–88.

1910 RICHTER, CARL. Chronologische Studien zur angelsächsischen Literatur auf Grund sprachlich-metrischer Kriterien. Halle, 1910. The Vercelli poems, pp. 37–43, 47–48, 65.

1910 SCHMITZ, THEODOR. Die Sechstakter in der altenglischen Dichtung. *Anglia* XXXIII, 1–76, 172–218. Textual notes on the Vercelli poems, pp. 5–7, 24–26, 58–63.

1911 SCHMITZ, THEODOR. Die Cynewulf-Forschung 1908 und 1909. *Anglia*, Beiblatt XXII, 337–341. Addenda to Jansen, Die Cynewulf-Forschung.

1912 KOCK, ERNST A. [Review of Holthausen, Cynewulfs Elene, 2d ed.] *Englische Studien* XLIV, 392–395.

1912 TUPPER, FREDERICK, JR. The Cynewulfian Runes of the Religious Poems. *Modern Language Notes* XXVII, 131–137.

1913 SARRAZIN, GREGOR. Von Kädmon bis Kynewulf. Eine litterarhistorische Studie. Berlin, 1913.

1913 TRAPP, WALTER. Zum Versbau Cynewulfs. Bonn, 1913. Textual notes, pp. 44–55.

1915 WUTH, ALFRED. Aktionsarten der Verba bei Cynewulf. Weida i. Thür., 1915.

1916 MONROE, B. S. Notes on the Anglo-Saxon Andreas. *Modern Language Notes* XXXI, 374–377.

1917 KERN, J. H. Altenglische Varia. *Englische Studien* LI, 1–15. Textual notes on Elene.

1917 HOLTHAUSEN, FERDINAND. Zu altenglischen Denkmälern. *Englische Studien* LI, 180–188. Textual notes on Elene.

1917 PERKINS, RUTH. On the Sources of the Fata Apostolorum. *Modern Language Notes* XXXII, 159–161.

1918 KOCK, ERNST A. Interpretations and Emendations of Early English Texts. IV. *Anglia* XLII, 99–124.

1918 KOCK, ERNST A. Jubilee Jaunts and Jottings. 250 Contributions to the Interpretation and Prosody of Old West Teutonic Alliterative Poetry. *Lunds Universitets Årsskrift*, NF., Avd. 1, Bd. 14, Nr. 26.

1919 COOK, ALBERT S. The Authorship of the OE. Andreas. *Modern Language Notes* XXXIV, 418–419.

1919 KOCK, ERNST A. Interpretations and Emendations of Early English Texts. V. *Anglia* XLIII, 298–312.

1920 HOLTHAUSEN, FERDINAND. Zu altenglischen Dichtungen. *Anglia*, Beiblatt XXXI, 25–32.

1920 KOCK, ERNST A. Interpretations and Emendations of Early English Texts. VI. *Anglia* XLIV, 97–114; VII. *Anglia* XLIV, 245–260.

1920 HAMILTON, GEORGE L. The Sources of the Fates of the Apostles and Andreas. *Modern Language Notes* XXXV, 385–395.

1920 HOLTHAUSEN, FERDINAND. Zu altenglischen Dichtungen. *Anglia* XLIV, 346–356.

1920 GRATTAN, J. H. G. [Review of Cook, The Old English Elene, Phoenix, and Physiologus.] *Modern Language Review* XV, 177–178.

1921 KOCK, ERNST A. Interpretations and Emendations of Early English Texts. VIII. *Anglia* XLV, 105–131.

1921 HOLTHAUSEN, FERDINAND. Zu altenglischen Gedichten. *Anglia*, Beiblatt XXXII, 136–138.

1921 KLAEBER, FR. [Review of Cook, The Old English Elene, Phoenix, and Physiologus.] *Englische Studien* LV, 280–285.

1922 EKWALL, EILERT. [Review of Cook, The Old English Elene, Phoenix, and Physiologus.] *Anglia*, Beiblatt XXXIII, 61–67.

1922 KOCK, ERNST A. Interpretations and Emendations of Early English Texts. IX. Anglia XLVI, 63–96; X. Anglia XLVI, 173–190.

1922 KOCK, ERNST A. Plain Points and Puzzles. Sixty Notes on Old English Poetry. *Lunds Universitets Årsskrift*, NF., Avd. 1, Bd. 17, Nr. 7.

1923 KOCK, ERNST A. Interpretations and Emendations of Early English Texts. XI. *Anglia* XLVII, 264–273.

1924 HOLTHAUSEN, FERDINAND. Zu altenglischen Dichtungen. *Anglia*, Beiblatt XXXV, 276–277. Note on El. 17.

1924 COOK, ALBERT S. The Old English Andreas and Bishop Acca of Hexham. Transactions of the Connecticut Academy of Arts and Sciences XXVI, 245–332.

1925 COOK, ALBERT S. Bitter Beer-Drinking. *Modern Language Notes* XL, 285–288.

1925 SIEVERS, EDUARD. Zu Cynewulf. *In* Neusprachliche Studien (*Die Neueren Sprachen*, 6. Beiheft), pp. 60–81.

TEXTS

ANDREAS

Hwæt! We gefrunan on fyrndagum
twelfe under tunglum tireadige hæleð,
þeodnes þegnas. No hira þrym alæg
camprædenne þonne cumbol hneotan,
5 syððan hie gedældon, swa him dryhten sylf,
heofona heahcyning, hlyt getæhte.
  Þæt wæron mære men ofer eorðan,
frome folctogan ond fyrdhwate,
rofe rincas, þonne rond ond hand
10 on herefelda helm ealgodon,
on meotudwange. Wæs hira Matheus sum,
se mid Iudeum ongan godspell ærest
wordum writan wundorcræfte.
  Þam halig god hlyt geteode
15 ut on þæt igland þær ænig þa git
ellþeodigra eðles ne mihte
blædes brucan. Oft him bonena hand
on herefelda hearde gesceode.
  Eal wæs þæt mearcland morðre bewunden,
20 feondes facne, folcstede gumena,
hæleða eðel. Næs þær hlafes wist
werum on þam wonge, ne wæteres drync
to bruconne, ah hie blod ond fel,
fira flæschoman, feorrancumenra,
25 ðegon geond þa þeode. Swelc wæs þeaw hira
þæt hie æghwylcne ellðeodigra
dydan him to mose meteþearfendum,
þara þe þæt ealand utan sohte.
  Swylc wæs þæs folces freoðoleas tacen,
30 unlædra eafoð, þæt hie eagena gesihð,
hettend heorogrimme, heafodgimmas

4 camprædenne] cam rædenne   6 hlyt] lyt   31 hettend] hetted
heafodgimmas] heafod gimme

agetton gealgmode   gara ordum.
Syððan him geblendan   bitere tosomne,
dryas þurh dwolcræft,   drync unheorne,
35 se onwende gewit,   wera ingeþanc,
heortan on hreðre,   (hyge wæs oncyrred),
þæt hie ne murndan   æfter mandreame,
hæleþ heorogrædige,   ac hie hig ond gærs
for meteleaste   meðe gedrehte.
40   þa wæs Matheus   to þære mæran byrig
cumen in þa ceastre.   þær wæs cirm micel
geond Mermedonia,   manfulra hloð,
fordenera gedræg,   syþþan deofles þegnas
geascodon   æðelinges sið.
45 Eodon him þa togenes,   garum gehyrsted,
lungre under linde,   (nalas late wæron),
eorre æscberend,   to þam orlege.
Hie þam halgan þær   handa gebundon
ond fæstnodon   feondes cræfte,
50 hæleð hellfuse,   ond his heafdes segl
abreoton mid billes ecge.   Hwæðre he in breostum þa git
herede in heortan   heofonrices weard,
þeah ðe he atres drync   atulne onfenge.
Eadig ond onmod,   he mid elne forð
55 wyrðode wordum   wuldres aldor,
heofonrices weard,   halgan stefne,
of carcerne.   Him wæs Cristes lof
on fyrhðlocan   fæste bewunden.
   He þa wepende   weregum tearum
60 his sigedryhten   sargan reorde
grette, gumena brego,   geomran stefne,
weoruda wilgeofan,   ond þus wordum cwæð:
"Hu me elþeodige   inwitwrasne
searonet seowað!   A ic symles wæs
65 on wega gehwam   willan þines
georn on mode;   nu ðurh geohða sceal
dæde fremman   swa þa dumban neat.

32 agetton] ageton   33 geblendan] geblondan   36 on] *Not in MS.*
43 þegnas] þegn *at end of page*   64 seowað] seoðað

þu ana canst ealra gehygdo,
meotud mancynnes, mod in hreðre.
70 Gif þin willa sie, wuldres aldor,
þæt me wærlogan wæpna ecgum,
sweordum, aswebban, ic beo sona gearu
to adreoganne þæt ðu, drihten min,
engla eadgifa, eðelleasum,
75 dugeða dædfruma, deman wille.
Forgif me to are, ælmihtig god,
leoht on þissum life, þy læs ic lungre scyle,
ablended in burgum, æfter billhete
þurh hearmcwide heorugrædigra,
80 laðra leodsceaðena, leng þrowian
edwitspræce. Ic to anum þe,
middangeardes weard, mod staþolige,
fæste fyrhðlufan, ond þe, fæder engla,
beorht blædgifa, biddan wille
85 ðæt ðu me ne gescyrige mid scyldhetum,
werigum wrohtsmiðum, on þone wyrrestan,
dugoða demend, deað ofer eorðan.''
Æfter þyssum wordum com wuldres tacen
halig of heofenum, swylce hadre segl
90 to þam carcerne. Þær gecyðed wearð
þæt halig god helpe gefremede,
ða wearð gehyred heofoncyninges stefn
wrætlic under wolcnum, wordhleoðres sweg
mæres þeodnes. He his maguþegne
95 under hearmlocan hælo ond frofre
beadurofum abead beorhtan stefne:
"Ic þe, Matheus, mine sylle
sybbe under swegle. Ne beo ðu on sefan to forht,
ne on mode ne murn. Ic þe mid wunige
100 ond þe alyse of þyssum leoðubendum,
ond ealle þa menigo þe þe mid wuniað
on nearonedum. Þe is neorxnawang,
blæda beorhtost, boldwela fægrost,

---

71 wærlogan] wær lo gan *with second* l *erased after* o   89 segl] sęgl
99 ne murn] ne ne murn   101 þe þe] *Second* þe *above the line*

hama hyhtlicost,   halegum mihtum
105 torht ontyned.   Þær ðu tyres most,
to widan feore   willan brucan.
Geþola þeoda þrea!   Nis seo þrah micel
þæt þe wærlogan   witebendum,
synnige ðurh searocræft,   swencan motan.
110 Ic þe Andreas   ædre onsende
to hleo ond to hroðre   in þas hæðenan burg.
He ðe alyseð   of þyssum leodhete.
Is to þære tide   tælmet hwile
emne mid soðe   seofon ond twentig
115 nihtgerimes,   þæt ðu of nede most,
sorgum geswenced,   sigore gewyrðod,
hweorfan of henðum   in gehyld godes."
    Gewat him þa se halga   helm ælwihta,
engla scyppend,   to þam uplican
120 eðelrice.   He is on riht cyning,
staðolfæst styrend,   in stowa gehwam.
    Ða wæs Matheus   miclum onbryrded
niwan stefne.   Nihthelm toglad,
lungre leorde.   Leoht æfter com,
125 dægredwoma.   Duguð samnade,
hæðne hildfrecan,   heapum þrungon,
(guðsearo gullon,   garas hrysedon),
bolgenmode,   under bordhreoðan.
Woldon cunnian   hwæðer cwice lifdon
130 þa þe on carcerne   clommum fæste
hleoleasan wic   hwile wunedon,
hwylcne hie to æte   ærest mihton
æfter fyrstmearce   feores berædan.
Hæfdon hie on rune   ond on rimcræfte
135 awriten, wælgrædige,   wera endestæf,
hwænne hie to mose   meteþearfendum
on þære werþeode   weorðan sceoldon.
    Cirmdon caldheorte,   (corðor oðrum getang),

---

109 synnige] synne   117 hweorfan] hweorfest   118 Gewat him] ge him
120 eðelrice] eðel rice, *the final* e *followed by* s, *partly erased, and by a comma*
136 hwænne] hwæne

reðe ræsboran. Rihtes ne gimdon,
140 meotudes mildse. Oft hira mod onwod
under dimscuan deofles larum,
þonne hie unlædra eafeðum gelyfdon.
Hie ða gemetton modes glawne,
haligne hæle, under heolstorlocan
145 bidan beadurofne þæs him beorht cyning,
engla ordfruma, unnan wolde.
Ða wæs first agan frumrædenne
þinggemearces butan þrim nihtum,
swa hit wælwulfas awriten hæfdon
150 þæt hie banhringas abrecan þohton,
lungre tolysan lic ond sawle,
ond þonne todælan duguðe ond geogoðe,
werum to wiste ond to wilþege,
fæges flæschoman. Feorh ne bemurndan,
155 grædige guðrincas, hu þæs gastes sið
æfter swyltcwale geseted wurde.
Swa hie symble ymb þritig þing gehedon
nihtgerimes; wæs him neod micel
þæt hie tobrugdon blodigum ceaflum
160 fira flæschoman him to foddorþege.
     Þa wæs gemyndig, se ðe middangeard
gestaðelode strangum mihtum,
hu he in ellþeódigum yrmðum wunode,
belocen leoðubendum, þe oft his lufan adreg
165 for Ebreum ond Israhelum;
swylce he Iudea galdorcræftum
wiðstod stranglice. Þa sio stefn gewearð
gehered of heofenum, þær se halga wer
in Achaia, Andreas, wæs,
170 (leode lærde on lifes weg),
þa him cirebaldum cininga wuldor,
meotud mancynnes, modhord onleac,
weoruda drihten, ond þus wordum cwæð:
     "Ðu scealt feran ond frið lædan,

142 eafeðum] eaueðum   145 þæs] wæs   164 oft] of

175 siðe gesecan,   þær sylfætan
    eard weardigað,   eðel healdaþ
    morðorcræftum.   Swa is þære menigo þeaw
    þæt hie uncuðra   ængum ne willað
    on þam folcstede   feores geunnan
180 syþþan manfulle   on Mermedonia
    onfindaþ feasceaftne.   þær sceall feorhgedal,
    earmlic ylda cwealm,   æfter wyrþan.
    Ðær ic seomian wat   þinne sigebroðor
    mid þam burgwarum   bendum fæstne.
185 Nu bið fore þreo niht   þæt he on þære þeode sceal
    fore hæðenra   handgewinne
    þurh gares gripe   gast onsendan,
    ellorfusne,   butan ðu ær cyme."
       Ædre him Andreas   agef andsware:
190 "Hu mæg ic, dryhten min,   ofer deop gelad
    fore gefremman   on feorne weg
    swa hrædlice,   heofona scyppend,
    wuldres waldend,   swa ðu worde becwist?
    Ðæt mæg engel þin   eað geferan,
195 halig of heofenum   con him holma begang,
    sealte sæstreamas   ond swanrade,
    waroðfaruða gewinn   ond wæterbrogan,
    wegas ofer widland.   Ne synt me winas cuðe,
    eorlas elþeodige,   ne þær æniges wat
200 hæleða gehygdo,   ne me herestræta
    ofer cald wæter   cuðe sindon."
       Him ða ondswarude   ece dryhten:
    "Eala, Andreas,   þæt ðu a woldest
    þæs siðfætes   sæne weorþan!
205 Nis þæt uneaðe   eallwealdan gode
    to gefremmanne   on foldwege,
    ðæt sio ceaster hider   on þas cneorisse
    under swegles gang   aseted wyrðe,
    breogostol breme,   mid þam burgwarum,
210 gif hit worde becwið   wuldres agend.

195 halig] *Not in MS.*   196 sealte] *A letter erased between* s *and* e
sæstreamas] *sæ stearmas*

Ne meaht ðu þæs siðfætes sæne weorðan,
ne on gewitte to wac, gif ðu wel þencest
wið þinne waldend wære gehealdan,
treowe tacen. Beo ðu on tid gearu;
215 ne mæg þæs ærendes ylding wyrðan.
  Ðu scealt þa fore geferan ond þin feorh beran
in gramra gripe, ðær þe guðgewinn
þurh hæðenra hildewoman,
beorna beaducræft, geboden wyrðeð.
220 Scealtu æninga mid ærdæge,
emne to morgene, æt meres ende
ceol gestigan ond on cald wæter
brecan ofer bæðweg. Hafa bletsunge
ofer middangeard mine, þær ðu fere!"
225 Gewat him þa se halga healdend ond wealdend,
upengla fruma, eðel secan,
middangeardes weard, þone mæran ham,
þær soðfæstra sawla moton
æfter lices hryre lifes brucan.
230 Þa wæs ærende æðelum cempan
aboden in burgum, ne wæs him bleað hyge,
ah he wæs anræd ellenweorces,
heard ond higerof, nalas hildlata,
gearo, guðe fram, to godes campe.
235 Gewat him þa on uhtan mid ærdæge
ofer sandhleoðu to sæs faruðe,
þriste on geþance, ond his þegnas mid,
gangan on greote. Garsecg hlynede,
beoton brimstreamas. Se beorn wæs on hyhte,
240 syðþan he on waruðe widfæðme scip
modig gemette. Þa com morgentorht
beacna beorhtost ofer breomo sneowan,
halig of heolstre. Heofoncandel blac
ofer lagoflodas. He ðær lidweardas,
245 þrymlice þry þegnas gemette,
modiglice menn, on merebate

219 wyrðeð] wyrdeð 227 weard] we^{a}rd 245 gemette] *Not in MS.*

sittan siðfrome,   swylce hie ofer sæ comon.
þæt wæs drihten sylf,   dugeða wealdend,
ece ælmihtig,   mid his englum twam.
250 Wæron hie on gescirplan   scipferendum,
eorlas onlice   ealiðendum,
þonne hie on flodes fæðm   ofer feorne weg
on cald wæter   ceolum lacað.
   Hie ða gegrette,   se ðe on greote stod,
255 fus on faroðe,   fægn reordade:
"Hwanon comon ge   ceolum liðan,
macræftige menn,   on mereþissan,
ane ægflotan?   Hwanon eagorstream
ofer yða gewealc   eowic brohte?"
260   Him ða ondswarode   ælmihti god,
swa þæt ne wiste,   se ðe þæs wordes bad,
hwæt se manna wæs   meðelhegendra,
þe he þær on waroðe   wiðþingode:
"We of Marmedonia   mægðe syndon
265 feorran geferede.   Us mid flode bær
on hranrade   heahstefn naca,
snellic sæmearh,   snude bewunden,
oðþæt we þissa leoda   land gesohton,
wære bewrecene,   swa us wind fordraf."
270   Him þa Andreas   eaðmod oncwæð:
"Wolde ic þe biddan,   þeh ic þe beaga lyt,
sincweorðunga,   syllan meahte,
þæt ðu us gebrohte   brante ceole,
hea hornscipe,   ofer hwæles eðel
275 on þære mægðe.   Bið ðe meorð wið god,
þæt ðu us on lade   liðe weorðe."
   Eft him ondswarode   æðelinga helm
of yðlide,   engla scippend:
"Ne magon þær gewunian   widferende,
280 ne þær elþeodige   eardes brucað,
ah in þære ceastre   cwealm þrowiað,
þa ðe feorran þyder   feorh gelædaþ,

---

255 fægn] frægn   268 þissa] þiss   271 biddan] *Inserted above the line*

ond þu wilnast nu   ofer widne mere
þæt ðu on þa fægðe   þine feore spilde."
285   Him þa Andreas   agef ondsware:
"Usic lust hweteð   on þa leodmearce,
mycel modes hiht,   to þære mæran byrig,
þeoden leofesta,   gif ðu us þine wilt
on merefaroðe   miltse gecyðan."
290   Him ondswarode   engla þeoden,
neregend fira,   of nacan stefne:
"We ðe estlice   mid us willað
ferigan freolice   ofer fisces bæð
efne to þam lande   þær þe lust myneð
295 to gesecanne,   syððan ge eowre
gafulrædenne   agifen habbað,
sceattas gescrifene,   swa eow scipweardas,
aras ofer yðbord,   unnan willað."
Him þa ofstlice   Andreas wið,
300 wineþearfende,   wordum mælde:
"Næbbe ic fæted gold   ne feohgestreon,
welan ne wiste   ne wira gespann,
landes ne locenra beaga,   þæt ic þe mæge lust ahwettan,
willan in worulde,   swa ðu worde becwist."
305   Him þa beorna breogo,   þær he on bolcan sæt,
ofer waroða geweorp   wiðþingode:
"Hu gewearð þe þæs,   wine leofesta,
ðæt ðu sæbeorgas   secan woldes,
merestreama gemet,   maðmum bedæled,
310 ofer cald cleofu   ceoles neosan?
Nafast þe to frofre   on faroðstræte
hlafes wiste   ne hlutterne
drync to dugoðe.   Is se drohtað strang
þam þe lagolade   lange cunnaþ."
315   Ða him Andreas   ðurh ondsware,
wis on gewitte,   wordhord onleac:
"Ne gedafenað þe,   nu þe dryhten geaf
welan ond wiste   ond woruldspede,

288 ðu us] ðus   309 bedæled] bedæleð   312 hlutterne] hluₜterne

ðæt ðu ondsware   mid oferhygdum,
320 sece sarcwide.   Selre við æghwam
þæt he eaðmedum   ellorfusne
oncnawe cuðlice,   swa þæt Crist bebead,
þeoden þrymfæst.   We his þegnas synd
gecoren to cempum.   He is cyning on riht,
325 wealdend ond wyrhta   wuldorþrymmes,
an ece god   eallra gesceafta,
swa he ealle befehð   anes cræfte,
hefon ond eorðan,   halgum mihtum,
sigora selost.   He ðæt sylfa cwæð,
330 fæder folca gehwæs,   ond us feran het
geond ginne grund   gasta streonan:
'Farað nu geond ealle   eorðan sceatas
emne swa wide   swa wæter bebugeð,
oððe stedewangas   stræte gelicgaþ.
335 Bodiað æfter burgum   beorhtne geleafan
ofer foldan fæðm.   Ic eow freoðo healde.
Ne ðurfan ge on þa fore   frætwe lædan,
gold ne seolfor.   Ic eow goda gehwæs
on eowerne agenne dom   est ahwette.'
340 Nu ðu seolfa miht   sið userne
gehyran hygeþancol.   Ic sceal hraðe cunnan
hwæt ðu us to duguðum   gedon wille."
       Him þa ondswarode   ece dryhten:
"Gif ge syndon þegnas   þæs þe þrym ahof
345 ofer middangeard,   swa ge me secgaþ,
ond ge geheoldon þæt eow   se halga bead,
þonne ic eow mid gefean   ferian wille
ofer brimstreamas,   swa ge benan sint."
       Þa in ceol stigon   collenfyrhðe,
350 ellenrofe,   æghwylcum wearð
on merefaroðe   mod geblissod.
Ða ofer yða geswing   Andreas ongann
mereliðendum   miltsa biddan
wuldres aldor,   ond þus wordum cwæð:

323 his] is   332 sceatas] c *corrected from* t   342 duguðum] dugudum
343 ece] ęce

355 "Forgife þe dryhten   domweorðunga,
     willan in worulde   ond in wuldre blæd,
     meotud manncynnes,   swa ðu me hafast
     on þyssum siðfæte   sybbe gecyðed!"
         Gesæt him þa se halga   helmwearde neah,
360 æðele be æðelum.   Æfre ic ne hyrde
     þon cymlicor   ceol gehladenne
     heahgestreonum.   Hæleð in sæton,
     þeodnas þrymfulle,   þegnas wlitige.
     Ða reordode   rice þeoden,
365 ece ælmihtig,   heht his engel gan,
     mærne maguþegn,   ond mete syllan,
     frefran feasceafte   ofer flodes wylm,
     þæt hie þe eað mihton   ofer yða geþring
     drohtaþ adreogan.   Þa gedrefed wearð,
370 onhrered hwælmere.   Hornfisc plegode,
     glad geond garsecg,   ond se græga mæw
     wælgifre wand.   Wedercandel swearc,
     windas weoxon,   wægas grundon,
     streamas styredon,   strengas gurron,
375 wædo gewætte.   Wæteregsa stod
     þreata þryðum.   Þegnas wurdon
     acolmode.   Ænig ne wende
     þæt he lifgende   land begete,
     þara þe mid Andreas   on eagorstream
380 ceol gesohte.   Næs him cuð þa gyt
     hwa þam sæflotan   sund wisode.
         Him þa se halga   on holmwege
     ofer argeblond,   Andreas þa git,
     þegn þeodenhold,   þanc gesægde,
385 ricum ræsboran,   þa he gereordod wæs:
         "Ðe þissa swæsenda   soðfæst meotud,
     lifes leohtfruma,   lean forgilde,
     weoruda waldend,   ond þe wist gife,
     heofonlicne hlaf,   swa ðu hyldo wið me
390 ofer firigendstream   freode gecyðdest!

359 helmwearde] holm wearde   367 feasceafte] fea sceaftne

Nu synt geþreade   þegnas mine,
geonge guðrincas.   Garsecg hlymmeð,
geofon geotende.   Grund is onhrered,
deope gedrefed,   duguð is geswenced,
395 modigra mægen   myclum gebysgod."
Him of helman oncwæð   hæleða scyppend:
"Læt nu geferian   flotan userne,
lid to lande   ofer lagufæsten,
ond þonne gebidan   beornas þine,
400 aras on earde,   hwænne ðu eft cyme."
Edre him þa eorlas   agefan ondsware,
þegnas þrohthearde,   þafigan ne woldon
ðæt hie forleton   æt lides stefnan
leofne lareow   ond him land curon:
405 "Hwider hweorfað we   hlafordlease,
geomormode,   gode orfeorme,
synnum wunde,   gif we swicað þe?
We bioð laðe   on landa gehwam,
folcum fracoðe,   þonne fira bearn,
410 ellenrofe,   æht besittaþ,
hwylc hira selost   symle gelæste
hlaforde æt hilde,   þonne hand ond rond
on beaduwange   billum forgrunden
æt niðplegan   nearu þrowedon."
415 Þa reordade   rice þeoden,
wærfæst cining,   word stunde ahof:
"Gif ðu þegn sie   þrymsittendes,
wuldorcyninges,   swa ðu worde becwist,
rece þa gerynu,   hu he reordberend
420 lærde under lyfte.   Lang is þes siðfæt
ofer fealuwne flod;   frefra þine
mæcgas on mode.   Mycel is nu gena
lad ofer lagustream,   land swiðe feorr
to gesecanne.   Sund is geblonden,
425 grund wið greote.   God eaðe mæg
heaðoliðendum   helpe gefremman."

393 geofon] heofon   394 duguð] dugud   396 helman] holme
413 forgrunden] fore grunden   424 Sund] sand

Ongan þa gleawlice   gingran sine,
wuldorspedige weras   wordum trymman:
"Ge þæt gehogodon,   þa ge on holm stigon,
430 þæt ge on fara folc   feorh gelæddon,
ond for dryhtnes lufan   deað þrowodon,
on Ælmyrcna   eðelrice
sawle gesealdon.   Ic þæt sylfa wat,
þæt us gescyldeð   scyppend engla,
435 weoruda dryhten.   Wæteregesa sceal,
geðyd ond geðreatod   þurh þryðcining,
lagu lacende,   liðra wyrðan.
Swa gesælde iu,   þæt we on sæbate
ofer waruðgewinn   wæda cunnedan,
440 faroðridende.   Frecne þuhton
egle ealada.   Eagorstreamas
beoton bordstæðu,   brim oft oncwæð,
yð oðerre.   Hwilum upp astod
of brimes bosme   on bates fæðm
445 egesa ofer yðlid.   Ælmihtig þær,
meotud mancynnes,   on mereþyssan
beorht basnode.   Beornas wurdon
forhte on mode,   friðes wilnedon,
miltsa to mærum.   Þa seo menigo ongan
450 clypian on ceole,   cyning sona aras,
engla eadgifa,   yðum stilde,
wæteres wælmum.   Windas þreade,
sæ sessade,   smylte wurdon
merestreama gemeotu.   Ða ure mod ahloh
455 syððan we gesegon   under swegles gang
windas ond wægas   ond wæterbrogan
forhte gewordne   for frean egesan.
Forþan ic eow to soðe   secgan wille,
þæt næfre forlæteð   lifgende god
460 eorl on eorðan,   gif his ellen deah."
Swa hleoðrode   halig cempa,
ðeawum geþancul.   Þegnas lærde

453 sæ sessade] sæs essade

eadig oreta, eorlas trymede,
oðð æt hie semninga slæp ofereode,
465 meðe be mæste. Mere sweoðerade,
yða ongin eft oncyrde,
hreoh holmþracu. Þa þam halgan wearð
æfter gryrehwile gast geblissod.
    Ongan ða reordigan rædum snottor,
470 wis on gewitte, wordlocan onspeonn:
"Næfre ic sælidan selran mette,
macræftigran, þæs ðe me þynceð,
rowend rofran, rædsnotterran,
wordes wisran. Ic wille þe,
475 eorl unforcuð, anre nu gena
bene biddan, þeah ic þe beaga lyt,
sincweorðunga, syllan mihte,
fætedsinces. Wolde ic freondscipe,
þeoden þrymfæst, þinne, gif ic mehte,
480 begitan godne. Þæs ðu gife hleotest,
haligne hyht on heofonþrymme,
gif ðu lidwerigum larna þinra
este wyrðest. Wolde ic anes to ðe,
cynerof hæleð, cræftes neosan,
485 ðæt ðu me getæhte, nu þe tir cyning
ond miht forgef, manna scyppend,
hu ðu wægflotan wære bestemdon,
sæhengeste, sund wisige.
    Ic wæs on gifeðe iu ond nu þa
490 syxtyne siðum on sæbate,
mere hrerendum mundum freorig,
eagorstreamas, (is ðys ane ma),
swa ic æfre ne geseah ænigne mann,
þryðbearn hæleða, þe gelicne,
495 steoran ofer stæfnan. Streamwelm hwileð,
beateþ brimstæðo. Is þes bat ful scrid,
færeð famigheals, fugole gelicost
glideð on geofone. Ic georne wat

479 þinne] þine   483 este] est   489 þa] *Not in MS.*   491 hrerendum]
r *erased before this word*   494 hæleða] hæleð   496 beateþ] beataþ

þæt ic æfre ne geseah   ofer yðlade
500 on sæleodan   syllicran cræft.
Is þon geliccost   swa he on landsceare
stille stande,   þær hine storm ne mæg,
wind awecgan,   ne wæterflodas
brecan brondstæfne,   hwæðere on brim snoweð
505 snel under segle.   Ðu eart seolfa geong,
wigendra hleo,   nalas wintrum frod,
hafast þe on fyrhðe,   faroðlacende,
eorles ondsware.   Æghwylces canst
worda for worulde   wislic andgit."
510   Him ondswarode   ece dryhten:
"Oft þæt gesæleð,   þæt we on sælade,
scipum under scealcum,   þonne sceor cymeð,
brecað ofer bæðweg,   brimhengestum.
Hwilum us on yðum   earfoðlice
515 gesæleð on sæwe,   þeh we sið nesan,
frecne geferan.   Flodwylm ne mæg
manna ænigne   ofer meotudes est
lungre gelettan;   ah him lifes geweald,
se ðe brimu bindeð,   brune yða
520 ðyð ond þreatað.   He þeodum sceal
racian mid rihte,   se ðe rodor ahof
ond gefæstnode   folmum sinum,
worhte ond wreðede,   wuldras fylde
beorhtne boldwelan,   swa gebledsod wearð
525 engla eðel   þurh his anes miht.
Forþan is gesyne,   soð orgete,
cuð oncnawen,   þæt ðu cyninges eart
þegen geþungen,   þrymsittendes,
forþan þe sona   sæholm oncneow,
530 garsecges begang,   þæt ðu gife hæfdes
haliges gastes.   Hærn eft onwand,
aryða geblond.   Egesa gestilde,
widfæðme wæg.   Wædu swæðorodon
seoðþan hie ongeton   þæt ðe god hæfde

499 yðlade] yð lafe   501 landsceare] lan sceare

535 wære bewunden, se ðe wuldres blæd
  gestaðolade strangum mihtum."
    Þa hleoðrade halgan stefne
  cempa collenferhð, cyning wyrðude,
  wuldres waldend, ond þus wordum cwæð:
540 "Wes ðu gebledsod, brego mancynnes,
  dryhten hælend! A þin dom lyfað!
  Ge neh ge feor is þin nama halig,
  wuldre gewlitegad ofer werþeoda,
  miltsum gemærsod. Nænig manna is
545 under heofonhwealfe, hæleða cynnes,
  ðætte areccan mæg oððe rim wite
  hu ðrymlice, þeoda baldor,
  gasta geocend, þine gife dælest.
  Huru is gesyne, sawla nergend,
550 þæt ðu þissum hysse hold gewurde
  ond hine geongne geofum wyrðodest,
  wis on gewitte ond wordcwidum.
  Ic æt efenealdum æfre ne mette
  on modsefan maran snyttro."
555   Him ða of ceole oncwæð cyninga wuldor,
  frægn fromlice fruma ond ende:
  "Saga, þances gleaw þegn, gif ðu cunne,
  hu ðæt gewurde be werum tweonum,
  þæt ða arleasan inwidþancum,
560 Iudea cynn wið godes bearne
  ahof hearmcwide. Hæleð unsælige
  no ðær gelyfdon in hira liffruman,
  grome gealgmode, þæt he god wære,
  þeah ðe he wundra feala weorodum gecyðde,
565 sweotulra ond gesynra. Synnige ne mihton
  oncnawan þæt cynebearn, se ðe acenned wearð
  to hleo ond to hroðre hæleða cynne,
  eallum eorðwarum. Æþelinge weox
  word ond wisdom, ah he þara wundra a,
570 domagende, dæl nænigne

---

535 bewunden] bewunde   570 nænigne] ænigne

frætre þeode   beforan cyðde."
   Him ða Andreas   agef andsware:
"Hu mihte þæt gewyrðan   in werþeode,
þæt ðu ne gehyrde   hælendes miht,
575 gumena leofost,   hu he his gif cyðde
geond woruld wide,   wealdendes bearn?
Sealde he dumbum gesprec,   deafe gehyrdon,
healtum ond hreofum   hyge blissode,
ða þe limseoce   lange wæron,
580 werige, wanhale,   witum gebundene,
æfter burhstedum   blinde gesegon.
Swa he on grundwæge   gumena cynnes
manige missenlice   men of deaðe
worde awehte.   Swylce he eac wundra feala
585 cynerof cyðde   þurh his cræftes miht.
He gehalgode   for heremægene
win of wætere   ond wendan het,
beornum to blisse,   on þa beteran gecynd.
Swylce he afedde   of fixum twam
590 ond of fif hlafum   fira cynnes
fif ðusendo.   Feðan sæton,
reonigmode,   reste gefegon,
werige æfter waðe,   wiste þegon,
menn on moldan,   swa him gemedost wæs.
595 Nu ðu miht gehyran,   hyse leofesta,
hu us wuldres weard   wordum ond dædum
lufode in life,   ond þurh lare speon
to þam fægeran gefean,   þær freo moton,
eadige mid englum,   eard weardigan,
600 þa ðe æfter deaðe   dryhten secað."
   Ða gen weges weard   wordhord onleac,
beorn ofer bolcan,   beald reordade:
"Miht ðu me gesecgan,   þæt ic soð wite,
hwæðer wealdend þin   wundor on eorðan,
605 þa he gefremede   nalas feam siðum,
folcum to frofre   beforan cyðde,

592 reonigmode] reomig mode

þær bisceopas   ond boceras
ond ealdormenn   æht besæton,
mæðelhægende?   Me þæt þinceð,
610 ðæt hie for æfstum   inwit syredon
þurh deopne gedwolan.   Deofles larum
hæleð hynfuse   hyrdon to georne,
wraðum wærlogan.   Hie seo wyrd beswac,
forleolc ond forlærde.   Nu hie lungre sceolon,
615 werige mid werigum,   wræce þrowian,
biterne bryne   on banan fæðme."
     Him ða Andreas   agef ondsware:
"Secge ic ðe to soðe   ðæt he swiðe oft
beforan fremede   folces ræswum
620 wundor æfter wundre   on wera gesiehðe,
swylce deogollice   dryhten gumena
folcræd fremede,   swa he to friðe hogode."
     Him ondswarode   æðelinga helm:
"Miht ðu, wis hæleð,   wordum gesecgan,
625 maga mode rof,   mægen þa he cyðde,
deormod on digle,   ða mid dryhten oft,
rodera rædend,   rune besæton?"
     "Him þa Andreas   ondsware agef:
"Hwæt frinest ðu me,   frea leofesta,
630 wordum wrætlicum,   ond þe wyrda gehwære
þurh snyttra cræft   soð oncnawest?"
     Ða git him wæges weard   wiðþingode:
"Ne frine ic ðe for tæle   ne ðurh teoncwide
on hranrade,   ac min hige blissað,
635 wynnum wridað,   þurh þine wordlæðe,
æðelum ecne.   Ne eom ic ana ðæt,
ac manna gehwam   mod bið on hyhte,
fyrhð afrefred,   þam þe feor oððe neah
on mode geman   hu se maga fremede,
640 godbearn on grundum.   Gastas hweorfon,
sohton siðfrome   swegles dreamas,
engla eðel   þurh þa æðelan miht."

633 ne] nu   637 gehwam] gehwǣm

Edre him Andreas   agef ondsware:
"Nu ic on þe sylfum   soð oncnawe,
645 wisdomes gewit,   wundorcræfte
sigesped geseald,   (snyttrum bloweð,
beorhtre blisse,   breost innanweard),
nu ic þe sylfum   secgan wille
oor ond ende,   swa ic þæs æðelinges
650 word ond wisdom   on wera gemote
þurh his sylfes muð   symle gehyrde.
Oft gesamnodon   side herigeas,
folc unmæte,   to frean dome,
þær hie hyrcnodon   haliges lare.
655 Ðonne eft gewat   æðelinga helm,
beorht blædgifa,   in bold oðer,
ðær him togenes,   god herigende,
to ðam meðelstede   manige comon,
snottre selerædend.   Symble gefegon,
660 beornas bliðheorte,   burhweardes cyme.
Swa gesælde iu   þæt se sigedema
ferde, frea mihtig.   Næs þær folces ma
on siðfate,   sinra leoda,
nemne ellefne   orettmæcgas,
665 geteled tireadige.   He wæs twelfta sylf.
Þa we becomon   to þam cynestole,
þær getimbred wæs   tempel dryhtnes,
heah ond horngeap,   hæleðum gefrege,
wuldre gewlitegod.   Huscworde ongan
670 þurh inwitðanc   ealdorsacerd
herme hyspan,   hordlocan onspeon,
wroht webbade.   He on gewitte oncneow
þæt we soðfæstes   swaðe folgodon,
læston larcwide.   He lungre ahof
675 woðe wiðerhydig   wean onblonden:
'Hwæt, ge syndon earme   ofer ealle menn!
Wadað widlastas,   weorn geferað
earfoðsiða,   ellþeodiges nu

672 gewitte] ge witte

butan leodrihte   larum hyrað,
680 eadiges orhlytte   æðeling cyðað,
secgað soðlice   þæt mid suna meotudes
drohtigen dæghwæmlice.   Þæt is duguðum cuð
hwanon þam ordfruman   æðelu onwocon.
He wæs afeded   on þysse folcsceare,
685 cildgeong acenned   mid his cneomagum.
Þus syndon haten   hamsittende,
fæder ond modur,   þæs we gefrægen habbað
þurh modgemynd,   Maria ond Ioseph.
Syndon him on æðelum   oðere twegen
690 beornas geborene,   broðorsybbum,
suna Iosephes,   Simon ond Iacob.'
Swa hleoðrodon   hæleða ræswan,
dugoð domgeorne,   dyrnan þohton
meotudes mihte.   Man eft gehwearf,
695 yfel endeleas,   þær hit ær aras.
    Þa se þeoden gewat   þegna heape
fram þam meðelstede   mihtum geswiðed,
dugeða dryhten,   secan digol land.
He þurh wundra feala   on þam westenne
700 cræfta gecyðde   þæt he wæs cyning on riht
ofer middangeard,   mægene geswiðed,
waldend ond wyrhta   wuldorþrymmes,
an ece god   eallra gesceafta.
Swylce he oðerra   unrim cyðde
705 wundorworca   on wera gesyhðe.
    Syþþan eft gewat   oðre siðe
getrume mycle,   þæt he in temple gestod,
wuldres aldor.   Wordhleoðor astag
geond heahræced.   Haliges lare
710 synnige ne swulgon,   þeah he soðra swa feala
tacna gecyðde,   þær hie to segon.
Swylce he wrætlice   wundor agræfene,
anlicnesse   engla sinra
geseh, sigora frea,   on seles wage,

682 drohtigen] drohtịgen   710 he] hie   712 agræfene] a^græfene

715 on twa healfe   torhte gefrætwed,
wlitige geworhte.   He worde cwæð:
'Ðis is anlicnes   engelcynna
þæs bremestan   þe mid þam burgwarum
in þære ceastre is.   Cheruphim et Seraphim
720 þa on swegeldreamum   syndon nemned.
Fore onsyne   ecan dryhtnes
standað stiðferðe,   stefnum herigað,
halgum hleoðrum,   heofoncyninges þrym,
meotudes mundbyrd.   Her amearcod is
725 haligra hiw,   þurh handmægen
awriten on wealle   wuldres þegnas.'
Þa gen worde cwæð   weoruda dryhten,
heofonhalig gast,   fore þam heremægene:
'Nu ic bebeode   beacen ætywan,
730 wundor geweorðan   on wera gemange,
ðæt þeos onlicnes   eorðan sece,
wlitig of wage,   ond word sprece,
secge soðcwidum,   (þy sceolon gelyfan
eorlas on cyððe),   hwæt min æðelo sien.'
735   Ne dorste þa forhylman   hælendes bebod
wundor fore weorodum,   ac of wealle ahleop,
frod fyrngeweorc,   þæt he on foldan stod,
stan fram stane.   Stefn æfter cwom,
hlud þurh heardne,   hleoðor dynede,
740 wordum wemde.   Wrætlic þuhte
stiðhycgendum   stanes ongin.
Septe sacerdas   sweotolum tacnum,
witig werede   ond worde cwæð:
'Ge synd unlæde,   earmra geþohta
745 searowum beswicene,   oððe sel nyton,
mode gemyrde.   Ge mon cigað
godes ece bearn,   þone þe grund ond sund,
heofon ond eorðan   ond hreo wægas,
salte sæstreamas   ond swegl uppe
750 amearcode   mundum sinum.

718 þe] *Not in MS.*   746 Ge mon cigað] ge monetigað   747 þone]
ond þone

þis is se ilca   ealwalda god
ðone on fyrndagum   fæderas cuðon.
He Abrahame   ond Isace
ond Iocobe   gife bryttode,
755 welum weorðode,   wordum sægde
ærest Habrahame   æðeles geþingu,
þæt of his cynne   cenned sceolde
weorðan wuldres god.   Is seo wyrd mid eow
open, orgete,   magan eagum nu
760 geseon sigores god,   swegles agend.'
Æfter þyssum wordum   weorud hlosnode
geond þæt side sel,   (swigodon ealle),
ða ða yldestan   eft ongunnon
secgan synfulle,   (soð ne oncneowan),
765 þæt hit drycræftum   gedon wære,
scingelacum,   þæt se scyna stan
mælde for mannum.   Man wridode
geond beorna breost,   brandhata nið
weoll on gewitte,   weorm blædum fag,
770 attor ælfæle.   þær orcnawe wearð
þurh teoncwide   tweogende mod,
mæcga misgehygd   morðre bewunden.
Ða se þeoden bebead   þryðweorc faran,
stan on stræte   of stedewange,
775 ond forð gan   foldweg tredan,
grene grundas,   godes ærendu
larum lædan   on þa leodmearce
to Channaneum,   cyninges worde
beodan Habrahame   mid his eaforum twæm
780 of eorðscræfe   ærest fremman,
lætan landreste,   leoðo gadrigean,
gaste onfon   ond geogoðhade,
edniwinga   andweard cuman,
frode fyrnweotan,   folce gecyðan,
785 hwylcne hie god mihtum   ongiten hæfdon.
Gewat he þa feran,   swa him frea mihtig,

770 wearð] *Not in MS.*   774 on] *Not in MS.*

scyppend wera,　gescrifen hæfde,
ofer mearcpaðu,　þæt he on Mambre becom
beorhte blican,　swa him bebead meotud,
790 þær þa lichoman　lange þrage,
heahfædera hra,　beheled wæron.
Het þa ofstlice　up astandan
Habraham ond Isaac,　æðeling þriddan
Iacob of greote　to godes geþinge,
795 sneome of slæpe þæm fæstan.　Het hie to þam siðe gyrwan,
faran to frean dome.　Sceoldon hie þam folce gecyðan
hwa æt frumsceafte　furðum teode
eorðan eallgrene　ond upheofon,
hwær se wealdend wære　þe þæt weorc staðolade.
800 Ne dorston þa gelettan　leng owihte
wuldorcyninges word.　Geweotan ða ða witigan þry
modige mearcland tredan.　Forlætan moldern wunigean
open eorðscræfu,　woldon hie ædre gecyðan
frumweorca fæder.　þa þæt folc gewearð
805 egesan geaclod,　þær þa æðelingas
wordum weorðodon　wuldres aldor.
Hie ða ricene het　rices hyrde
to eadwelan　oþre siðe
secan mid sybbe　swegles dreamas,
810 ond þæs to widan feore　willum neotan.
　　　Nu ðu miht gehyran,　hyse leofesta,
hu he wundra worn　wordum cyðde,
swa þeah ne gelyfdon　larum sinum
modblinde menn.　Ic wat manig nu gyt
815 mycel mære spell　ðe se maga fremede,
rodera rædend,　ða ðu aræfnan ne miht,
hreðre behabban,　hygeþances gleaw.''
　　　þus Andreas　ondlangne dæg
herede hleoðorcwidum　haliges lare,
820 oððæt hine semninga　slæp ofereode
on hronrade　heofoncyninge neh.
Ða gelædan het　lifes brytta
ofer yða geþræc　englas sine,
fæðmum ferigean　on fæder wære

825 leofne mid lissum   ofer lagufæsten,
oððæt sæwerige   slæp ofereode.
Þurh lyftgelac   on land becwom
to þære ceastre   þe him cining engla
*   *   *
ða þa aras siðigean,
830 eadige on upweg,   eðles neosan.
Leton þone halgan   be herestræte
swefan on sybbe   under swegles hleo,
bliðne bidan   burhwealle neh,
his niðhetum,   nihtlangne fyrst,
835 oðþæt dryhten forlet   dægcandelle
scire scinan.   Sceadu sweðerodon,
wonn under wolcnum.   Þa com wederes blæst,
hador heofonleoma,   ofer hofu blican.
Onwoc þa wiges heard,   (wang sceawode),
840 fore burggeatum.   Beorgas steape,
hleoðu hlifodon,   ymbe harne stan
tigelfagan trafu,   torras stodon,
windige weallas.   Þa se wisa oncneow
þæt he Marmedonia   mægðe hæfde
845 siðe gesohte,   swa him sylf bebead,
þa he him fore gescraf,   fæder mancynnes.
Geseh he þa on greote   gingran sine,
beornas beadurofe,   biryhte him
swefan on slæpe.   He sona ongann
850 wigend weccean,   ond worde cwæð:
"Ic eow secgan mæg   soð orgete,
þæt us gystrandæge   on geofones stream
ofer arwelan   æðeling ferede.
In þam ceole wæs   cyninga wuldor,
855 waldend werðeode.   Ic his word oncneow,
þeh he his mægwlite   bemiðen hæfde."
Him þa æðelingas   ondsweorodon,
geonge gencwidum,   gastgerynum:
"We ðe, Andreas,   eaðe gecyðað

838 heofonleoma] heofon leⁿma   843 wisa] wis   846 þa] þā = þam
852 gystrandæge] gyrstran dæge   855 werðeode] weorðode

860 sið userne,   þæt ðu sylfa miht
    ongitan gleawlice   gastgehygdum.
    Us sæwerige   slæp ofereode.
    Þa comon earnas   ofer yða wylm
    faran on flyhte,   feðerum hremige,
865 us ofslæpendum   sawle abrugdon,
    mid gefean feredon   flyhte on lyfte,
    brehtmum bliðe,   beorhte ond liðe.
    Lissum lufodon   ond in lofe wunedon,
    þær wæs singal sang   ond swegles gong,
870 wlitig weoroda heap   ond wuldres þreat.
    Utan ymbe æðelne   englas stodon,
    þegnas ymb þeoden,   þusendmælum,
    heredon on hehðo   halgan stefne
    dryhtna dryhten.   Dream wæs on hyhte.
875   We ðær heahfæderas   halige oncneowon
    ond martyra   mægen unlytel,
    sungon sigedryhtne   soðfæstlic lof,
    dugoð domgeorne.   Þær wæs Dauid mid,
    eadig oretta,   Essages sunu,
880 for Crist cumen,   cining Israhela.
    Swylce we gesegon   for suna meotudes,
    æðelum ecne,   eowic standan,
    twelfe getealde,   tireadige hæleð.
    Eow þegnodon   þrymsittende,
885 halige heahenglas.   Ðam bið hæleða well
    þe þara blissa   brucan moton.
    Þær wæs wuldres wynn,   wigendra þrym,
    æðelic onginn,   næs þær ænigum gewinn.
    Þam bið wræcsið witod,   wite geopenad,
890 þe þara gefeana sceal   fremde weorðan,
    hean hwearfian,   þonne heonon gangaþ.''
       Þa wæs modsefa   myclum geblissod
    haliges on hreðre,   syðþan hleoðorcwide
    gingran gehyrdon,   þæt hie god wolde
895 onmunan swa mycles   ofer menn ealle,

864 faran] *Not in MS.*   890 þe] *Preceded by a second* þe *erased in the MS.*
gefeana] *Not in MS.*

ond þæt word gecwæð   wigendra hleo:
   "Nu ic, god dryhten,   ongiten hæbbe
þæt ðu on faroðstræte   feor ne wære,
cyninga wuldur,   þa ic on ceol gestah,
900 ðeh ic on yðfare,   engla þeoden,
gasta geocend,   ongitan ne cuðe.
Weorð me nu milde,   meotud ælmihtig,
bliðe, beorht cyning!   Ic on brimstreame
spræc worda worn,   wat æfter nu
905 hwa me wyrðmyndum   on wudubate
ferede ofer flodas.   Þæt is frofre gast
hæleða cynne.   Þær is help gearu,
milts æt mærum,   manna gehwylcum,
sigorsped geseald,   þam þe seceð to him."
910   Ða him fore eagum   onsyne wearð
æðeling oðywed   in þa ilcan tid,
cining cwicera gehwæs,   þurh cnihtes had.
Þa he worde cwæð,   wuldres aldor:
   "Wes ðu, Andreas, hal,   mid þas willgedryht,
915 ferðgefeonde!   Ic þe friðe healde,
þæt þe ne moton   mangeniðlan,
grame grynsmiðas,   gaste gesceððan."
   Feoll þa to foldan,   frioðo wilnode
wordum wis hæleð,   winedryhten frægn:
920 "Hu geworhte ic þæt,   waldend fira,
synnig wið seolfne,   sawla nergend,
þæt ic þe swa godne   ongitan ne meahte
on wægfære,   þær ic worda gespræc
minra for meotude   ma þonne ic sceolde?"
925   Him andswarode   ealwalda god:
   "No ðu swa swiðe   synne gefremedest
swa ðu in Achaia   ondsæc dydest,
ðæt ðu on feorwegas   feran ne cuðe
ne in þa ceastre   becuman mehte,
930 þing gehegan   þreora nihta
fyrstgemearces,   swa ic þe feran het

907 is] *Above the line in the MS.*   910 wearð] werð
927 Achaia] ach^{a}ia

ofer wega gewinn. Wast nu þe gearwor
þæt ic eaðe mæg anra gehwylcne
fremman ond fyrþran freonda minra
935 on landa gehwylc, þær me leofost bið.
Aris nu hrædlice, ræd ædre ongit,
beorn gebledsod, swa þe beorht fæder
geweorðað wuldorgifum to widan aldre,
cræfte ond mihte. Ðu in þa ceastre gong
940 under burglocan, þær þin broðor is.
Wat ic Matheus þurh mænra hand
hrinen heorudolgum, heafodmagan
searonettum beseted. Þu hine secan scealt,
leofne alysan of laðra hete,
945 ond eal þæt mancynn þe him mid wunige,
elþeodigra inwitwrasnum,
bealuwe gebundene. Him sceal bot hraðe
weorþan in worulde ond in wuldre lean,
swa ic him sylfum ær secgende wæs.
950   Nu ðu, Andreas, scealt edre geneðan
in gramra gripe. Is þe guð weotod,
heardum heoruswengum scel þin hra dæled
wundum weorðan, wættre geliccost
faran flode blod. Hie þin feorh ne magon
955 deaðe gedælan, þeh ðu drype ðolie,
synnigra slege. Ðu þæt sar aber;
ne læt þe ahweorfan hæðenra þrym,
grim gargewinn, þæt ðu gode swice,
dryhtne þinum. Wes a domes georn;
960 læt ðe on gemyndum hu þæt manegum wearð
fira gefrege geond feala landa,
þæt me bysmredon bennum fæstne
weras wansælige. Wordum tyrgdon,
slogon ond swungon, synnige ne mihton
965 þurh sarcwide soð gecyðan.
Þa ic mid Iudeum gealgan þehte,
(rod wæs aræred), þær rinca sum

942 hrinen] hrinan   heafodmagan] heafod magū   943 searonettum]
searo mettū   952 dæled] dælan

of minre sidan   swat ut forlet,
dreor to foldan.   Ic adreah feala
970 yrmþa ofer eorðan.   Wolde ic eow on ðon
þurh bliðne hige   bysne onstellan,
swa on ellþeode   ywed wyrðeð.
Manige syndon   in þysse mæran byrig
þara þe ðu gehweorfest   to heofonleohte
975 þurh minne naman,   þeah hie morðres feala
in fyrndagum   gefremed habban."
    Gewat him þa se halga   heofonas secan,
eallra cyninga cining,   þone clænan ham,
eaðmedum upp,   þær is ar gelang
980 fira gehwylcum,   þam þe hie findan cann.
    Ða wæs gemyndig   modgeþyldig,
beorn beaduwe heard,   eode in burh hraðe,
anræd oretta,   elne gefyrðred,
maga mode rof,   meotude getreowe,
985 stop on stræte,   (stig wisode),
swa him nænig gumena   ongitan ne mihte,
synfulra geseon.   Hæfde sigora weard
on þam wangstede   wære betolden
leofne leodfruman   mid lofe sinum.
990 Hæfde þa se æðeling   in geþrungen,
Cristes cempa,   carcerne neh.
Geseh he hæðenra   hloð ætgædere,
fore hlindura   hyrdas standan,
seofone ætsomne.   Ealle swylt fornam,
995 druron domlease.   Deaðræs forfeng
hæleð heorodreorige.   Ða se halga gebæd
bilwytne fæder,   breostgehygdum
herede on hehðo   heofoncyninges þrym,
godes dryhtendom.   Duru sona onarn
1000 þurh handhrine   haliges gastes,
ond þær in eode,   elnes gemyndig,
hæle hildedeor.   Hæðene swæfon,
dreore druncne,   deaðwang rudon.

996 heorodreorige] heoro deorig   998 þrym] *Not in MS.*   999 godes]
god   1000 handhrine] han hrine

Geseh he Matheus in þam morðorcofan,
1005 hæleð higerofne under heolstorlocan,
secgan dryhtne lof, domweorðinga
engla ðeodne. He ðær ana sæt
geohðum geomor in þam gnornhofe.
Geseh þa under swegle swæsne geferan,
1010 halig haligne. Hyht wæs geniwad.
Aras þa togenes, gode þancade
þæs ðe hie onsunde æfre moston
geseon under sunnan. Syb wæs gemæne
bam þam gebroðrum, blis edniwe.
1015 Æghwæðer oðerne earme beþehte,
cyston hie ond clypton. Criste wæron begen
leofe on mode. Hie leoht ymbscan
halig ond heofontorht. Hreðor innan wæs
wynnum awelled. þa worde ongan
1020 ærest Andreas æðelne geferan
on clustorcleofan mid cwide sinum
gretan godfyrhtne, sæde him guðgeðingu,
feohtan fara monna: "Nu is þis folc on luste,
hæleð hyder on
                    *   *   *
1025   gewyrht eardes neosan."
Æfter þyssum wordum wuldres þegnas,
begen þa gebroðor, to gebede hyldon,
sendon hira bene fore bearn godes.
Swylce se halga in þam hearmlocan
1030 his god grette ond him geoce bæd,
hælend helpe, ær þan hra crunge
fore hæðenra hildeþrymme,
ond þa gelædde of leoðobendum
fram þam fæstenne on frið dryhtnes
1035 tu ond hundteontig geteled rime,
swylce feowertig,
generede fram niðe, (þær he nænigne forlet
under burglocan bennum fæstne),

1023 þis] þin   1030 grette] grete   1037 nænigne] nænige

ond þær wifa þa gyt,   weorodes to eacan,
1040 anes wana þe fiftig
forhte gefreoðode.   Fægen wæron siðes,
lungre leordan,   nalas leng bidon
in þam gnornhofe   guðgeþingo.
  Gewat þa Matheus   menigo lædan
1045 on gehyld godes,   swa him se halga bebead.
Weorod on wilsið   wolcnum beþehte,
þe læs him scyldhatan   scyððan comon
mid earhfare,   ealdgeniðlan.
Þær þa modigan mid him   mæðel gehedan,
1050 treowgeþoftan,   ær hie on tu hweorfan.
Ægðer þara eorla   oðrum trymede
heofonrices hyht,   helle witu
wordum werede.   Swa ða wigend mid him,
hæleð higerofe,   halgum stefnum
1055 cempan coste   cyning weorðadon,
wyrda waldend,   þæs wuldres ne bið
æfre mid eldum   ende befangen.
  Gewat him þa Andreas   inn on ceastre
glædmod gangan,   to þæs ðe he gramra gemot,
1060 fara folcmægen,   gefrægen hæfde,
oððæt he gemette   be mearcpaðe
standan stræte neah   stapul ærenne.
Gesæt him þa be healfe,   hæfde hluttre lufan,
ece upgemynd   engla blisse;
1065 þanon basnode   under burhlocan
hwæt him guðweorca   gifeðe wurde.
  Þa gesamnedon   side herigeas,
folces frumgaras.   To þam fæstenne
wærleasra werod   wæpnum comon,
1070 hæðne hildfrecan,   to þæs þa hæftas ær
under hlinscuwan   hearm þrowedon.
Wendan ond woldon   wiðerhycgende
þæt hie on elþeodigum   æt geworhton,
weotude wiste.   Him seo wen gelah,

1039 ond] on   1064 ece] Eçce   1066 gifeðe] *Two letters erased before
this word*

1075 syððan mid corðre   carcernes duru
eorre æscberend   opene fundon,
onhliden hamera geweorc,   hyrdas deade.
Hie þa unhyðige   eft gecyrdon,
luste belorene,   laðspell beran,
1080 sægdon þam folce   þæt ðær feorrcundra,
ellreordigra,   ænigne to lafe
in carcerne   cwicne ne gemetton,
ah þær heorodreorige   hyrdas lagan,
gæsne on greote,   gaste berofene,
1085 fægra flæschaman.   þa wearð forht manig
for þam færspelle   folces ræswa,
hean, hygegeomor,   hungres on wenum,
blates beodgastes.   Nyston beteran ræd,
þonne hie þa belidenan   him to lifnere
1090 deade gefeormedon.   Duruþegnum wearð
in ane tid   eallum ætsomne
þurh heard gelac   hildbedd styred.
        Ða ic lungre gefrægn   leode tosomne
burgwaru bannan.   Beornas comon,
1095 wiggendra þreat,   wicgum gengan,
on mearum modige,   mæðelhegende,
æscum dealle.   þa wæs eall geador
to þam þingstede   þeod gesamnod.
Leton him þa betweonum   taan wisian
1100 hwylcne hira ærest   oðrum sceolde
to foddurþege   feores ongyldan;
hluton hellcræftum,   hæðengildum
teledon betwinum.   Ða se tan gehwearf
efne ofer ænne   ealdgesiða,
1105 se wæs uðweota   eorla dugoðe,
heriges on ore.   Hraðe siððan wearð
fetorwrasnum fæst,   feores orwena.
Cleopode þa collenferhð   cearegan reorde,
cwæð he his sylfes sunu   syllan wolde

1082 ne] *Not in MS.*   gemetton] gemette   1089 belidenan] be hlidenan
1090 deade] *Not in MS.*   1099 taan] tá an   1102 hellcræftum] hell
cræftum   1109 sunu] *Preceded by a word* (sunu ?) *erased*

1110 on æhtgeweald,   eaforan geongne,
     lifes to lisse. Hie ða lac hraðe
     þegon to þance. Þeod wæs oflysted,
     metes modgeomre,   næs him to maðme wynn,
     hyht to hordgestreonum. Hungre wæron
1115 þearle geþreatod,   swa se ðeodsceaða
     reow ricsode. Þa wæs rinc manig,
     guðfrec guma,   ymb þæs geongan feorh
     breostum onbryrded. To þam beadulace
     wæs þæt weatacen   wide gefrege,
1120 geond þa burh bodad   beorne manegum,
     þæt hie þæs cnihtes cwealm   corðre gesohton,
     duguðe ond eogoðe,   dæl onfengon
     lifes to leofne. Hie lungre to þæs,
     hæðene herigweardas,   here samnodan
1125 ceastrewarena. Cyrm upp astah
     ða se geonga ongann   geomran stefne,
     gehæfted for herige,   hearmleoð galan,
     freonda feasceaft,   friðes wilnian.
     Ne mihte earmsceapen   are findan,
1130 freoðe æt þam folce,   þe him feores wolde,
     ealdres geunnan. Hæfdon æglæcan
     sæcce gesohte. Sceolde sweordes ecg,
     scerp ond scurheard,   of sceaðan folme,
     fyrmælum fag,   feorh acsigan.
1135   Ða þæt Andrea   earmlic þuhte,
     þeodbealo þearlic   to geðolianne,
     þæt he swa unscyldig   ealdre sceolde
     lungre linnan. Wæs se leodhete
     þrist ond þrohtheard. Þrymman sceocan,
1140 modige maguþegnas,   morðres on luste,
     woldon æninga,   ellenrofe,
     on þam hysebeorðre   heafolan gescenan,
     garum agetan. Hine god forstod,
     halig of hehðo,   hæðenum folce.
1145 Het wæpen wera   wexe gelicost

1110 geongne] geone   1116 reow] Hreow   1132 Sceolde] sceolde
1139 þrist ond] *Not in MS.*

on þam orlege   eall formeltan,
þy læs scyldhatan   sceððan mihton,
egle ondsacan,   ecga þryðum.
Swa wearð alysed   of leodhete,
1150 geong of gyrne.   Gode ealles þanc,
dryhtna dryhtne,   þæs ðe he dom gifeð
gumena gehwylcum,   þara þe geoce to him
seceð mid snytrum.   Þær bið symle gearu
freod unhwilen,   þam þe hie findan cann.
1155   Þa wæs wop hæfen   in wera burgum,
hlud heriges cyrm.   Hreopon friccan,
mændon meteleaste,   meðe stodon,
hungre gehæfte.   Hornsalu wunedon,
weste winræced,   welan ne benohton
1160 beornas to brucanne   on þa bitran tid,
gesæton searuþancle   sundor to rune
ermðu eahtigan.   Næs him to eðle wynn.
    Fregn þa gelome   freca oðerne:
"Ne hele se ðe hæbbe   holde lare,
1165 on sefan snyttro!   Nu is sæl cumen,
þrea ormæte,   is nu þearf mycel
þæt we wisfæstra   wordum hyran."
    Þa for þære dugoðe   deoful ætywde,
wann ond wliteleas,   hæfde weriges hiw.
1170 Ongan þa meldigan   morþres brytta,
hellehinca,   þone halgan wer
wiðerhycgende,   ond þæt word gecwæð:
"Her is gefered   ofer feorne weg
æðelinga sum   innan ceastre,
1175 ellþeodigra,   þone ic Andreas
nemnan herde.   He eow neon gesceod
ða he aferede   of fæstenne
manncynnes ma   þonne gemet wære.
Nu ge magon eaðe   oncyðdæda
1180 wrecan on gewyrhtum.   Lætað wæpnes spor

1147 sceððan] sceaðan   1154 freod] freond   1180 gewyrhtum] gwyrhtum
wæpnes] *Not in MS.*

iren ecgheard, ealdorgeard sceoran,
fæges feorhhord. Gað fromlice
þæt ge wiðerfeohtend wiges gehnægan."
    Him þa Andreas agef ondsware:
1185 "Hwæt, ðu þristlice þeode lærest,
bældest to beadowe! Wæst þe bæles cwealm,
hatne in helle, ond þu here fysest,
feðan to gefeohte. Eart ðu fag wið god,
dugoða demend. Hwæt, ðu deofles stræl,
1190 icest þine yrmðo. Ðe se ælmihtiga
heanne gehnægde, ond on heolstor besceaf,
þær þe cyninga cining clamme belegde,
ond þe syððan a Satan nemdon,
ða ðe dryhtnes a deman cuðon."
1195   Ða gyt se wiðermeda wordum lærde
folc to gefeohte, feondes cræfte:
"Nu ge gehyrað hæleða gewinnan,
se ðyssum herige mæst hearma gefremede.
Ðæt is Andreas, se me on fliteð
1200 wordum wrætlicum for wera menigo."
    Ða wæs beacen boden burhsittendum.
Ahleopon hildfrome heriges brehtme
ond to weallgeatum wigend þrungon,
cene under cumblum, corðre mycle
1205 to ðam orlege, ordum ond bordum.
Þa worde cwæð weoroda dryhten,
meotud mihtum swið sægde his magoþegne:
"Scealt ðu, Andreas, ellen fremman!
Ne mið ðu for menigo, ah þinne modsefan
1210 staðola wið strangum! Nis seo stund latu
þæt þe wælreowe witum belecgaþ,
cealdan clommum. Cyð þe sylfne,
herd hige þinne, heortan staðola,
þæt hie min on ðe mægen oncnawan.
1215 Ne magon hie ond ne moton ofer mine est
þinne lichoman, lehtrum scyldige,
deaðe gedælan, ðeah ðu drype þolige,

mirce manslaga. Ic þe mid wunige."
    Æfter þam wordum com   werod unmæte,
1220 lyswe larsmeoðas,   mid lindgecrode,
bolgenmode;   bæron ut hræðe
ond þam halgan þær   handa gebundon.
Siþþan geypped wæs   æðelinga wynn,
ond hie andweardne   eagum meahton
1225 gesion sigerofne,   þær wæs sec manig
on þam welwange   wiges oflysted
leoda duguðe. Lyt sorgodon
hwylc him þæt edlean   æfter wurde.
Heton þa lædan   ofer landsceare,
1230 ðragmælum teon,   torngeniðlan,
swa hie hit frecnost   findan meahton.
Drogon deormodne   æfter dunscræfum,
ymb stanhleoðo,   stærcedferþne,
efne swa wide swa   wegas to lagon,
1235 enta ærgeweorc,   innan burgum,
stræte stanfage. Storm upp aras
æfter ceasterhofum,   cirm unlytel
hæðnes heriges. Wæs þæs halgan lic
sarbennum soden,   swate bestemed,
1240 banhus abrocen. Blod yðum weoll,
hatan heolfre. Hæfde him on innan
ellen untweonde,   wæs þæt æðele mod
asundrad fram synnum,   þeah he sares swa feala
deopum dolgslegum   dreogan sceolde.
1245 Swa wæs ealne dæg   oððæt æfen com
sigetorht swungen. Sar eft gewod
ymb þæs beornes breost,   oðþæt beorht gewat
sunne swegeltorht   to sete glidan.
Læddan þa leode   laðne gewinnan
1250 to carcerne. He wæs Criste swa þeah
leof on mode. Him wæs leoht sefa
halig heortan neh,   hige untyddre.

1232 deormodne] deormode   1233 stærcedferþne] stærced ferþþe
1241 hatan heolfre] hat of heolfre   1242 untweonde] untweodne   1246
sigetorht] sigel torht

þa se halga wæs   under heolstorscuwan,
eorl ellenheard,   ondlange niht
1255 searoþancum beseted.   Snaw eorðan band
wintergeworpum.   Weder coledon
heardum hægelscurum,   swylce hrim ond forst,
hare hildstapan,   hæleða eðel
lucon, leoda gesetu.   Land wæron freorig
1260 cealdum cylegicelum,   clang wæteres þrym
ofer eastreamas,   is brycgade
blæce brimrade.   Bliðheort wunode
eorl unforcuð,   elnes gemyndig,
þrist ond þrohtheard   in þreanedum
1265 wintercealdan niht.   No on gewitte blon,
acol for þy egesan,   þæs þe he ær ongann,
þæt he a domlicost   dryhten herede,
weorðade wordum,   oððæt wuldres gim
heofontorht onhlad.   Ða com hæleða þreat
1270 to ðære dimman ding,   duguð unlytel,
wadan wælgifre   weorodes brehtme.
Heton ut hræðe   æðeling lædan
in wraðra geweald,   wærfæstne hæleð.
Ða wæs eft swa ær   ondlangne dæg
1275 swungen sarslegum.   Swat yðum weoll
þurh bancofan,   blodlifrum swealg,
hatan heolfre.   Hra weorces ne sann,
wundum werig.   Þa cwom wopes hring
þurh þæs beornes breost,   blat ut faran,
1280 weoll waðuman stream,   ond he worde cwæð:
    "Geseoh nu, dryhten god,   drohtað minne,
weoruda willgeofa!   Þu wæst ond const
anra gehwylces   earfeðsiðas.
Ic gelyfe to ðe,   min liffruma,
1285 þæt ðu mildheort me   for þinum mægenspedum,
nerigend fira,   næfre wille,
ece ælmihtig,   anforlætan,
swa ic þæt gefremme,   þenden feorh leofað,

1253 þa] A *with preceding* S *erased, but no other letter supplied*   1286
                                                               i
wille] welle

min on moldan,　þæt ic, meotud, þinum
1290 larum leofwendum　lyt geswice.
　　Þu eart gescyldend　wið sceaðan wæpnum,
ece eadfruma,　eallum þinum;
ne læt nu bysmrian　banan manncynnes,
facnes frumbearn,　þurh feondes cræft
1295 leahtrum belecgan　þa þin lof berað."
　　Ða ðær ætywde　se atola gast,
wrað wærloga.　Wigend lærde
for þam heremægene　helle dioful
awerged in witum,　ond þæt word gecwæð:
1300 "Sleað synnigne　ofer seolfes muð,
folces gewinnan!　Nu to feala reordaþ."
　　Þa wæs orlege　eft onhrered,
niwan stefne.　Nið upp aras
oþðæt sunne gewat　to sete glidan
1305 under niflan næs.　Niht helmade,
brunwann oferbræd　beorgas steape,
ond se halga wæs　to hofe læded,
deor ond domgeorn,　in þæt dimme ræced;
sceal þonne in neadcofan　nihtlangne fyrst
1310 wærfæst wunian　wic unsyfre.
　　Þa com seofona sum　to sele geongan,
atol æglæca　yfela gemyndig,
morðres manfrea　myrce gescyrded,
deoful deaðreow　duguðum bereafod,
1315 ongan þa þam halgan　hospword sprecan:
　　"Hwæt hogodest ðu, Andreas,　hidercyme þinne
on wraðra geweald?　Hwæt is wuldor þin,
þe ðu oferhigdum　upp arærdest,
þa ðu goda ussa　gild gehnægdest?
1320 Hafast nu þe anum　eall getihhad
land ond leode,　swa dyde lareow þin.
Cyneþrym ahof,　þam wæs Crist nama,
ofer middangeard,　þynden hit meahte swa.
Þone Herodes　ealdre besnyðede,

1291 gescyldend] gescylded　　1319 gild] gilp

1325 forcom æt campe   cyning Iudea,
rices berædde,   ond hine rode befealg,
þæt he on gealgan   his gast onsende.
Swa ic nu bebeode   bearnum minum,
þegnum þryðfullum,   ðæt hie ðe hnægen,
1330 gingran æt guðe.   Lætað gares ord,
earh ættre gemæl,   in gedufan
in fæges ferð.   Gað fromlice,
ðæt ge guðfrecan   gylp forbegan."
    Hie wæron reowe,   ræsdon on sona
1335 gifrum grapum.   Hine god forstod,
staðulfæst steorend,   þurh his strangan miht.
Syððan hie oncneowon   Cristes rode
on his mægwlite,   mære tacen,
wurdon hie ða acle   on þam onfenge,
1340 forhte, afærde,   ond on fleam numen.
Ongan eft swa ær   ealdgeniðla,
helle hæftling,   hearmleoð galan:
"Hwæt wearð eow swa rofum,   rincas mine,
lindgesteallan,   þæt eow swa lyt gespeow?"
1345   Him þa earmsceapen   agef ondsware,
fah fyrnsceaþa,   ond his fæder oncwæð:
"Ne magan we him lungre   lað ætfæstan,
swilt þurh searwe.   Ga þe sylfa to!
Þær þu gegninga   guðe findest,
1350 frecne feohtan,   gif ðu furður dearst
to þam anhagan   aldre geneðan.
    We ðe magon eaðe,   eorla leofost,
æt þam secgplegan   selre gelæran;
ær ðu gegninga   guðe fremme,
1355 wiges woman,   weald, hu ðe sæle
æt þam gegnslege.   Utan gangan eft,
þæt we bysmrigen   bendum fæstne,
oðwitan him his wræcsið.   Habbað word gearu
wið þam æglæcan   eall getrahtod!"

1337 rode] rade   1345 Him þa] *Not in MS.*   earmsceapen] Hearm
sceapen

1360   þa hleoðrade   hludan stefne,
        witum bewæled,   ond þæt word gecwæð:
        "Þu þe, Andreas,   aclæccræftum
        lange feredes!   Hwæt, ðu leoda feala
        forleolce ond forlærdest!   Nu leng ne miht
1365 gewealdan þy weorce.   Þe synd witu þæs grim
        weotud be gewyrhtum.   Þu scealt werigmod,
        hean, hroðra leas,   hearm þrowigan,
        sare swyltcwale.   Secgas mine
        to þam guðplegan   gearwe sindon,
1370   þa þe æninga   ellenweorcum
        unfyrn faca   feorh ætþringan.
        Hwylc is þæs mihtig   ofer middangeard,
        þæt he þe alyse   of leoðubendum,
        manna cynnes,   ofer mine est?"
1375   Him þa Andreas   agef ondsware:
        "Hwæt, me eaðe   ælmihtig god,
        niða neregend,   se ðe in niedum iu
        gefæstnode   fyrnum clommum!
        Þær ðu syððan a,   susle gebunden,
1380 in wræc wunne,   wuldres blunne,
        syððan ðu forhogedes   heofoncyninges word.
        Þær wæs yfles or,   ende næfre
        þines wræces weorðeð.   Ðu scealt widan feorh
        ecan þine yrmðu.   Þe bið a symble
1385 of dæge on dæg   drohtaþ strengra."
        Ða wearð on fleame   se ðe ða fæhðo iu
        wið god geara   grimme gefremede.
            Com þa on uhtan   mid ærdæge
        hæðenra hloð   haliges neosan
1390 leoda weorude.   Heton lædan ut
        þrohtheardne þegn   þriddan siðe,
        woldon aninga   ellenrofes
        mod gemyltan.   Hit ne mihte swa!
        Ða wæs niowinga   nið onhrered,
1395 heard ond hetegrim.   Wæs se halga wer

1377 niedum] medum

sare geswungen,   searwum gebunden,
dolgbennum þurhdrifen,   ðendon dæg lihte.
Ongan þa geomormod   to gode cleopian,
heard of hæfte,   halgan stefne
1400 weop werigferð,   ond þæt word gecwæð:
"Næfre ic geferde   mid frean willan
under heofonhwealfe   heardran drohtnoð,
þær ic dryhtnes æ   deman sceolde.
Sint me leoðu tolocen,   lic sare gebrocen,
1405 banhus blodfag,   benne weallað,
seonodolg swatige.   Hwæt, ðu sigora weard,
dryhten hælend,   on dæges tide
mid Iudeum   geomor wurde
ða ðu of gealgan,   god lifigende,
1410 fyrnweorca frea,   to fæder cleopodest,
cininga wuldor,   ond cwæde ðus:
'Ic ðe, fæder engla,   frignan wille,
lifes leohtfruma,   hwæt forlætest ðu me?'
Ond ic nu þry dagas   þolian sceolde
1415 wælgrim witu.   Bidde ic, weoroda god,
þæt ic gast minne   agifan mote,
sawla symbelgifa,   on þines sylfes hand.
Ðu ðæt gehete   þurh þin halig word,
þa ðu us twelfe   trymman ongunne,
1420 þæt us heterofra   hild ne gesceode,
ne lices dæl   lungre oððeoded,
ne synu ne ban   on swaðe lagon,
ne loc of heafde   to forlore wurde,
gif we þine lare   læstan woldon.
1425 Nu sint sionwe toslopen,   is min swat adropen,
licgað æfter lande   loccas todrifene,
fex on foldan.   Is me feorhgedal
leofre mycle   þonne þeos lifcearo."
    Him þa stefn oncwæð,   stiðhycgendum,
1430 wuldorcyninges   word hloðrode:
"Ne wep þone wræcsið,   wine leofesta,

1400 werigferð] ferð *above the line*   1404 leoðu] leoð   1425 adropen]
d *altered from* ð

nis þe to frecne. Ic þe friðe healde,
minre mundbyrde mægene besette.
Me is miht ofer eall,
1435 sigorsped geseald. Soð þæt gecyðeð
mænig æt meðle on þam myclan dæge,
þæt ðæt geweorðeð, þæt ðeos wlitige gesceaft,
heofon ond eorðe, hreosaþ togadore,
ær awæged sie worda ænig
1440 þe ic þurh minne muð meðlan onginne.
Geseoh nu seolfes swæðe, swa þin swat aget
þurh bangebrec blodige stige,
lices lælan. No þe laðes ma
þurh daroða gedrep gedon motan,
1445 þa þe heardra mæst hearma gefremedan."
Þa on last beseah leoflic cempa
æfter wordcwidum wuldorcyninges.
Geseh he geblowene bearwas standan
blædum gehrodene, swa he ær his blod aget.
1450 Ða worde cwæð wigendra hleo:
"Sie ðe ðanc ond lof, þeoda waldend,
to widan feore wuldor on heofonum,
ðæs ðu me on sare, sigedryhten min,
ellþeodigne, an ne forlæte."
1455 Swa se dædfruma dryhten herede
halgan stefne oððæt hador sægl
wuldortorht gewat under waðu scriðan.
Þa þa folctogan feorðan siðe,
egle ondsacan, æðeling læddon
1460 to þam carcerne, woldon cræfta gehygd,
magorædendes mod oncyrran
on þære deorcan niht. Þa com dryhten god
in þæt hlinræced, hæleða wuldor,
ond þa wine synne wordum grette
1465 ond frofre gecwæð, fæder manncynnes,
lifes lareow, heht his lichoman
hales brucan: "Ne scealt ðu in henðum a leng

1443 lices] lic

searohæbbendra   sar þrowian."
    Aras þa mægene rof,   sægde meotude þanc,
1470 hal of hæfte   heardra wita.
    Næs him gewemmed wlite,   ne wloh of hrægle
lungre alysed,   ne loc of heafde,
ne ban gebrocen,   ne blodig wund
lice gelenge,   ne laðes dæl,
1475 þurh dolgslege   dreore bestemed,
ac wæs eft swa ær   þurh þa æðelan miht
lof lædende,   ond on his lice trum.
    Hwæt, ic hwile nu   haliges lare,
leoðgiddinga,   lof þæs þe worhte,
1480 wordum wemde,   wyrd undyrne
ofer min gemet.   Mycel is to secganne,
langsum leornung,   þæt he in life adreag,
eall æfter orde.   Þæt scell æglæwra
mann on moldan   þonne ic me tælige
1485 findan on ferðe,   þæt fram fruman cunne
eall þa earfeðo   þe he mid elne adreah,
grimra guða.   Hwæðre git sceolon
lytlum sticcum   leoðworda dæl
furður reccan.   Þæt is fyrnsægen,
1490 hu he weorna feala   wita geðolode,
heardra hilda,   in þære hæðenan byrig.
    He be wealle geseah   wundrum fæste
under sælwage   sweras unlytle,
stapulas standan,   storme bedrifene,
1495 eald enta geweorc.   He wið anne þæra,
mihtig ond modrof,   mæðel gehede,
wis, wundrum gleaw,   word stunde ahof:
"Geher ðu, marmanstan,   meotudes rædum,
fore þæs onsyne   ealle gesceafte
1500 forhte geweorðað,   þonne hie fæder geseoð
heofonas ond eorðan   herigea mæste
on middangeard   mancynn secan.

1468 sar] sas   1472 alysed] alysde   1474 lice] lic   1478 Hwæt] HÆT
1490 geðolode] geðolǫde   1492 fæste] fæstne   1493 sælwage] sæl wange
1496 modrof] mod rofe

Læt nu of þinum staþole   streamas weallan,
ea inflede,   nu ðe ælmihtig
1505 hateð, heofona cyning,   þæt ðu hrædlice
on þis fræte folc   forð onsende
wæter widrynig   to wera cwealme,
geofon geotende.   Hwæt, ðu golde eart,
sincgife, sylla!   On ðe sylf cyning
1510 wrat, wuldres god,   wordum cyðde
recene geryno,   ond ryhte æ
getacnode   on tyn wordum,
meotud mihtum swið.   Moyse sealde,
swa hit soðfæste   syðþan heoldon,
1515 modige magoþegnas,   magas sine,
godfyrhte guman,   Iosua ond Tobias.
Nu ðu miht gecnawan   þæt þe cyning engla
gefrætwode   furður mycle
giofum geardagum   þonne eall gimma cynn.
1520 Þurh his halige hæs   þu scealt hræðe cyðan
gif ðu his ondgitan   ænige hæbbe.''
     Næs þa wordlatu   wihte þon mare
þæt se stan togan.   Stream ut aweoll,
fleow ofer foldan.   Famige walcan
1525 mid ærdæge   eorðan þehton,
myclade mereflod.   Meoduscerwen wearð
æfter symbeldæge,   slæpe tobrugdon
searuhæbbende.   Sund grunde onfeng,
deope gedrefed.   Duguð wearð afyrhted
1530 þurh þæs flodes fær.   Fæge swulton,
geonge on geofene   guðræs fornam
þurh sealtne weg.   Þæt wæs sorgbyrþen,
biter beorþegu.   Byrlas ne gældon,
ombehtþegnas.   Þær wæs ælcum genog
1535 fram dæges orde   drync sona gearu.
Weox wæteres þrym.   Weras cwanedon,

1508 geofon] heofon   1514 heoldon] *One or two letters erased before this
word*   1516 Iosua] iosau   1527 tobrugdon] tobrǔgdon   1528 sea-
ruhæbbende] searu *above the line, and* hæbende   1532 sealtne] scealtes
weg] sweg

ealde æscberend. Wæs him ut myne
fleon fealone stream, woldon feore beorgan,
to dunscræfum drohtað secan,
1540 eorðan ondwist. Him þæt engel forstod,
se ða burh oferbrægd blacan lige,
hatan heaðowælme. Hreoh wæs þær inne
beatende brim. Ne mihte beorna hloð
of þam fæstenne fleame spowan.
1545 Wægas weoxon, wadu hlynsodon,
flugon fyrgnastas, flod yðum weoll.
Ðær wæs yðfynde innan burgum
geomorgidd wrecen. Gehðo mændan
forhtferð manig, fusleoð golon.
1550 Egeslic æled eagsyne wearð,
heardlic hereteam, hleoðor gryrelic.
þurh lyftgelac leges blæstas
weallas ymbwurpon, wæter mycladon.
    þær wæs wop wera wide gehyred,
1555 earmlic ylda gedræg. þa þær an ongann,
feasceaft hæleð, folc gadorigean,
hean, hygegeomor, heofende spræc:
"Nu ge magon sylfe soð gecnawan,
þæt we mid unrihte ellþeodigne
1560 on carcerne clommum belegdon,
witebendum. Us seo wyrd scyðeð,
heard ond hetegrim. þæt is her swa cuð,
is hit mycle selre, þæs þe ic soð talige,
þæt we hine alysan of leoðobendum,
1565 ealle anmode, (ofost is selost),
ond us þone halgan helpe biddan,
geoce ond frofre. Us bið gearu sona
sybb æfter sorge, gif we secaþ to him."
    þa þær Andrea orgete wearð
1570 on fyrhðlocan folces gebæro,
þær wæs modigra mægen forbeged,
wigendra þrym. Wæter fæðmedon,

1545 wadu] wudu   1548 mændan] mænan   1549 golon] galen
1562 her] *Not in MS.*   1571 mægen] *Not in MS.*

fleow firgendstream, flod wæs on luste,
oþþæt breost oferstag, brim weallende,
1575 eorlum oð exle. Þa se æðeling het
streamfare stillan, stormas restan
ymbe stanhleoðu. Stop ut hræðe
cene collenferð, carcern ageaf,
gleawmod, gode leof. Him wæs gearu sona
1580 þurh streamræce stræt gerymed.
Smeolt wæs se sigewang, symble wæs dryge
folde fram flode, swa his fot gestop.
Wurdon burgware bliðe on mode,
ferhðgefeonde. Þa wæs forð cumen
1585 geoc æfter gyrne. Geofon swaðrode
þurh haliges hæs, hlyst yst forgeaf,
brimrad gebad. Þa se beorg tohlad,
eorðscræf egeslic, ond þær in forlet
flod fæðmian, fealewe wægas,
1590 geotende gegrind grund eall forswealg.
Nalas he þær yðe ane bisencte,
ach þæs weorodes eac ða wyrrestan,
faa folcsceaðan, feowertyne
gewiton mid þy wæge in forwyrd sceacan
1595 under eorþan grund. Þa wearð acolmod,
forhtferð manig folces on laste.
Wendan hie wifa ond wera cwealmes,
þearlra geþinga ðrage hnagran,
syððan mane faa, morðorscyldige,
1600 guðgelacan under grund hruron.
     Hie ða anmode ealle cwædon:
"Nu is gesyne ðæt þe soð meotud,
cyning eallwihta, cræftum wealdeð,
se ðisne ar hider onsende
1605 þeodum to helpe. Is nu þearf mycel
þæt we gumcystum georne hyran."
     Þa se halga ongann hæleð blissigean,
wigendra þreat wordum retan:

1579 wæs] *Not in MS.*   1585 Geofon] heofon   1597 wifa] *Not in*
MS.   1601 Hie] Hi̹e

"Ne beoð ge to forhte, þeh þe fell curen
1610 synnigra cynn. Swylt þrowode,
witu be gewyrhtum. Eow is wuldres leoht
torht ontyned, gif ge teala hycgað."
Sende þa his bene fore bearn godes,
bæd haligne helpe gefremman
1615 gumena geogoðe, þe on geofene ær
þurh flodes fæðm feorh gesealdon,
ðæt þa gastas, gode orfeorme,
in wita forwyrd, wuldre bescyrede,
in feonda geweald gefered ne wurdan.
1620 Þa ðæt ærende ealwealdan gode
æfter hleoðorcwidum haliges gastes
wæs on þanc sprecen, ðeoda ræswan.
Het þa onsunde ealle arisan,
geonge of greote, þa ær geofon cwealde.
1625 Þa þær ofostlice upp astodon
manige on meðle, mine gefrege,
eaforan unweaxne, ða wæs eall eador
leoðolic ond gastlic, þeah hie lungre ær
þurh flodes fær feorh aleton.
1630 Onfengon fulwihte ond freoðuwære,
wuldres wedde witum aspedde,
mundbyrd meotudes. Þa se modiga het,
cyninges cræftiga, ciricean getimbran,
gerwan godes tempel, þær sio geogoð aras
1635 þurh fæder fulwiht ond se flod onsprang.
Þa gesamnodon secga þreate
weras geond þa winburg wide ond side,
eorlas anmode, ond hira idesa mid,
cwædon holdlice hyran woldon,
1640 onfon fromlice fullwihtes bæð
dryhtne to willan, ond diofolgild,
ealde eolhstedas, anforlætan.
Þa wæs mid þy folce fulwiht hæfen,
æðele mid eorlum, ond æ godes

1619 ne] *Not in MS.* 1622 ræswan] ræswum 1643 fulwiht] *Two
letters* (fo ?) *erased before this word*

1645 riht aræred,   ræd on lande
     mid þam ceasterwarum,   cirice gehalgod.
     Þær se ar godes   anne gesette,
     wisfæstne wer,   wordes gleawne,
     in þære beorhtan byrig   bisceop þam leodum,
1650 ond gehalgode   fore þam heremægene
     þurh apostolhad,   Platan nemned,
     þeodum on þearfe,   ond þriste bebead
     þæt hie his lare   læston georne,
     feorhræd fremedon.   Sægde his fusne hige,
1655 þæt he þa goldburg   ofgifan wolde,
     secga seledream   ond sincgestreon,
     beorht beagselu,   ond him brimþisan
     æt sæs faroðe   secan wolde.
     Þæt wæs þam weorode   weorc to geþoligenne,
1660 þæt hie se leodfruma   leng ne wolde
     wihte gewunian.   Þa him wuldres god
     on þam siðfæte   sylfum ætywde,
     ond þæt word gecwæð,   weoruda dryhten:
                  *   *   *
     "folc of firenum?   Is him fus hyge
1665 gað geomriende,   geohðo mænað
     weras wif samod.   Hira wop becom,
     murnende mod
                  *   *   *
                      fore sneowan.
     Ne scealt ðu þæt eowde   anforlætan
1670 on swa niowan gefean,   ah him naman minne
     on ferðlocan   fæste getimbre.
     Wuna in þære winbyrig,   wigendra hleo,
     salu sinchroden,   seofon nihta fyrst.
     Syððan ðu mid mildse   minre ferest."
1675   Þa eft gewat   oðre siðe
     modig, mægene rof,   Marmedonia
     ceastre secan.   Cristenra weox
     word ond wisdom,   syððan wuldres þegn,

1647 se] sio   1653 hie] he   1658 faroðe] foroðe   1659 weorc] weor
1664 Is] his   1676 modig] *Followed by* e *erased*

æþelcyninges ar,   eagum sawon.
1680 Lærde þa þa leode   on geleafan weg,
trymede torhtlice,   tireadigra
wenede to wuldre   weorod unmæte,
to þam halgan ham   heofona rices,
þær fæder ond sunu   ond frofre gast
1685 in þrinnesse   þrymme wealdeð
in woruld worulda   wuldorgestealda.
Swylce se halga   herigeas þreade,
deofulgild todraf   ond gedwolan fylde.
Þæt wæs Satane   sar to geþolienne,
1690 mycel modes sorg,   þæt he ða menigeo geseah
hweorfan higebliðe   fram helltrafum
þurh Andreas   este lare
to fægeran gefean,   þær næfre feondes ne bið,
gastes gramhydiges,   gang on lande.
1695   Þa wæron gefylde   æfter frean dome
dagas on rime,   swa him dryhten bebead,
þæt he þa wederburg   wunian sceolde.
Ongan hine þa fysan   ond to flote gyrwan,
blissum hremig,   wolde on brimþisan
1700 Achaie   oðre siðe
sylfa gesecan,   þær he sawulgedal,
beaducwealm gebad.   Þæt þam banan ne wearð
hleahtre behworfen,   ah in helle ceafl
sið asette,   ond syððan no,
1705 fah, freonda leas,   frofre benohte.
    Ða ic lædan gefrægn   leoda weorode
leofne lareow   to lides stefnan,
mæcgas modgeomre.   Þær manegum wæs
hat æt heortan   hyge weallende.
1710 Hie ða gebrohton   æt brimes næsse
on wægþele   wigan unslawne.
Stodon him ða on ofre   æfter reotan
þendon hie on yðum   æðelinga wunn
ofer seolhpaðu   geseon mihton,
1715 ond þa weorðedon   wuldres agend,

1704 syððan] syð

cleopodon on corðre, ond cwædon þus:
"An is ece god eallra gesceafta!
Is his miht ond his æht ofer middangeard
breme gebledsod, ond his blæd ofer eall
1720 in heofonþrymme halgum scineð,
wlitige on wuldre to widan ealdre,
ece mid englum. Þæt is æðele cyning!"

FATES OF THE APOSTLES

Hwæt! Ic þysne sang siðgeomor fand
on seocum sefan, samnode wide
hu þa æðelingas ellen cyðdon,
torhte ónd tireadige. Twelfe wæron,
5 dædum domfæste, dryhtne gecorene,
leofe on life. Lof wide sprang,
miht ond mærðo, ofer middangeard,
þeodnes þegna, þrym unlytel.
Halgan heape hlyt wisode
10 þær hie dryhtnes æ deman sceoldon,
reccan fore rincum. Sume on Romebyrig,
frame, fyrdhwate, feorh ofgefon
þurg Nerones nearwe searwe,
Petrus ond Paulus. Is se apostolhad
15 wide geweorðod ofer werþeoda!
Swylce Andreas in Achagia
for Egias aldre geneðde.
Ne þreodode he fore þrymme ðeodcyninges,
æniges on eorðan, ac him ece geceas
20 langsumre lif, leoht unhwilen,
syþþan hildeheard, heriges byrhtme,
æfter guðplegan gealgan þehte.
Hwæt, we eac gehyrdon be Iohanne
æglæawe menn æðelo reccan!
25 Se manna wæs, mine gefrege,

1 Hwæt] WÆT *with space vacant for an initial capital*   4 wæron] woron
13 nearwe] neawe   18 he] *Added above the line*

þurh cneorisse   Criste leofast
on weres hade,   syððan wuldres cyning,
engla ordfruma,   eorðan sohte
þurh fæmnan hrif,   fæder manncynnes.
30 He in Effessia   ealle þrage
leode lærde,   þanon lifes weg
siðe gesohte,   swegle dreamas,
beorhtne boldwelan.   Næs his broðor læt,
siðes sæne,   ac ðurh sweordes bite
35 mid Iudeum   Iacob sceolde
fore Herode   ealdre gedælan,
feorh wið flæsce.   Philipus wæs
mid Asseum,   þanon ece lif
þurh rode cwealm   ricene gesohte,
40 syððan on galgan   in Gearapolim
ahangen wæs   hildecorðre.
      Huru, wide wearð   wurd undyrne
þæt to Indeum   aldre gelædde
beaducræftig beorn,   Bartholameus!
45 Þone heht Astrias   in Albano,
hæðen ond hygeblind,   heafde beneotan,
forþan he ða hæðengild   hyran ne wolde,
wig weorðian.   Him wæs wuldres dream,
lifwela leofra   þonne þas leasan godu.
50   Swylce Thomas eac   þriste geneðde
on Indea   oðre dælas,
þær manegum wearð   mod onlihted,
hige onhyrded,   þurh his halig word.
Syððan collenferð   cyninges broðor
55 awehte for weorodum,   wundorcræfte,
þurh dryhtnes miht,   þæt he of deaðe aras,
geong ond guðhwæt,   ond him wæs Gad nama,
ond ða þæm folce   feorg gesealde,
sin æt sæcce.   Sweordræs fornam
60 þurh hæðene hand,   þær se halga gecrang,
wund for weorudum,   þonon wuldres leoht
sawle gesohte   sigores to leane.

43 gelædde] *Altered from* gelæððe   52 onlihted] i *corrected from* u

Hwæt, we þæt gehyrdon   þurg halige bec,
þæt mid Sigelwarum   soð yppe wearð,
65 dryhtlic dom godes!   Dæges or onwoc,
leohtes geleafan,   land wæs gefælsod
þurh Matheus   mære lare.
Þone het Irtacus   ðurh yrne hyge,
wælreow cyning,   wæpnum aswebban.
70   Hyrde we þæt Iacob   in Ierusalem
fore sacerdum   swilt þrowode.
Ðurg stenges sweng   stiðmod gecrang,
eadig for æfestum.   Hafað nu ece lif
mid wuldorcining,   wiges to leane.
75   Næron ða twegen   tohtan sæne,
lindgelaces,   land Persea
sohton siðfrome,   Simon ond Thaddeus,
beornas beadorofe!   Him wearð bam samod
an endedæg.   Æðele sceoldon
80 ðurh wæpenhete   weorc þrowigan,
sigelean secan,   ond þone soðan gefean,
dream æfter deaðe,   þa gedæled wearð
lif wið lice,   ond þas lænan gestreon,
idle æhtwelan,   ealle forhogodan.
85   Ðus ða æðelingas   ende gesealdon,
XII tilmodige.   Tir unbræcne
wegan on gewitte   wuldres þegnas.
      Nu ic þonne bidde   beorn se ðe lufige
þysses giddes begang   þæt he geomrum me
90 þone halgan heap   helpe bidde,
friðes ond fultomes.   Hu, ic freonda beþearf
liðra on lade,   þonne ic sceal langne ham,
eardwic uncuð,   ana gesecan,
lætan me on laste   lic, eorðan dæl,
95 wælreaf wunigean   weormum to hroðre.
      Her mæg findan   foreþances gleaw,
se ðe hine lysteð   leoðgiddunga,

77 Thaddeus] tḥaddeus   84 ealle] ealne   90 halgan] halga
93 gesecan] gesece   94 lætan] læt   96–122] *For the MS. readings,*
see Notes

hwa þas fitte fegde. ᚠ þær on ende standeþ,
eorlas þæs on eorðan brucaþ. Ne moton hie awa ætsomne,
woruldwunigende; ᚹ sceal gedreosan,
ᚢ on eðle, æfter tohreosan
læne lices frætewa, efne swa ᛚ toglideð.
Þonne ᚳ ond ᚣ cræftes neosað
nihtes nearowe, on him ᚾ ligeð,
cyninges þeodom. Nu ðu cunnon miht
hwa on þam wordum wæs werum oncyðig.
 Sie þæs gemyndig, mann se ðe lufige
þisses galdres begang, þæt he geoce me
ond frofre fricle. Ic sceall feor heonan,
an elles forð, eardes neosan,
sið asettan, nat ic sylfa hwær,
of þisse worulde. Wic sindon uncuð,
eard ond eðel, swa bið ælcum menn
nemþe he godcundes gastes bruce.
 Ah utu we þe geornor to gode cleopigan,
sendan usse bene on þa beorhtan gesceaft,
þæt we þæs botles brucan motan,
hames in hehðo, þær is hihta mæst,
þær cyning engla clænum gildeð
lean unhwilen. Nu a his lof standeð,
mycel ond mære, ond his miht seomaþ,
ece ond edgiong, ofer ealle gesceaft. Finit.

SOUL AND BODY I

 Huru, ðæs behofað hæleða æghwylc
þæt he his sawle sið sylfa geþence,
hu þæt bið deoplic þonne se deað cymeð,
asyndreð þa sybbe þe ær samod wæron,
lic ond sawle! Lang bið syððan
þæt se gast nimeð æt gode sylfum
swa wite swa wuldor, swa him on worulde ær
efne þæt eorðfæt ær geworhte.

2 sið] sið sið

Sceal se gast cuman   geohðum hremig,
10 symble ymbe seofon niht   sawle findan
þone lichoman   þe hie ær lange wæg,
þreo hund wintra,   butan ær þeodcyning,
ælmihtig god,   ende worulde
wyrcan wille,   weoruda dryhten.
15   Cleopað þonne swa cearful   cealdan reorde,
spreceð grimlice   se gast to þam duste:
"Hwæt, druh ðu dreorega,   to hwan drehtest ðu me,
eorðan fulnes   eal forwisnad,
lames gelicnes!   Lyt ðu gemundest
20 to hwan þinre sawle þing   siðþan wurde,
syððan of lichoman   læded wære!
Hwæt, wite ðu me, weriga!   Hwæt, ðu huru wyrma gyfl
lyt geþohtest,   þa ðu lustgryrum eallum
ful geeodest,   hu ðu on eorðan scealt
25 wyrmum to wiste!   Hwæt, ðu on worulde ær
lyt geþohtest   hu þis is þus lang hider!
Hwæt, þe la engel   ufan of roderum
sawle onsende   þurh his sylfes hand,
meotod ælmihtig,   of his mægenþrymme,
30 ond þe gebohte   blode þy halgan,
ond þu me mid þy heardan   hungre gebunde
ond gehæftnedest   helle witum!
   Eardode iç þe on innan.   Ne meahte ic ðe of cuman,
flæsce befangen,   ond me fyrenlustas
35 þine geþrungon.   Þæt me þuhte ful oft
þæt hit wære XXX   þusend wintra
to þinum deaððæge.   A ic uncres gedales onbad
earfoðlice.   Nis nu huru se ende to god!
   Wære þu þe wiste wlanc   ond wines sæd,
40 þrymful þunedest,   ond ic ofþyrsted wæs
godes lichoman,   gastes dryncces.
Forðan þu ne hogodest   her on life,
syððan ic ðe on worulde   wunian sceolde,
þæt ðu wære þurh flæsc   ond þurh fyrenlustas

22a ðu] ðuðu   24 geeodest] geodest   36 wære] wær   38 god] goð
40 ic] *Not in MS.*

45 strange gestryned   ond gestaðolod þurh me,
   ond ic wæs gast on ðe   fram gode sended.
   Næfre ðu me wið swa heardum   helle witum
   ne generedest   þurh þinra nieda lust.
   Scealt ðu minra gesynta   sceame þrowian
50 on ðam myclan dæge   þonne eall manna cynn
   se ancenneda   ealle gesamnað.
   Ne eart ðu þon leofra   nænigum lifigendra
   men to gemæccan,   ne meder ne fæder
   ne nænigum gesybban,   þonne se swearta hrefen,
55 syððan ic ana of ðe   ut siðode
   þurh þæs sylfes hand   þe ic ær onsended wæs.
   Ne magon þe nu heonon adon   hyrsta þa readan
   ne gold ne seolfor   ne þinra goda nan,
   ne þinre bryde beag   ne þin boldwela,
60 ne nan þara goda   þe ðu iu ahtest,
   ac her sceolon onbidan   ban bereafod,
   besliten synum,   ond þe þin sawl sceal
   minum unwillum   oft gesecan,
   wemman þe mid wordum,   swa ðu worhtest to me.
65   Eart ðu nu dumb ond deaf,   ne synt þine dreamas
                                              awiht.
   Sceal ic ðe nihtes swa þeah   nede gesecan,
   synnum gesargod,   ond eft sona fram þe
   hweorfan on hancred,   þonne halige men
   lifiendum gode   lofsang doð,
70 secan þa hamas   þe ðu me her scrife,
   ond þa arleasan   eardungstowe,
   ond þe sculon her moldwyrmas   manige ceowan,
   slitan sarlice   swearte wihta,
   gifre ond grædige.   Ne synt þine æhta awihte
75 þe ðu her on moldan   mannum eowdest.
   Forðan þe wære selre   swiðe mycle
   þonne þe wæron ealle   eorðan speda,

47 wið] mid   48 nieda] meda   51 ancenneda] acenneda   54 þonne]
þonn *with* e *crowded in before the next word*   57 magon] mæg   þa] þy
59 boldwela] gold wela   62 sceal] *Followed by abbreviation for* ond, *partly*
obliterated   63 unwillum] unwillu

(butan þu hie gedælde   dryhtne sylfum),
þær ðu wurde æt frymðe fugel   oððe fisc on sæ,
80 oððe on eorðan neat   ætes tilode,
feldgangende   feoh butan snyttro,
oððe on westenne   wildra deora
þæt wyrreste,   þær swa god wolde,
ge þeah ðu wære   wyrma cynna
85 þæt grimmeste,   þær swa god wolde,
þonne ðu æfre on moldan   man gewurde
oððe æfre fulwihte   onfon sceolde.
    Þonne ðu for unc bæm   andwyrdan scealt
on ðam miclan dæge,   þonne mannum beoð
90 wunda onwrigene,   þa ðe on worulde ær
fyrenfulle men   fyrn geworhton,
ðonne wyle dryhten sylf   dæda gehyran
hæleða gehwylces,   heofena scippend,
æt ealra manna gehwæs   muðes reorde
95 wunde wiðerlean.   Ac hwæt wylt ðu þær
on þam domdæge   dryhtne secgan?
Þonne ne bið nan na to þæs lytel lið   on lime aweaxen,
þæt ðu ne scyle for anra   gehwylcum onsundrum
riht agildan,   þonne reðe bið
100 dryhten æt þam dome.   Ac hwæt do wyt unc?
Sculon wit þonne eft ætsomne   siððan brucan
swylcra yrmða,   swa ðu unc her ær scrife!"
    Fyrnað þus þæt flæschord,   sceall þonne feran onweg,
secan hellegrund,   nallæs heofondreamas,
105 dædum gedrefed.   Ligeð dust þær hit wæs,
ne mæg him ondsware   ænige gehatan,
geomrum gaste,   geoce oððe frofre.
Bið þæt heafod tohliden,   handa toliðode,
geaglas toginene,   goman toslitene,
110 sina beoð asocene,   swyra becowen,
fingras tohrorene.
    Rib reafiað   reðe wyrmas,
beoð hira tungan totogenne   on tyn healfa

82 wildra deora] wild deora   84 wyrma] wyrm   103 onweg] on weg
with a w *erased before* on   105 Ligeð] liget

hungregum to frofre;   forþan hie ne magon huxlicum
115 wordum wrixlian   wið þone werian gast.
    Gifer hatte se wyrm,   þe þa eaglas beoð
    nædle scearpran.   Se genydde to
    ærest eallra   on þam eorðscræfe,
    þæt he þa tungan totyhð   ond þa teð þurhsmyhð
120 ond þa eagan þurheteð   ufan on þæt heafod
    ond to ætwelan   oðrum gerymeð,
    wyrmum to wiste,   þonne þæt werie
    lic acolod bið   þæt he lange ær
    werede mid wædum.   Bið þonne wyrma gifel,
125 æt on eorþan.   Þæt mæg æghwylcum
    men to gemynde,   modsnotra gehwam!
        Ðonne bið hyhtlicre   þæt sio halige sawl
    færeð to ðam flæsce,   frofre bewunden.
    Bið þæt ærende   eadiglicre
130 funden on ferhðe.   Mid gefean seceð
    lustum þæt lamfæt   þæt hie ær lange wæg.
    þonne þa gastas   gode word sprecað,
    snottre, sigefæste,   ond þus soðlice
    þone lichoman   lustum gretaþ:
135 "Wine leofesta,   þeah ðe wyrmas gyt
    gifre gretaþ,   nu is þin gast cumen,
    fægere gefrætewod,   of mines fæder rice,
    arum bewunden.   Eala, min dryhten,
    þær ic þe moste   mid me lædan,
140 þæt wyt englas   ealle gesawon,
    heofona wuldor,   swylc swa ðu me ær her scrife!
    Fæstest ðu on foldan   ond gefyldest me
    godes lichoman,   gastes dryncces.
    Wære ðu on wædle,   sealdest me wilna geniht.
145 Forðan ðu ne þearft sceamian,   þonne sceadene beoþ
    þa synfullan   ond þa soðfæstan
    on þam mæran dæge,   þæs ðu me geafe,
    ne ðe hreowan þearf   her on life
    ealles swa mycles   swa ðu me sealdest

---

117 to] to me   123 he] *Not in MS.*   125 æt] *Not in MS.*
132 sprecað] sprecat   135 þeah ðe] ah ðæ   138 arum] earum

150 on gemotstede   manna ond engla.
      Bygdest ðu þe for hæleðum   ond ahofe me on ecne
                                        dream.
      Forþan me a langaþ,   leofost manna,
      on minum hige hearde,   þæs þe ic þe on þyssum hynðum
                                            wat
      wyrmum to wiste,   ac þæt wolde god,
155 þæt þu æfre þus laðlic   legerbed cure.
      Wolde ic þe ðonne secgan   þæt ðu ne sorgode,
      forðan wyt bioð gegæderode   æt godes dome.
      Moton wyt þonne ætsomne   syþan brucan
      ond unc on heofonum   heahþungene beon.
160 Ne þurfon wyt beon cearie   æt cyme dryhtnes,
      ne þære andsware   yfele habban
      sorge in hreðre,   ac wyt sylfe magon
      æt ðam dome þær   dædum agilpan,
      hwylce earnunga   uncre wæron.
165 Wat ic þæt þu wære   on woruldrice
      geþungen þrymlice   þysses"
             *   *   *

HOMILETIC FRAGMENT I

                 sorh cymeð
      manig ond mislic   in manna dream.
      Eorl oðerne   mid æfþancum
      ond mid teonwordum   tæleð behindan,
  5 spreceð fægere beforan,   ond þæt facen swa þeah
      hafað in his heortan,   hord unclæne.
      Byð þonne þæs wommes gewita   weoruda dryhten.
      Forðan se witiga cwæð:
      "Ne syle ðu me ætsomne   mid þam synfullum
 10 in wita forwyrd,   weoruda dryhten,
      ne me on life forleos   mid þam ligewyrhtum,
      þam þe ful smeðe   spræce habbað,
      ond in gastcofan   grimme geþohtas,

---

151 ahofe] *Followed by another* me *erased*   162 hreðre] reðre
5 swa] swa swa

gehataðð holdlice,   swa hyra hyht ne gæð,
15 wære mid welerum." Wea bið in mode,
siofa synnum fah,   sare geblonden,
gefylled mid facne,   þeah he fæger word
utan ætywe. Ænlice beoð,
swa ða beon berað   buta ætsomne
20 arlicne anleofan,   ond ætterne tægel
hafað on hindan,   hunig on muðe,
wynsume wist. Hwilum wundiaþ
sare mid stinge,   þonne se sæl cymeð.
    Swa bioð gelice   þa leasan men,
25 þa ðe mid tungan   treowa gehataþ
fægerum wordum,   facenlice þencaþ,
þonne hie æt nehstan   nearwe beswicaþ,
hafað on gehatum   hunigsmæccas,
smeðne sybcwide,   ond in siofan innan
30 þurh deofles cræft   dyrne wunde.
    Swa is nu þes middangeard   mane geblonden,
wanað ond weaxeð. Wacað se ealda,
dweleð ond drefeð   dæges ond nihtes
miltse mid mane,   mægene getryweð,
35 ehteð æfestra,   inwit saweð,
nið mid geneahe. Nænig oðerne
freoð in fyrhðe   nimþe feara hwylc,
þæt he soðlice   sybbe healde,
gastlice lufe,   swa him god bebead.
40 Forþan eallunga   hyht geceoseð,
woruld wynsume,   se ðe wis ne bið,
snottor, searocræftig   sawle rædes.
    Uton to þam beteran,   nu we bot cunnon,
hycgan ond hyhtan,   þæt we heofones leoht
45 uppe mid englum   agan moton
gastum to geoce,   þonne god wile
eorðan lifes   ende gewyrcan!

---

23 stinge] *Not in MS.*   39 bebead] *One or two letters erased between* be *and*
bead   43 bot] *Not in MS.*

DREAM OF THE ROOD

Hwæt! Ic swefna cyst   secgan wylle,
hwæt me gemætte   to midre nihte,
syðþan reordberend   reste wunedon!
   Þuhte me þæt ic gesawe   syllicre treow
5 on lyft lædan,   leohte bewunden,
beama beorhtost.   Eall þæt beacen wæs
begoten mid golde.   Gimmas stodon
fægere æt foldan sceatum,   swylce þær fife wæron
uppe on þam eaxlegespanne.   Beheoldon þær engel dryht-
                           nes ealle,
10 fægere þurh forðgesceaft.   Ne wæs ðær huru fracodes
                           gealga,
ac hine þær beheoldon   halige gastas,
men ofer moldan,   ond eall þeos mære gesceaft.
   Syllic wæs se sigebeam,   ond ic synnum fah,
forwunded mid wommum.   Geseah ic wuldres treow,
15 wædum geweorðode,   wynnum scinan,
gegyred mid golde;   gimmas hæfdon
bewrigene weorðlice   wealdendes treow.
Hwæðre ic þurh þæt gold   ongytan meahte
earmra ærgewin,   þæt hit ærest ongan
20 swætan on þa swiðran healfe.   Eall ic wæs mid sorgum
                           gedrefed,
forht ic wæs for þære fægran gesyhðe.   Geseah ic þæt fuse
                           beacen
wendan wædum ond bleom;   hwilum hit wæs mid wætan
                           bestemed,
beswyled mid swates gange,   hwilum mid since gegyrwed.
   Hwæðre ic þær licgende   lange hwile
25 beheold hreowcearig   hælendes treow,
oððæt ic gehyrde   þæt hit hleoðrode.
Ongan þa word sprecan   wudu selesta:
   "Þæt wæs geara iu,   (ic þæt gyta geman),
þæt ic wæs aheawen   holtes on ende,

2 hwæt] hæt   17 wealdendes] wealdes   20 sorgum] surgum

30 astyred of stefne minum.   Genaman me ðær strange
                                              feondas,
    geworhton him þær to wæfersyne,   heton me heora wergas
                                              hebban.
    Bæron me ðær beornas on eaxlum,   oððæt hie me on beorg
                                              asetton,
    gefæstnodon me þær feondas genoge.   Geseah ic þa frean
                                              mancynnes
    efstan elne mycle   þæt he me wolde on gestigan.
35 þær ic þa ne dorste   ofer dryhtnes word
    bugan oððe berstan,   þa ic bifian geseah
    eorðan sceatas.   Ealle ic mihte
    feondas gefyllan,   hwæðre ic fæste stod.
    Ongyrede hine þa geong hæleð, (þæt wæs god ælmihtig),
40 strang ond stiðmod.   Gestah he on gealgan heanne,
    modig on manigra gesyhðe,   þa he wolde mancyn lysan.
    Bifode ic þa me se beorn ymbclypte.   Ne dorste ic hwæðre
                                              bugan to eorðan,
    feallan to foldan sceatum,   ac ic sceolde fæste standan.
    Rod wæs ic aræred.   Ahof ic ricne cyning,
45 heofona hlaford,   hyldan me ne dorste.
    Þurhdrifan hi me mid deorcan næglum.   On me syndon þa
                                              dolg gesiene,
    opene   inwidhlemmas.   Ne dorste ic hira nænigum
                                              sceððan.
    Bysmeredon hie unc butu ætgædere.   Eall ic wæs mid
                                              blode bestemed,
    begoten of þæs guman sidan,   siððan he hæfde his gast
                                              onsended.
50   Feala ic on þam beorge   gebiden hæbbe
    wraðra wyrda.   Geseah ic weruda god
    þearle þenian.   Þystro hæfdon
    bewrigen mid wolcnum   wealdendes hræw,
    scirne sciman,   sceadu forðeode,
55 wann under wolcnum.   Weop eal gesceaft,
    cwiðdon cyninges fyll.   Crist wæs on rode.
        Hwæðere þær fuse   feorran cwoman
    to þam æðelinge.   Ic þæt eall beheold.

Sare ic wæs mid sorgum gedrefed,   hnag ic hwæðre þam
                  secgum to handa,
60 eaðmod elne mycle.   Genamon hie þær ælmihtigne god,
   ahofon hine of ðam hefian wite.   Forleton me þa hilde-
                  rincas
   standan steame bedrifenne;   eall ic wæs mid strælum
                  forwundod.
   Aledon hie ðær limwerigne,   gestodon him æt his lices
                  heafdum,
   beheoldon hie ðær heofenes dryhten,   ond he hine ðær
                  hwile reste,
65 meðe æfter ðam miclan gewinne.   Ongunnon him þa
                  moldern wyrcan
   beornas on banan gesyhðe;   curfon hie ðæt of beorhtan
                  stane,
   gesetton hie ðæron sigora wealdend.   Ongunnon him þa
                  sorhleoð galan
   earme on þa æfentide,   þa hie woldon eft siðian,
   meðe fram þam mæran þeodne.   Reste he ðær mæte
                  weorode.
70   Hwæðere we ðær greotende   gode hwile
   stodon on staðole,   syððan stefn up gewat
   hilderinca.   Hræw colode,
   fæger feorgbold.   Þa us man fyllan ongan
   ealle to eorðan.   Þæt wæs egeslic wyrd!
75 Bedealf us man on deopan seaþe.   Hwæðre me þær
                  dryhtnes þegnas,
   freondas gefrunon,
   ond gyredon me   golde ond seolfre.
    Nu ðu miht gehyran,   hæleð min se leofa,
   þæt ic bealuwara weorc   gebiden hæbbe,
80 sarra sorga.   Is nu sæl cumen
   þæt me weorðiað   wide ond side
   menn ofer moldan,   ond eall þeos mære gesceaft,
   gebiddaþ him to þyssum beacne.   On me bearn godes
   þrowode hwile.   Forþan ic þrymfæst nu

59 sorgum] *Not in MS.*   65 moldern] moldærn   70 greotende] reotende
71 stefn] *Not in MS.*   77a ond] *Not in MS.*

85 hlifige under heofenum,   ond ic hælan mæg
   æghwylcne anra,   þara þe him bið egesa to me.
   Iu ic wæs geworden   wita heardost,
   leodum laðost,   ærþan ic him lifes weg
   rihtne gerymde,   reordberendum.
90 Hwæt, me þa geweorðode   wuldres ealdor
   ofer holmwudu,   heofonrices weard!
   Swylce swa he his modor eac,   Marian sylfe,
   ælmihtig god   for ealle menn
   geweorðode   ofer eall wifa cynn.
95   Nu ic þe hate,   hæleð min se leofa,
   þæt ðu þas gesyhðe   secge mannum,
   onwreoh wordum   þæt hit is wuldres beam,
   se ðe ælmihtig god   on þrowode
   for mancynnes   manegum synnum
100 ond Adomes   ealdgewyrhtum.
   Deað he þær byrigde,   hwæðere eft dryhten aras
   mid his miclan mihte   mannum to helpe.
   He ða on heofenas astag.   Hider eft fundaþ
   on þysne middangeard   mancynn secan
105 on domdæge   dryhten sylfa,
   ælmihtig god,   ond his englas mid,
   þæt he þonne wile deman,   se ah domes geweald,
   anra gehwylcum   swa he him ærur her
   on þyssum lænum   life geearnaþ.
110 Ne mæg þær ænig   unforht wesan
   for þam worde   þe se wealdend cwyð.
   Frineð he for þære mænige   hwær se man sie,
   se ðe for dryhtnes naman   deaðes wolde
   biteres onbyrigan,   swa he ær on ðam beame dyde.
115 Ac hie þonne forhtiað,   ond fea þencaþ
   hwæt hie to Criste   cweðan onginnen.
   Ne þearf ðær þonne ænig   anforht wesan
   þe him ær in breostum bereð   beacna selest,
   ac ðurh ða rode sceal   rice gesecan
120 of eorðwege   æghwylc sawl,

113 wolde] wolde *preceded by an erasure, probably of* þro   117 anforht]
unforht

seo þe mid wealdende   wunian þenceð."
   Gebæd ic me þa to þan beame   bliðe mode,
elne mycle,   þær ic ana wæs
mæte werede.   Wæs modsefa
125 afysed on forðwege,   feala ealra gebad
langunghwila.   Is me nu lifes hyht
þæt ic þone sigebeam   secan mote
ana oftor   þonne ealle men,
well weorþian.   Me is willa to ðam
130 mycel on mode,   ond min mundbyrd is
geriht to þære rode.   Nah ic ricra feala
freonda on foldan,   ac hie forð heonon
gewiton of worulde dreamum,   sohton him wuldres cyn-
                                                               ing,
lifiaþ nu on heofenum   mid heahfædere,
135 wuniaþ on wuldre,   ond ic wene me
daga gehwylce   hwænne me dryhtnes rod,
þe ic her on eorðan   ær sceawode,
on þysson lænan   life gefetige
ond me þonne gebringe   þær is blis mycel,
140 dream on heofonum,   þær is dryhtnes folc
geseted to symle,   þær is singal blis,
ond me þonne asette   þær ic syþþan mot
wunian on wuldre,   well mid þam halgum
dreames brucan.   Si me dryhten freond,
145 se ðe her on eorþan   ær þrowode
on þam gealgtreowe   for guman synnum.
He us onlysde   ond us lif forgeaf,
heofonlicne ham.   Hiht wæs geniwad
mid bledum ond mid blisse   þam þe þær bryne þolodan.
150 Se sunu wæs sigorfæst   on þam siðfate,
mihtig ond spedig,   þa he mid manigeo com,
gasta weorode,   on godes rice,
anwealda ælmihtig,   englum to blisse
ond eallum ðam halgum   þam þe on heofonum ær
155 wunedon on wuldre,   þa heora wealdend cwom,
ælmihtig god,   þær his eðel wæs.

127 ic] *Added above the line*   132 foldan] *Erasure of two letters after* foldan
142 me] he   152 on] *o erased before this word*

ELENE

Þa wæs agangen   geara hwyrftum
tu hund ond þreo   geteled rimes,
swylce XXX eac,   þinggemearces,
wintra for worulde,   þæs þe wealdend god
5 acenned wearð,   cyninga wuldor,
in middangeard   þurh mennisc heo,
soðfæstra leoht.   Þa wæs syxte gear
Constantines   caserdomes,
þæt he Romwara   in rice wearð
10 ahæfen, hildfruma,   to hereteman.
    Wæs se leodhwata   lindgeborga
eorlum arfæst.   Æðelinges weox
rice under roderum.   He wæs riht cyning,
guðweard gumena.   Hine god trymede
15 mærðum ond mihtum,   þæt he manegum wearð
geond middangeard   mannum to hroðer,
werþeodum to wræce,   syððan wæpen ahof
wið hetendum.   Him wæs hild boden,
wiges woma.   Werod samnodan
20 Huna leode   ond Hreðgotan,
foron fyrdhwate   Francan ond Hugas.
Wæron hwate weras,
gearwe to guðe.   Garas lixtan,
wriðene wælhlencan.   Wordum ond bordum
25 hofon herecombol.   Þa wæron heardingas
sweotole gesamnod   ond eal sib geador.
For folca gedryht.   Fyrdleoð agol
wulf on wealde,   wælrune ne mað.
Urigfeðera   earn sang ahof,
30 laðum on laste.   Lungre scynde
ofer burg enta   beaduþreata mæst,
hergum to hilde,   swylce Huna cyning
ymbsittendra   awer meahte

---

12 Æðelinges] æðelnges   14 guðweard] guð wearð   16 middangeard]
middan g̃   21 foron] foro *with* n *crowded in at end*   Hugas] hunas   26
ond] *The abbreviation crowded in*   sib] *Not in MS.*

abannan to beadwe   burgwigendra.
35 For fyrda mæst. Feðan trymedon
eoredcestum,   þæt on ælfylce
deareðlacende   on Danubie,
stærcedfyrhðe,   stæðe wicedon
ymb þæs wæteres wylm.   Werodes breahtme
40 woldon Romwara   rice geþringan,
hergum ahyðan.   Þær wearð Huna cyme
cuð ceasterwarum.   Þa se casere heht
ongean gramum   guðgelæcan
under earhfære   ofstum myclum
45 bannan to beadwe,   beran ut þræce
rincas under roderum.   Wæron Romware,
secgas sigerofe,   sona gegearwod
wæpnum to wigge,   þeah hie werod læsse
hæfdon to hilde   þonne Huna cining;
50 ridon ymb rofne,   þonne rand dynede,
campwudu clynede,   cyning þreate for,
herge to hilde.   Hrefen uppe gol,
wan ond wælfel.   Werod wæs on tyhte.
Hleopon hornboran,   hreopan friccan,
55 mearh moldan træd.   Mægen samnode,
cafe to cease.   Cyning wæs afyrhted,
egsan geaclad,   siððan elþeodige,
Huna ond Hreða   here sceawede,
ðæt he on Romwara   rices ende
60 ymb þæs wæteres stæð   werod samnode,
mægen unrime.   Modsorge wæg
Romwara cyning,   rices ne wende
for werodleste,   hæfde wigena to lyt,
eaxlgestealna   wið ofermægene,
65 hrora to hilde.   Here wicode,
eorlas ymb æðeling,   egstreame neah
on neaweste   nihtlangne fyrst,
þæs þe hie feonda gefær   fyrmest gesægon.
    Þa wearð on slæpe   sylfum ætywed
70 þam casere,   þær he on corðre swæf,

49 þonne] þone   58 sceawede] sceawedon   68 hie] he

sigerofum gesegen   swefnes woma.
þuhte him wlitescyne   on weres hade
hwit ond hiwbeorht   hæleða nathwylc
geywed ænlicra   þonne he ær oððe sið
75 gesege under swegle.   He of slæpe onbrægd,
eofurcumble beþeaht.   Him se ar hraðe,
wlitig wuldres boda,   wið þingode
ond be naman nemde,   (nihthelm toglad):
"Constantinus,   heht þe cyning engla,
80 wyrda wealdend,   wære beodan,
duguða dryhten.   Ne ondræd þu ðe,
ðeah þe elþeodige   egesan hwopan,
heardre hilde.   Þu to heofenum beseoh
on wuldres weard,   þær ðu wraðe findest,
85 sigores tacen."   He wæs sona gearu
þurh þæs halgan hæs,   hreðerlocan onspeon,
up locade,   swa him se ar abead,
fæle friðowebba.   Geseah he frætwum beorht
wliti wuldres treo   ofer wolcna hrof,
90 golde geglenged,   (gimmas lixtan);
wæs se blaca beam   bocstafum awriten,
beorhte ond leohte: "Mid þys beacne ðu
on þam frecnan fære   feond oferswiðesð,
geletest lað werod."   Þa þæt leoht gewat,
95 up siðode,   ond se ar somed,
on clænra gemang.   Cyning wæs þy bliðra
ond þe sorgleasra,   secga aldor,
on fyrhðsefan,   þurh þa fægeran gesyhð.
   Heht þa onlice   æðelinga hleo,
100 beorna beaggifa,   swa he þæt beacen geseah,
heria hildfruma,   þæt him on heofonum ær
geiewed wearð,   ofstum myclum,
Constantinus,   Cristes rode,
tireadig cyning,   tacen gewyrcan.
105 Heht þa on uhtan   mid ærdæge
wigend wreccan,   ond wæpenþræce
hebban heorucumbul,   ond þæt halige treo

90 geglenged] gelenged   91 awriten] *About two letters erased before this word*

him beforan ferian   on feonda gemang,
beran beacen godes.   Byman sungon
110 hlude for hergum.   Hrefn weorces gefeah,
urigfeðra,   earn sið beheold,
wælhreowra wig.   Wulf sang ahof,
holtes gehleða.   Hildegesa stod.
Þær wæs borda gebrec   ond beorna geþrec,
115 heard handgeswing   ond herga gring,
syððan heo earhfære   ærest metton.
On þæt fæge folc   flana scuras,
garas ofer geolorand   on gramra gemang,
hetend heorugrimme,   hildenædran,
120 þurh fingra geweald   forð onsendan.
Stopon stiðhidige,   stundum wræcon,
bræcon bordhreðan,   bil in dufan,
þrungon þræchearde.   Þa wæs þuf hafen,
segn for sweotum,   sigeleoð galen.
125 Gylden grima,   garas lixtan
on herefelda.   Hæðene grungon,
feollon friðelease.   Flugon instæpes
Huna leode,   swa þæt halige treo
aræran heht   Romwara cyning,
130 heaðofremmende.   Wurdon heardingas
wide towrecene.   Sume wig fornam.
Sume unsofte   aldor generedon
on þam heresiðe.   Sume healfcwice
flugon on fæsten   ond feore burgon
135 æfter stanclifum,   stede weardedon
ymb Danubie.   Sume drenc fornam
on lagostreame   lifes æt ende.
Ða wæs modigra   mægen on luste,
ehton elþeoda   oð þæt æfen forð
140 fram dæges orde.   Daroðæsc flugon,
hildenædran.   Heap wæs gescyrded,
laðra lindwered.   Lythwon becwom
Huna herges   ham eft þanon.

119 heorugrimme] heora grimme   124 sweotum] sweotolū   126 here-
felda] hera felda

Þa wæs gesyne   þæt sige forgeaf
145 Constantino   cyning ælmihtig
    æt þam dægweorce,   domweorðunga,
    rice under roderum,   þurh his rode treo.
        Gewat þa heriga helm   ham eft þanon,
    huðe hremig,   (hild wæs gesceaden),
150 wigge geweorðod.   Com þa wigena hleo
    þegna þreate   þryðbold secan,
    beadurof cyning   burga neosan.
    Heht þa wigena weard   þa wisestan
    snude to sionoðe,   þa þe snyttro cræft
155 þurh fyrngewrito   gefrigen hæfdon,
    heoldon higeþancum   hæleða rædas.
    Ða þæs fricggan ongan   folces aldor,
    sigerof cyning,   ofer sid weorod,
    wære þær ænig   yldra oððe gingra
160 þe him to soðe   secggan meahte,
    galdrum cyðan,   hwæt se god wære,
    boldes brytta,   "þe þis his beacen wæs
    þe me swa leoht oðywde   ond mine leode generede,
    tacna torhtost,   ond me tir forgeaf,
165 wigsped wið wraðum,   þurh þæt wlitige treo."
    Hio him ondsware   ænige ne meahton
    agifan togenes,   ne ful geare cuðon
    sweotole gesecggan   be þam sigebeacne.
        Þa þa wisestan   wordum cwædon
170 for þam heremægene   þæt hit heofoncyninges
    tacen wære,   ond þæs tweo nære.
    Þa þæt gefrugnon   þa þurh fulwihte
    lærde wæron,   (him wæs leoht sefa,
    ferhð gefeonde,   þeah hira fea wæron),
175 ðæt hie for þam casere   cyðan moston
    godspelles gife,   hu se gasta helm,
    in þrynesse   þrymme geweorðad,
    acenned wearð,   cyninga wuldor,
    ond hu on galgan wearð   godes agen bearn
180 ahangen for hergum   heardum witum.

151 þryðbold secan] þryð bord stenan

Alysde leoda bearn   of locan deofla,
geomre gastas,   ond him gife sealde
þurh þa ilcan gesceaft   þe him geywed wearð
sylfum on gesyhðe,   sigores tacen,
185 wið þeoda þræce.   Ond hu ðy þriddan dæge
of byrgenne   beorna wuldor
of deaðe aras,   dryhten ealra
hæleða cynnes,   ond to heofonum astah.
   Ðus gleawlice   gastgerynum
190 sægdon sigerofum,   swa fram Siluestre
lærde wæron.   Æt þam se leodfruma
fulwihte onfeng   ond þæt forð geheold
on his dagana tid,   dryhtne to willan.
   Ða wæs on sælum   sinces brytta,
195 niðheard cyning.   Wæs him niwe gefea
befolen in fyrhðe,   wæs him frofra mæst
ond hyhta nihst   heofonrices weard.
   Ongan þa dryhtnes æ   dæges ond nihtes
þurh gastes gife   georne cyðan,
200 ond hine soðlice   sylfne getengde
goldwine gumena   in godes þeowdom,
æscrof, unslaw.   Þa se æðeling fand,
leodgebyrga,   þurh larsmiðas,
guðheard, garþrist,   on godes bocum
205 hwær ahangen wæs   heriges beorhtme
on rode treo   rodora waldend
æfstum þurh inwit,   swa se ealda feond
forlærde ligesearwum,   leode fortyhte,
Iudea cyn,   þæt hie god sylfne
210 ahengon, herga fruman.   Þæs hie in hynðum sculon
to widan feore   wergðu dreogan!
   Þa wæs Cristes lof   þam casere
on firhðsefan,   forð gemyndig
ymb þæt mære treo,   ond þa his modor het
215 feran foldwege   folca þreate
to Iudeum,   georne secan
wigena þreate   hwær se wuldres beam,

184 tacen] tacne   197 hyhta] hyht

halig under hrusan, hyded wære,
æðelcyninges rod. Elene ne wolde
220 þæs siðfates sæne weorðan,
ne ðæs wilgifan word gehyrwan,
hiere sylfre suna, ac wæs sona gearu,
wif on willsið, swa hire weoruda helm,
byrnwiggendra, beboden hæfde.
225 Ongan þa ofstlice eorla mengu
to flote fysan. Fearoðhengestas
ymb geofenes stæð gearwe stodon,
sælde sæmearas, sunde getenge.
Ða wæs orcnæwe idese siðfæt,
230 siððan wæges helm werode gesohte.
Þær wlanc manig æt Wendelsæ
on stæðe stodon. Stundum wræcon
ofer mearcpaðu, mægen æfter oðrum,
ond þa gehlodon hildesercum,
235 bordum ond ordum, byrnwigendum,
werum ond wifum, wæghengestas.
Leton þa ofer fifelwæg famige scriðan
bronte brimþisan. Bord oft onfeng
ofer earhgeblond yða swengas;
240 sæ swinsade. Ne hyrde ic sið ne ær
on egstreame idese lædan,
on merestræte, mægen fægerre.
Þær meahte gesion, se ðone sið beheold,
brecan ofer bæðweg, brimwudu snyrgan
245 under swellingum, sæmearh plegean,
wadan wægflotan. Wigan wæron bliðe,
collenferhðe, cwen siðes gefeah,
syþþan to hyðe hringedstefnan
ofer lagofæsten geliden hæfdon
250 on Creca land. Ceolas leton
æt sæfearoðe, sande bewrecene,

---

221 gehyrwan] ge hyr^wan   222 wæs] *First written* æs, *the beginning word*
of a line, with w *added in the margin*   237 Leton] ton *on an erasure*
famige] a *altered from* æ (*Wülker*)   242 fægerre] fægrre   245 swellingum]
spellingum, *or perhaps* w *altered from* p

ald yðhofu, oncrum fæste
on brime bidan beorna geþinges,
hwonne heo sio guðcwen gumena þreate
255 ofer eastwegas eft gesohte.
    Ðær wæs on eorle eðgesyne
brogden byrne ond bill gecost,
geatolic guðscrud, grimhelm manig,
ænlic eoforcumbul. Wæron æscwigan,
260 secggas ymb sigecwen, siðes gefysde.
Fyrdrincas frome foron on luste
on Creca land, caseres bodan,
hilderincas, hyrstum gewerede.
Þær wæs gesyne sincgim locen
265 on þam hereþreate, hlafordes gifu.
Wæs seo eadhreðige Elene gemyndig,
þriste on geþance, þeodnes willan
georn on mode þæt hio Iudeas
ofer herefeldas heape gecoste
270 lindwigendra land gesohte,
secga þreate. Swa hit siððan gelamp
ymb lytel fæc þæt ðæt leodmægen,
guðrofe hæleþ to Hierusalem
cwomon in þa ceastre corðra mæste,
275 eorlas æscrofe, mid þa æðelan cwen.
    Heht ða gebeodan burgsittendum
þam snoterestum side ond wide
geond Iudeas, gumena gehwylcum,
meðelhegende, on gemot cuman,
280 þa ðe deoplicost dryhtnes geryno
þurh rihte æ reccan cuðon.
Ða wæs gesamnod of sidwegum
mægen unlytel, þa ðe Moyses æ
reccan cuðon. Þær on rime wæs
285 þreo M þæra leoda
alesen to lare. Ongan þa leoflic wif
weras Ebrea wordum negan:

---

252 yðhofu] yð liofu   254 hwonne] hwone   279 meðelhegende] meðel
hengende   285 M] .m̄.

"Ic þæt gearolice   ongiten hæbbe
þurg witgena   wordgeryno
290 on godes bocum   þæt ge geardagum
wyrðe wæron   wuldorcyninge,
dryhtne dyre   ond dædhwæte.
Hwæt, ge ealle snyttro   unwislice,
wraðe wiðweorpon,   þa ge wergdon þane
295 þe eow of wergðe   þurh his wuldres miht,
fram ligcwale,   lysan þohte,
of hæftnede.   Ge mid horu speowdon
on þæs ondwlitan   þe eow eagena leoht,
fram blindnesse   bote gefremede
300 edniowunga   þurh þæt æðele spald,
ond fram unclænum   oft generede
deofla gastum.   Ge to deaþe þone
deman ongunnon,   se ðe of deaðe sylf
woruld awehte   on wera corþre
305 in þæt ærre lif   eowres cynnes.
Swa ge modblinde   mengan ongunnon
lige wið soðe,   leoht wið þystrum,
æfst wið are,   inwitþancum
wroht webbedan.   Eow seo wergðu forðan
310 sceðþeð scyldfullum.   Ge þa sciran miht
deman ongunnon,   ond gedweolan lifdon,
þeostrum geþancum,   oð þysne dæg.
Gangaþ nu snude,   snyttro geþencaþ,
weras wisfæste,   wordes cræftige,
315 þa ðe eowre æ   æðelum cræftige
on ferhðsefan   fyrmest hæbben,
þa me soðlice   secgan cunnon,
ondsware cyðan   for eowic forð
tacna gehwylces   þe ic him to sece."
320   Eodan þa on geruman   reonigmode
eorlas æcleawe,   egesan geþreade,
gehðum geomre,   georne sohton

293 ealle] þære   295 wuldres] wuldre *at the end of a line*   302 to] *Not in MS*.   310 sciran] scịran   318 eowic] eow   320 geruman] gerū
322 georne] eorne

þa wisestan   wordgeryno,
þæt hio þære cwene   oncweðan meahton
325 swa tiles swa trages,   swa hio him to sohte.
Hio þa on þreate   M manna
fundon ferhðgleawra,   þa þe fyrngemynd
mid Iudeum   gearwast cuðon.
Þrungon þa on þreate   þær on þrymme bad
330 in cynestole   caseres mæg,
geatolic guðcwen   golde gehyrsted.
     Elene maþelode   ond for eorlum spræc:
"Gehyrað, higegleawe,   halige rune,
word ond wisdom.   Hwæt, ge witgena
335 lare onfengon,   hu se liffruma
in cildes had   cenned wurde,
mihta wealdend.   Be þam Moyses sang,
ond þæt word gecwæð   weard Israhela:
'Eow acenned bið   cniht on degle,
340 mihtum mære,   swa þæs modor ne bið
wæstmum geeacnod   þurh weres frige.'
Be ðam Dauid cyning   dryhtleoð agol,
frod fyrnweota,   fæder Salomones,
ond þæt word gecwæþ   wigona baldor:
345 'Ic frumþa god   fore sceawode,
sigora dryhten.   He on gesyhðe wæs,
mægena wealdend,   min on þa swiðran,
þrymmes hyrde.   Þanon ic ne wende
æfre to aldre   onsion mine.'
350 Swa hit eft be eow   Essaias,
witga for weorodum,   wordum mælde,
deophycggende   þurh dryhtnes gast:
'Ic up ahof   eaforan gingne
ond bearn cende,   þam ic blæd forgeaf,
355 halige higefrofre,   ac hie hyrwdon me,
feodon þurh feondscipe,   nahton foreþances,
wisdomes gewitt;   ond þa weregan neat,
þe man daga gehwam   drifeð ond þirsceð,
ongitaþ hira goddend,   nales gnyrnwræcum

326 M] .m̄.   338 word] *Not in MS.*   348 wende] weno   355 me] þe

360 feogað frynd hiera þe him fodder gifað,
ond me Israhela æfre ne woldon
folc oncnawan, þeah ic feala for him
æfter woruldstundum wundra gefremede.'
　　Hwæt, we þæt gehyrdon þurh halige bec
365 þæt eow dryhten geaf dom unscyndne,
meotod mihta sped, Moyse sægde
hu ge heofoncyninge hyran sceoldon,
lare læstan. Eow þæs lungre aþreat,
ond ge þam ryhte wiðroten hæfdon,
370 onscunedon þone sciran scippend eallra,
dryhtna dryhten, ond gedwolan fylgdon
ofer riht godes. Nu ge raþe gangaþ
ond findaþ gen þa þe fyrngewritu
þurh snyttro cræft selest cunnen,
375 æriht eower, þæt me ondsware
þurh sidne sefan secgan cunnen."
　　Eodan ða mid mengo modcwanige,
collenferhðe, swa him sio cwen bead.
Fundon þa D forþsnottera
380 alesen leodmæga, þa ðe leornungcræft
þurh modgemynd mæste hæfdon,
on sefan snyttro. Heo to salore eft
ymb lytel fæc laðode wæron,
ceastre weardas. Hio sio cwen ongan
385 wordum genegan, (wlat ofer ealle):
"Oft ge dyslice dæd gefremedon,
werge wræcmæcggas, ond gewritu herwdon,
fædera lare, næfre furður þonne nu,
ða ge blindnesse bote forsegon,
390 ond ge wiðsocon soðe ond rihte,
þæt in Bethleme bearn wealdendes,
cyning anboren, cenned wære,
æðelinga ord. þeah ge þa æ cuðon,
witgena word, ge ne woldon þa,

360 gifað] gifeð　371 dryhtna] *Not in MS.*　379 Fundon] funden
392 wære] *Written twice, at the end and at the beginning of a line*　394
witgena] witg̦na

395 synwyrcende, soð oncnawan."
    Hie þa anmode ondsweredon:
"Hwæt, we Ebreisce æ leornedon,
þa on fyrndagum fæderas cuðon
æt godes earce, ne we geare cunnon
400 þurh hwæt ðu ðus hearde, hlæfdige, us
eorre wurde. We ðæt æbylgð nyton
þe we gefremedon on þysse folcscere,
þeodenbealwa, wið þec æfre."
    Elene maðelade ond for eorlum spræc,
405 undearninga ides reordode
hlude for herigum: "Ge nu hraðe gangað,
sundor asecaþ þa ðe snyttro mid eow,
mægn ond modcræft, mæste hæbben,
þæt me þinga gehwylc þriste gecyðan,
410 untraglice, þe ic him to sece."
    Eodon þa fram rune, swa him sio rice cwen,
bald in burgum, beboden hæfde,
geomormode, georne smeadon,
sohton searoþancum, hwæt sio syn wære
415 þe hie on þam folce gefremed hæfdon
wið þam casere, þe him sio cwen wite.
Þa þær for eorlum an reordode,
gidda gearosnotor, (ðam wæs Iudas nama,
wordes cræftig): "Ic wat geare
420 þæt hio wile secan be ðam sigebeame
on ðam þrowode þeoda waldend,
eallra gnyrna leas, godes agen bearn,
þone orscyldne eofota gehwylces
þurh hete hengon on heanne beam
425 in fyrndagum fæderas usse.
    Þæt wæs þrealic geþoht! Nu is þearf mycel
þæt we fæstlice ferhð staðelien,
þæt we ðæs morðres meldan ne weorðen
hwær þæt halige trio beheled wurde
430 æfter wigþræce, þy læs toworpen sien

396 ondsweredon] 7 sweř 399 geare] eare 401 æbylgð] *A letter erased after y* 422 gnyrna] gnyrnra 423 orscyldne] scyldū

frod fyrngewritu   ond þa fæderlican
lare forleten.   Ne bið lang ofer ðæt
þæt Israhela   æðelu moten
ofer middangeard   ma ricsian,
435 æcræft eorla,   gif ðis yppe bið,
swa þa þæt ilce gio   min yldra fæder
sigerof sægde,   (þam wæs Sachius nama),
frod fyrnwiota,   fæder minum,
*   *   *
eaferan,
440 wende hine of worulde   ond þæt word gecwæð:
'Gif þe þæt gelimpe   on lifdagum
þæt ðu gehyre   ymb þæt halige treo
frode frignan,   ond geflitu ræran
be ðam sigebeame   on þam soðcyning
445 ahangen wæs,   heofonrices weard,
eallre sybbe bearn,   þonne þu snude gecyð,
min swæs sunu,   ær þec swylt nime.
Ne mæg æfre ofer þæt   Ebrea þeod
rædþeahtende   rice healdan,
450 duguðum wealdan,   ac þara dom leofað
ond hira dryhtscipe,
in woruld weorulda   willum gefylled,
ðe þone ahangnan cyning   heriaþ ond lofiað.'
Þa ic fromlice   fæder minum,
455 ealdum æwitan,   ageaf ondsware:
'Hu wolde þæt geweorðan   on woruldrice
þæt on þone halgan   handa sendan
to feorhlege   fæderas usse
þurh wrað gewitt,   gif hie wiston ær
460 þæt he Crist wære,   cyning on roderum,
soð sunu meotudes,   sawla nergend?'
Ða me yldra min   ageaf ondsware,
frod on fyrhðe   fæder reordode:
'Ongit, guma ginga,   godes heahmægen,
465 nergendes naman.   Se is niða gehwam
unasecgendlic,   þone sylf ne mæg

432 forleten] forleton   453 ðe] *Above the line*

on moldwege man aspyrigean.
Næfre ic þa geþeahte þe þeos þeod ongan
secan wolde, ac ic symle mec
470 asced þara scylda, nales sceame worhte
gaste minum. Ic him georne oft
þæs unrihtes ondsæc fremede,
þonne uðweotan æht bisæton,
on sefan sohton hu hie sunu meotudes
475 ahengon, helm wera, hlaford eallra
engla ond elda, æðelust bearna.
Ne meahton hie swa disige deað oðfæstan,
weras wonsælige, swa hie wendon ær,
sarum settan, þeah he sume hwile
480 on galgan his gast onsende,
sigebearn godes. Þa siððan wæs
of rode ahæfen rodera wealdend,
eallra þrymma þrym, þreo niht siððan
in byrgenne bidende wæs
485 under þeosterlocan, ond þa þy þriddan dæg
ealles leohtes leoht lifgende aras,
ðeoden engla, ond his þegnum hine,
soð sigora frea, seolfne geywde,
beorht on blæde. Þonne broðor þin
490 onfeng æfter fyrste fulwihtes bæð,
leohtne geleafan. Þa for lufan dryhtnes
Stephanus wæs stanum worpod;
ne geald he yfel yfele, ac his ealdfeondum
þingode þrohtherd, bæd þrymcyning
495 þæt he him þa weadæd to wræce ne sette,
þæt hie for æfstum unscyldigne,
synna leasne, Sawles larum
feore beræddon, swa he þurh feondscipe
to cwale monige Cristes folces
500 demde to deaþe. Swa þeah him dryhten eft
miltse gefremede, þæt he manegum wearð
folca to frofre, syððan him frymða god,
niða nergend, naman oncyrde,

487 hine] *Not in MS.* 496 hie] he 501 wearð] *Not in MS.*

    ond he syðða waes   sanctus Paulus
505 be naman haten,   ond him naenig waes
    aelaerendra   oðer betera
    under swegles hleo   syðþan aefre,
    þara þe wif oððe wer   on woruld cendan,
    þeah he Stephanus   stanum hehte
510 abreotan on beorge,   broðor þinne.
     Nu ðu meaht gehyran,   haeleð min se leofa,
    hu arfaest is   ealles wealdend,
    þeah we aebylgð wið hine   oft gewyrcen,
    synna wunde,   gif we sona eft
515 þara bealudaeda   bote gefremmaþ
    ond þaes unrihtes   eft geswicaþ.
    Forðan ic soðlice   ond min swaes faeder
    syðþan gelyfdon
    þaet geþrowade   eallra þrymma god,
520 lifes lattiow,   laðlic wite
    for oferþearfe   ilda cynnes.
    Forðan ic þe laere   þurh leoðorune,
    hyse leofesta,   þaet ðu hospcwide,
    aefst ne eofulsaec   aefre ne fremme,
525 grimne geagncwide,   wið godes bearne.
    Þonne ðu geearnast   þaet þe bið ece lif,
    selust sigeleana,   seald in heofonum.'
     Ðus mec faeder min   on fyrndagum
    unweaxenne   wordum laerde,
530 septe soðcwidum,   (þam waes Symon nama),
    guma gehðum frod.   Nu ge geare cunnon
    hwaet eow þaes on sefan   selest þince
    to gecyðanne,   gif ðeos cwen usic
    frigneð ymb ðaet treo,   nu ge fyrhðsefan
535 ond modgeþanc   minne cunnon."
     Him þa togenes   þa gleawestan
    on wera þreate   wordum maeldon:
    "Naefre we hyrdon   haeleð aenigne

---

524 fremme] *A letter erased after this word*   526 ece] *Two letters* (fa?)
erased before this word   531 gehðum] gehdū   frod] *A letter erased
after this word*

on þysse þeode, butan þec nu ða,
540 þegn oðerne þyslic cyðan
ymb swa dygle wyrd. Do swa þe þynce,
fyrngidda frod, gif ðu frugnen sie
on wera corðre. Wisdomes beðearf,
worda wærlicra ond witan snyttro,
545 se ðære æðelan sceal ondwyrde agifan
for þyslicne þreat on meþle."
    Weoxan word cwidum, weras þeahtedon
on healfa gehwær, sume hyder, sume þyder,
þrydedon ond þohton. Þa cwom þegna heap
550 to þam heremeðle. Hreopon friccan,
caseres bodan: "Eow þeos cwen laþaþ,
secgas to salore, þæt ge seonoðdomas
rihte reccen. Is eow rædes þearf
on meðelstede, modes snyttro."
555 Heo wæron gearwe, geomormode
leodgebyrgean, þa hie laðod wæron
þurh heard gebann; to hofe eodon,
cyðdon cræftes miht. Þa sio cwen ongan
weras Ebresce wordum negan,
560 fricggan fyrhðwerige ymb fyrngewritu,
hu on worulde ær witgan sungon,
gasthalige guman, be godes bearne,
hwær se þeoden geþrowade,
soð sunu meotudes, for sawla lufan.
565 Heo wæron stearce, stane heardran,
noldon þæt geryne rihte cyðan,
ne hire andsware ænige secgan,
torngeniðlan, þæs hio him to sohte,
ac hio worda gehwæs wiðersæc fremedon,
570 fæste on fyrhðe, þæt heo frignan ongan,
cwædon þæt hio on aldre owiht swylces
ne ær ne sið æfre hyrdon.
    Elene maþelade ond him yrre oncwæð:
"Ic eow to soðe secgan wille,
575 ond þæs in life lige ne wyrðeð,

561 witgan] witga

gif ge þissum lease   leng gefylgað
mid fæcne gefice,   þe me fore standaþ,
þæt eow in beorge   bæl fornimeð,
hattost heaðowelma,   ond eower hra bryttað,
580 lacende lig,   þæt eow sceal þæt leas
apundrad weorðan   to woruldgedale.
Ne magon ge ða word geseðan   þe ge hwile nu on unriht
wrigon under womma sceatum,   ne magon ge þa wyrd
bemiðan,
bedyrnan þa deopan mihte." Ða wurdon hie deaðes on
wenan,
585 ades ond endelifes,   ond þær þa ænne betæhton
giddum gearusnottorne,   (þam wæs Iudas nama
cenned for cneomagum),   þone hie þære cwene agefon,
sægdon hine sundorwisne: "He þe mæg soð gecyðan,
onwreon wyrda geryno,   swa ðu hine wordum frignest,
590 æriht from orde   oð ende forð.
He is for eorðan   æðeles cynnes,
wordcræftes wis   ond witgan sunu,
bald on meðle;   him gebyrde is
þæt he gencwidas   gleawe hæbbe,
595 cræft in breostum.   He gecyðeð þe
for wera mengo   wisdomes gife
þurh þa myclan miht,   swa þin mod lufaþ."
Hio on sybbe forlet   secan gehwylcne
agenne eard,   ond þone ænne genam,
600 Iudas to gisle,   ond þa georne bæd
þæt he be ðære rode   riht getæhte
þe ær in legere wæs   lange bedyrned,
ond hine seolfne   sundor acigde.
Elene maþelode   to þam anhagan,
605 tireadig cwen: "Þe synt tu gearu,
swa lif swa deað,   swa þe leofre bið
to geceosanne.   Cyð ricene nu
hwæt ðu þæs to þinge   þafian wille."
Iudas hire ongen þingode   (ne meahte he þa gehðu
bebugan,

590 orde] ord

610 oncyrran rex geniðlan;   he wæs on þære cwene ge-
             wealdum):
"Hu mæg þæm geweorðan   þe on westenne
meðe ond meteleas   morland tryðeð,
hungre gehæfted,   ond him hlaf ond stan
on gesihðe bu   samod geweorðað,
615 streac ond hnesce,   þæt he þone stan nime
wið hungres hleo,   hlafes ne gime,
gewende to wædle,   ond þa wiste wiðsæce,
beteran wiðhyccge,   þonne he bega beneah?"
 Him þa seo eadige   ondwyrde ageaf
620 Elene for eorlum   undearnunga:
"Gif ðu in heofonrice   habban wille
eard mid englum   ond on eorðan lif,
sigorlean in swegle,   saga ricene me
hwær seo rod wunige   radorcyninges,
625 halig under hrusan,   þe ge hwile nu
þurh morðres man   mannum dyrndun."
 Iudas maðelade,   (him wæs geomor sefa,
hat æt heortan,   ond gehwæðres wa,
ge he heofonrices   hyht swa mode
630 ond þis ondwearde   anforlete,
rice under roderum,   ge he ða rode ne tæhte):
"Hu mæg ic þæt findan   þæt swa fyrn gewearð
wintra gangum?   Is nu worn sceacen,
CC oððe ma   geteled rime.
635 Ic ne mæg areccan,   nu ic þæt rim ne can.
Is nu feala siðþan   forðgewitenra
frodra ond godra   þe us fore wæron,
gleawra gumena.   Ic on geogoðe wearð
on siðdagum   syððan acenned,
640 cnihtgeong hæleð.   Ic ne can þæt ic nat,
findan on fyrhðe   þæt swa fyrn gewearð."
 Elene maðelade   him on ondsware:
"Hu is þæt geworden   on þysse werþeode

---

614 samod] *Not in MS.* 629 hyht] *Not in MS.* 636 feala] feale
637 us] *Followed by an erasure of two letters* 640 ic] *The second* ic *added
above the line*

þæt ge swa monigfeald   on gemynd witon,
645 alra tacna gehwylc   swa Troiana
þurh gefeoht fremedon?   Þæt wæs fyr mycle,
open ealdgewin,   þonne þeos æðele gewyrd,
geara gongum.   Ge þæt geare cunnon
edre gereccan,   hwæt þær eallra wæs
650 on manrime   morðorslehtes,
dareðlacendra   deadra gefeallen
under bordhagan.   Ge þa byrgenna
under stanhleoðum,   ond þa stowe swa some,
ond þa wintergerim   on gewritu setton."
655 Iudas maðelade,   gnornsorge wæg:
"We þæs hereweorces,   hlæfdige min,
for nydþearfe   nean myndgiaþ,
ond þa wiggþræce   on gewritu setton,
þeoda gebæru,   ond þis næfre
660 þurh æniges mannes   muð gehyrdon
hæleðum cyðan,   butan her nu ða."
    Him seo æðele cwen   ageaf ondsware:
"Wiðsæcest ðu to swiðe   soðe ond rihte
ymb þæt lifes treow,   ond nu lytle ær
665 sægdest soðlice   be þam sigebeame
leodum þinum,   ond nu on lige cyrrest."
    Iudas hire ongen þingode,   cwæð þæt he þæt on gehðu
                                              gespræce
ond on tweon swiðost,   wende him trage hnagre.
    Him oncwæð hraðe   caseres mæg:
670 "Hwæt, we ðæt hyrdon   þurh halige bec
hæleðum cyðan   þæt ahangen wæs
on Caluarie   cyninges freobearn,
godes gastsunu.   Þu scealt geagninga
wisdom onwreon,   swa gewritu secgaþ,
675 æfter stedewange   hwær seo stow sie
Caluarie,   ær þec cwealm nime,
swilt for synnum,   þæt ic hie syððan mæge
geclænsian   Criste to willan,

646 fyr mycle] fær mycel   661 hæleðum] hæleðu   668 on] *Not in MS.*
671 ahangen] ahaⁿgen   676 Caluarie] caluare

hæleðum to helpe,   þæt me halig god
680 gefylle, frea mihtig,   feores ingeþanc,
weoruda wuldorgeofa,   willan minne,
gasta geocend."   Hire Iudas oncwæð
stiðhycgende: "Ic þa stowe ne can,
ne þæs wanges wiht   ne þa wisan cann."
685   Elene maðelode   þurh eorne hyge:
"Ic þæt geswerige   þurh sunu meotodes,
þone ahangnan god,   þæt ðu hungre scealt
for cneomagum   cwylmed weorðan,
butan þu forlæte   þa leasunga
690 ond me sweotollice   soð gecyðe."
   Heht þa swa cwicne   corðre lædan,
scufan scyldigne   (scealcas ne gældon)
in drygne seað,   þær he duguða leas
siomode in sorgum   VII nihta fyrst
695 under hearmlocan   hungre geþreatod,
clommum beclungen,   ond þa cleopigan ongan
sarum besylced   on þone seofeðan dæg,
meðe ond meteleas,   (mægen wæs geswiðrod):
"Ic eow healsie   þurh heofona god
700 þæt ge me of ðyssum earfeðum   up forlæten,
heanne fram hungres geniðlan.   Ic þæt halige treo
lustum cyðe,   nu ic hit leng ne mæg
helan for hungre.   Is þes hæft to ðan strang,
þreanyd þæs þearl   ond þes þroht to ðæs heard
705 dogorrimum.   Ic adreogan ne mæg,
ne leng helan   be ðam lifes treo,
þeah ic ær mid dysige   þurhdrifen wære
ond ðæt soð to late   seolf gecneowe."
   Þa ðæt gehyrde   sio þær hæleðum scead,
710 beornes gebæro,   hio bebead hraðe
þæt hine man of nearwe   ond of nydcleofan,
fram þam engan hofe,   up forlete.
Hie ðæt ofstlice   efnedon sona,
ond hine mid arum   up gelæddon
715 of carcerne,   swa him seo cwen bebead.

715 bebead] be *inserted between* cwen *and* bead

Stopon þa to þære stowe   stiðhycgende
on þa dune up   ðe dryhten ær
ahangen wæs,   heofonrices weard,
godbearn on galgan,   ond hwæðre geare nyste,
720 hungre gehyned,   hwær sio halige rod,
þurh feondes searu   foldan getyned,
lange legere fæst   leodum dyrne
wunode wælreste.   Word stunde ahof
elnes oncyðig,   ond on Ebrisc spræc:
725   "Dryhten hælend,   þu ðe ahst doma geweald,
ond þu geworhtest   þurh þines wuldres miht
heofon ond eorðan   ond holmþræce,
sæs sidne fæðm,   samod ealle gesceaft,
ond þu amæte   mundum þinum
730 ealne ymbhwyrft   ond uprador,
ond þu sylf sitest,   sigora waldend,
ofer þam æðelestan   engelcynne,
þe geond lyft farað   leohte bewundene,
mycle mægenþrymme.   Ne mæg þær manna gecynd
735 of eorðwegum   up geferan
in lichoman   mid þa leohtan gedryht,
wuldres aras.   Þu geworhtest þa
ond to þegnunge   þinre gesettest,
halig ond heofonlic.   Þara on hade sint
740 in sindreame   syx genemned,
þa ymbsealde synt   mid syxum eac
fiðrum gefrætwad,   fægere scinaþ.
Þara sint IIII   þe on flihte a
þa þegnunge   þrymme beweotigaþ
745 fore onsyne   eces deman,
singallice   singaþ in wuldre
hædrum stefnum   heofonciningis lof,
woða wlitegaste,   ond þas word cweðaþ
clænum stefnum,   (þam is ceruphin nama):

---

716 stowe stiðhycgende] *With* stowe stið *on an erasure*   718 wæs] *A second* wæs *erased after this word*   720 halige] halig   721 feondes] *Not in MS.*   731 sigora] sig°ra *preceded by* on *erased*   734 mægenþrymme] mægen þrȳme, *added above the line*   743 sint] sit   749 ceruphin] *With* cer *on an erasure*

750 'Halig is se halga   heahengla god,
  weoroda wealdend!   Is ðæs wuldres ful
  heofun ond eorðe   ond eall heahmægen,
  tire getacnod.'   Syndon tu on þam,
  sigorcynn on swegle,   þe man seraphin
755 be naman hateð.   He sceal neorxnawang
  ond lifes treo   legene sweorde
  halig healdan.   Heardecg cwacaþ,
  beofaþ brogdenmæl,   ond bleom wrixleð
  grapum gryrefæst.   Þæs ðu, god dryhten,
760 wealdest widan fyrhð,   ond þu womfulle
  scyldwyrcende   sceaðan of radorum
  awurpe wonhydige.   Þa sio werge sceolu
  under heolstorhofu   hreosan sceolde
  in wita forwyrd,   þær hie in wylme nu
765 dreogaþ deaðcwale   in dracan fæðme,
  þeostrum forþylmed.   He þinum wiðsoc
  aldordome.   Þæs he in ermðum sceal,
  ealra fula ful,   fah þrowian,
  þeowned þolian.   Þær he þin ne mæg
770 word aweorpan,   is in witum fæst,
  ealre synne fruma,   susle gebunden.
    Gif þin willa sie,   wealdend engla,
  þæt ricsie   se ðe on rode wæs,
  ond þurh Marian   in middangeard
775 acenned wearð   in cildes had,
  þeoden engla,   (gif he þin nære
  sunu synna leas,   næfre he soðra swa feala
  in woruldrice   wundra gefremede
  dogorgerimum;   no ðu of deaðe hine
780 swa þrymlice,   þeoda wealdend,
  aweahte for weorodum,   gif he in wuldre þin
  þurh ða beorhtan   bearn ne wære),
  gedo nu, fæder engla,   forð beacen þin.
  Swa ðu gehyrdest   þone halgan wer

757 Heardecg] *With* ecg *added above the line*   765 deaðcwale] ð *altered
from* t   771 susle] sule *with a second* s *inserted between* u *and* l   774
middangeard] middanḡ   784 gehyrdest] *A letter erased after this word*

785 Moyses on meðle,   þa ðu, mihta god,
    geywdest þam eorle   on þa æðelan tid
    under beorhhliðe   ban Iosephes,
    swa ic þe, weroda wyn,   gif hit sie willa þin,
    þurg þæt beorhte gesceap   biddan wille
790 þæt me þæt goldhord,   gasta scyppend,
    geopenie,   þæt yldum wæs
    lange behyded.   Forlæt nu, lifes fruma,
    of ðam wangstede   wynsumne up
    under radores ryne   rec astigan
795 lyftlacende.   Ic gelyfe þe sel
    ond þy fæstlicor   ferhð staðelige,
    hyht untweondne,   on þone ahangnan Crist,
    þæt he sie soðlice   sawla nergend,
    ece ælmihtig,   Israhela cining,
800 walde widan ferhð   wuldres on heofenum,
    a butan ende   ecra gestealda."
        Ða of ðære stowe   steam up aras
    swylce rec under radorum.   Þær aræred wearð
    beornes breostsefa.   He mid bæm handum,
805 eadig ond ægleaw,   upweard plegade.
    Iudas maþelode,   gleaw in geþance:
    "Nu ic þurh soð hafu   seolf gecnawen
    on heardum hige   þæt ðu hælend eart
    middangeardes.   Sie ðe, mægena god,
810 þrymsittendum   þanc butan ende,
    þæs ðu me swa meðum   ond swa manweorcum
    þurh þin wuldor inwrige   wyrda geryno.
    Nu ic þe, bearn godes,   biddan wille,
    weoroda willgifa,   nu ic wat þæt ðu eart
815 gecyðed ond acenned   allra cyninga þrym,
    þæt ðu ma ne sie   minra gylta,
    þara þe ic gefremede   nalles feam siðum,
    metud, gemyndig.   Læt mec, mihta god,
    on rimtale   rices þines
820 mid haligra   hlyte wunigan

786 geywdest] ge hywdest   788 wyn] .w.   810 þrymsittendum] þrym
sittendum *with another* m *erased after* þrym

in þære beorhtan byrig,   þær is broðor min
geweorðod in wuldre,   þæs he wære wið þec,
Stephanus, heold,   þeah he stangreopum
worpod wære.   He hafað wigges lean,
825 blæd butan blinne.   Sint in bocum his
wundor þa he worhte   on gewritum cyðed."
    Ongan þa wilfægen   æfter þam wuldres treo,
elnes anhydig,   eorðan delfan
under turfhagan,   þæt he on XX
830 fotmælum feor   funde behelede,
under neolum niðer   næsse gehydde
in þeostorcofan.   He ðær III mette
in þam reonian hofe   roda ætsomne,
greote begrauene,   swa hio geardagum
835 arleasra sceolu   eorðan beþeahton,
Iudea cynn.   Hie wið godes bearne
nið ahofun,   swa hie no sceoldon,
þær hie leahtra fruman   larum ne hyrdon.
Þa wæs modgemynd   myclum geblissod,
840 hige onhyrded,   þurh þæt halige treo,
inbryrded breostsefa,   syððan beacen geseh,
halig under hrusan.   He mid handum befeng
wuldres wynbeam,   ond mid weorode ahof
of foldgræfe.   Feðegestas
845 eodon, æðelingas,   in on þa ceastre.
    Asetton þa on gesyhðe   sigebeamas III
eorlas anhydige   fore Elenan cneo,
collenferhðe.   Cwen weorces gefeah
on ferhðsefan,   ond þa frignan ongan
850 on hwylcum þara beama   bearn wealdendes,
hæleða hyhtgifa,   hangen wære:
"Hwæt, we þæt hyrdon   þurh halige bec
tacnum cyðan,   þæt twegen mid him
geþrowedon,   ond he wæs þridda sylf
855 on rode treo.   Rodor eal geswearc
on þa sliðan tid.   Saga, gif ðu cunne,

836 cynn] *Not in MS.*   841 geseh] ḡ *with* seh *added above the line*   847
cneo] cⁿeo   855 treo] *Erasure of four or five letters before this word*

on hwylcre þyssa þreora   þeoden engla
geþrowode,   þrymmes hyrde."
   Ne meahte hire Iudas,   ne ful gere wiste,
860 sweotole gecyþan   be ðam sigebeame,
on hwylcne se hælend   ahafen wære,
sigebearn godes,   ær he asettan heht
on þone middel   þære mæran byrig
beamas mid bearhtme,   ond gebidan þær
865 oððæt him gecyðde   cyning ælmihtig
wundor for weorodum   be ðam wuldres treo.
Gesæton sigerofe,   sang ahofon,
rædþeahtende,   ymb þa roda þreo
oð þa nigoðan tid,   hæfdon neowne gefean
870 mærðum gemeted.   þa þær menigo cwom,
folc unlytel,   ond gefærenne man
brohton on bære   beorna þreate
on neaweste,   (wæs þa nigoðe tid),
gingne gastleasne.   þa ðær Iudas wæs
875 on modsefan   miclum geblissod.
Heht þa asettan   sawlleasne,
life belidenes   lic on eorðan,
unlifgendes,   ond up ahof
rihtes wemend   þara roda twa
880 fyrhðgleaw on fæðme   ofer þæt fæge hus,
deophycgende.   Hit wæs dead swa ær,
lic legere fæst.   Leomu colodon
þreanedum beþeaht.   þa sio þridde wæs
ahafen halig.   Hra wæs on anbide
885 oððæt him uppan   æðelinges wæs
rod aræred,   rodorcyninges beam,
sigebeacen soð.   He sona aras
gaste gegearwod,   geador bu samod
lic ond sawl.   þær wæs lof hafen
890 fæger mid þy folce.   Fæder weorðodon,
ond þone soðan   sunu wealdendes
wordum heredon.   Sie him wuldor ond þanc
a butan ende   eallra gesceafta!

861 hwylcne] hwylcre   877 belidenes] *Four letters erased after this word*

Ða wæs þam folce on ferhðsefan,
895 ingemynde, swa him a scyle,
wundor þa þe worhte weoroda dryhten
to feorhnere fira cynne,
lifes lattiow. Þa þær ligesynnig
on lyft astah lacende feond.
900 Ongan þa hleoðrian helledeofol,
eatol æclæca, yfela gemyndig:
"Hwæt is þis, la, manna, þe minne eft
þurh fyrngeflit folgaþ wyrdeð,
iceð ealdne nið, æhta strudeð?
905 Þis is singal sacu. Sawla ne moton
manfremmende in minum leng
æhtum wunigan. Nu cwom elþeodig,
þone ic ær on firenum fæstne talde,
hafað mec bereafod rihta gehwylces,
910 feohgestreona. Nis ðæt fæger sið.
Feala me se hælend hearma gefremede,
niða nearolicra, se ðe in Nazareð
afeded wæs. Syððan furþum weox
of cildhade, symle cirde to him
915 æhte mine. Ne mot ænige nu
rihte spowan. Is his rice brad
ofer middangeard. Min is geswiðrod
ræd under roderum. Ic þa rode ne þearf
hleahtre herigean. Hwæt, se hælend me
920 in þam engan ham oft getynde,
geomrum to sorge! Ic þurh Iudas ær
hyhtful gewearð, ond nu gehyned eom,
goda geasne, þurh Iudas eft,
fah ond freondleas. Gen ic findan can
925 þurh wrohtstafas wiðercyr siððan
of ðam wearhtreafum, ic awecce wið ðe
oðerne cyning, se ehteð þin,
ond he forlæteð lare þine
ond manþeawum minum folgaþ,

915 Ne] e *altered from* a? 916 spowan] w *altered from* n? 924 findan
can] findan ne can 925 siððan] wiððan 926 awecce] ǣwecce

930 ond þec þonne sendeð in þa sweartestan
ond þa wyrrestan witebrogan,
þæt ðu, sarum forsoht, wiðsæcest fæste
þone ahangnan cyning, þam ðu hyrdest ær."
     Him ða gleawhydig Iudas oncwæð,
935 hæleð hildedeor, (him wæs halig gast
befolen fæste, fyrhat lufu,
weallende gewitt þurh witgan snyttro),
ond þæt word gecwæð, wisdomes ful:
"Ne þearft ðu swa swiðe, synna gemyndig,
940 sar niwigan ond sæce ræran,
morðres manfrea, þæt þe se mihtiga cyning
in neolnesse nyðer bescufeð,
synwyrcende, in susla grund
domes leasne, se ðe deadra feala
945 worde awehte. Wite ðu þe gearwor
þæt ðu unsnyttrum anforlete
leohta beorhtost ond lufan dryhtnes,
þone fægran gefean, ond on fyrbæðe
suslum beþrungen syððan wunodest,
950 ade onæled, ond þær awa scealt,
wiðerhycgende, wergðu dreogan,
yrmðu butan ende." Elene gehyrde
hu se feond ond se freond geflitu rærdon,
tireadig ond trag, on twa halfa,
955 synnig ond gesælig. Sefa wæs þe glædra
þæs þe heo gehyrde þone hellesceaþan
oferswiðedne, synna bryttan,
ond þa wundrade ymb þæs weres snyttro,
hu he swa geleafful on swa lytlum fæce
960 ond swa uncyðig æfre wurde,
gleawnesse þurhgoten. Gode þancode,
wuldorcyninge, þæs hire se willa gelamp
þurh bearn godes bega gehwæðres,
ge æt þære gesyhðe þæs sigebeames,

937 witgan] wigan   941 þe] *Not in MS.*   952 ende] *A letter erased
before this word*   954 halfa] ha^lfa   957 oferswiðedne] ofer swiðende
958 ymb þæs] ym_bþæs

965 ge ðæs geleafan   þe hio swa leohte oncneow,
    wuldorſæste gife   in þæs weres breostum.
       Ða wæs gefrege   in þære folcsceare,
    geond þa werþeode   wide læded,
    mære morgenspel   manigum on andan
970 þara þe dryhtnes æ   dyrnan woldon,
    boden æfter burgum,   swa brimo fæðmeð,
    in ceastra gehwære,   þæt Cristes rod,
    fyrn foldan begræfen,   funden wære,
    selest sigebeacna   þara þe sið oððe ær
975 halig under heofenum   ahafen wurde,
    ond wæs Iudeum   gnornsorga mæst,
    werum wansæligum,   wyrda laðost,
    þær hie.hit for worulde   wendan meahton,
    cristenra gefean.   Ða sio cwen bebead
980 ofer eorlmægen   aras fysan
    ricene to rade.   Sceoldon Romwarena
    ofer heanne holm   hlaford secean
    ond þam wiggende   wilspella mæst
    seolfum gesecgan,   þæt ðæt sigorbeacen
985 þurh meotodes est   meted wære,
    funden in foldan,   þæt ær feala mæla
    behyded wæs   halgum to teonan,
    cristenum folce.   Þa ðam cininge wearð
    þurh þa mæran word   mod geblissod,
990 ferhð gefeonde.   Næs þa fricgendra
    under goldhoman   gad in burgum,
    feorran geferede.   Wæs him frofra mæst
    geworden in worlde   æt ðam willspelle,
    hlihende hyge,   þe him hereræswan
995 ofer eastwegas,   aras brohton,
    hu gesundne sið   ofer swonrade
    secgas mid sigecwen   aseted hæfdon
    on Creca land.   Hie se casere heht
    ofstum myclum   eft gearwian
1000 sylfe to siðe.   Secgas ne gældon

971 boden] bodan   972 rod] *Not in MS.*   974 sigebeacna] sige be^acna
984 þæt ðæt] þe ðæt   996 swonrade] spon rade   997 aseted] aseten

syððan andsware   edre gehyrdon,
æðelinges word.   Heht he Elenan hæl
abeodan beadurofre,   gif hie brim nesen
ond gesundne sið   settan mosten,
1005 hæleð hwætmode,   to þære halgan byrig.
Heht hire þa aras   eac gebeodan
Constantinus   þæt hio cirican þær
on þam beorhhliðe   begra rædum
getimbrede,   tempel dryhtnes
1010 on Caluarie   Criste to willan,
hæleðum to helpe,   þær sio halige rod
gemeted wæs,   mærost beama
þara þe gefrugnen   foldbuende
on eorðwege.   Hio geefnde swa,
1015 siððan winemagas   westan brohton
ofer lagufæsten   leofspell manig.
   Ða seo cwen bebead   cræftum getyde
sundor asecean   þa selestan,
þa þe wrætlicost   wyrcan cuðon
1020 stangefogum,   on þam stedewange
girwan godes tempel,   swa hire gasta weard
reord of roderum.   Heo þa rode heht
golde beweorcean   ond gimcynnum,
mid þam æðelestum   eorcnanstanum
1025 besettan searocræftum   ond þa in seolfren fæt
locum belucan.   þær þæt lifes treo,
selest sigebeama,   siððan wunode
æðelum anbræce.   þær bið a gearu
wraðu wannhalum   wita gehwylces,
1030 sæce ond sorge.   Hie sona þær
þurh þa halgan gesceaft   helpe findaþ,
godcunde gife.   Swylce Iudas onfeng
æfter fyrstmearce   fulwihtes bæð,
ond geclænsod wearð   Criste getrywe,
1035 lifwearde leof.   His geleafa wearð
fæst on ferhðe,   siððan frofre gast

1019 cuðon] cuðoⁿ,   1025 besettan] Be setton   1028 æðelum] æðelu
at end of a line   anbræce] anbręce

wic gewunode   in þæs weres breostum,
bylde to bote.   He þæt betere geceas,
wuldres wynne,   ond þam wyrsan wiðsoc,
1040 deofulgildum,   ond gedwolan fylde,
unrihte æ.   Him wearð ece rex,
meotud milde, god,   mihta wealdend.
   Þa wæs gefulwad   se ðe ær feala tida
leoht gearu
                    *   *   *
1045 inbryrded breostsefa   on þæt betere lif,
gewended to wuldre.   Huru, wyrd gescreaf
þæt he swa geleaffull   ond swa leof gode
in worldrice   weorðan sceolde,
Criste gecweme.   Þæt gecyðed wearð,
1050 siððan Elene heht   Eusebium
on rædgeþeaht,   Rome bisceop,
gefetian on fultum,   forðsnoterne,
hæleða gerædum   to þære halgan byrig,
þæt he gesette   on sacerdhad
1055 in Ierusalem   Iudas þam folce
to bisceope   burgum on innan,
þurh gastes gife   to godes temple
cræftum gecorene,   ond hine Cyriacus
þurh snyttro geþeaht   syððan nemde
1060 niwan stefne.   Nama wæs gecyrred
beornes in burgum   on þæt betere forð,
æ hælendes.   Þa gen Elenan wæs
mod gemynde   ymb þa mæran wyrd,
geneahhe for þam næglum   þe ðæs nergendes
1065 fet þurhwodon   ond his folme swa some,
mid þam on rode wæs   rodera wealdend
gefæstnod, frea mihtig.   Be ðam frignan ongan
cristenra cwen,   Cyriacus bæd
þæt hire þa gina   gastes mihtum
1070 ymb wundorwyrd   willan gefylde,
onwrige wuldorgifum,   ond þæt word acwæð
to þam bisceope,   bald reordode:
   "Þu me, eorla hleo,   þone æðelan beam,

rode rodera cininges   ryhte getæhtesð,
1075 on þa ahangen wæs   hæðenum folmum
gasta geocend,   godes agen bearn,
nerigend fira.   Mec þæra nægla gen
on fyrhðsefan   fyrwet myngaþ.
Wolde ic þæt ðu funde   þa ðe in foldan gen
1080 deope bedolfen   dierne sindon,
heolstre behyded.   A min hige sorgað,
reonig reoteð,   ond geresteð no
ærþan me gefylle   fæder ælmihtig,
wereda wealdend,   willan minne,
1085 niða nergend,   þurh þara nægla cyme,
halig of hiehða.   Nu ðu hrædlice
eallum eaðmedum,   ar selesta,
þine bene onsend   in ða beorhtan gesceaft,
on wuldres wyn.   Bide wigena þrym
1090 þæt þe gecyðe,   cyning ælmihtig,
hord under hrusan   þæt gehyded gen,
duguðum dyrne,   deogol bideð."
Þa se halga ongan   hyge staðolian,
breostum onbryrded,   bisceop þæs folces.
1095 Glædmod eode   gumena þreate
god hergendra,   ond þa geornlice
Cyriacus   on Caluarie
hleor onhylde,   hygerune ne mað,
gastes mihtum   to gode cleopode
1100 eallum eaðmedum,   bæd him engla weard
geopenigean   uncuðe wyrd,
niwan on nearwe,   hwær he þara nægla swiðost
on þam wangstede   wenan þorfte.
Leort ða tacen forð,   þær hie to sægon,
1105 fæder, frofre gast,   ðurh fyres bleo
up eðigean   þær þa æðelestan
hæleða gerædum   hydde wæron
þurh nearusearwe,   næglas on eorðan.
Ða cwom semninga   sunnan beorhtra

1074 cininges] cining *at end of page*   1089 wyn] .w.
1097 Caluarie] caluarię

1110 lacende lig. Leode gesawon
    hira willgifan wundor cyðan,
    ða ðær of heolstre, swylce heofonsteorran
    oððe goldgimmas, grunde getenge,
    næglas of nearwe neoðan scinende
1115 leohte lixton. Leode gefægon,
    weorud willhreðig, sægdon wuldor gode
    ealle anmode, þeah hie ær wæron
    þurh deofles spild in gedwolan lange,
    acyrred fram Criste. Hie cwædon þus:
1120   "Nu we seolfe geseoð sigores tacen,
    soðwundor godes, þeah we wiðsocun ær
    mid leasingum. Nu is in leoht cymen,
    onwrigen, wyrda bigang. Wuldor þæs age
    on heannesse heofonrices god!"
1125   Ða wæs geblissod se ðe to bote gehwearf
    þurh bearn godes, bisceop þara leoda,
    niwan stefne. He þam næglum onfeng,
    egesan geaclod, ond þære arwyrðan
    cwene brohte. Hæfde Ciriacus
1130 eall gefylled, swa him seo æðele bebead,
    wifes willan. Þa wæs wopes hring,
    hat heafodwylm ofer hleor goten,
    (nalles for torne tearas feollon
    ofer wira gespon), wuldres gefylled
1135 cwene willa. Heo on cneow sette
    leohte geleafan, lac weorðode,
    blissum hremig, þe hire brungen wæs
    gnyrna to geoce. Gode þancode,
    sigora dryhtne, þæs þe hio soð gecneow
1140 ondweardlice þæt wæs oft bodod
    feor ær beforan fram fruman worulde,
    folcum to frofre. Heo gefylled wæs
    wisdomes gife, ond þa wic beheold
    halig heofonlic gast, hreðer weardode,
1145 æðelne innoð, swa hie ælmihtig
    sigebearn godes sioððan freoðode.

1113 goldgimmas] god gimmas   1127 þam næglum] þan næglan

Ongan þa geornlice   gastgerynum
on sefan secean   soðfæstnesse
weg to wuldre.   Huru, weroda god
1150 gefullæste,   fæder on roderum,
cining ælmihtig,   þæt seo cwen begeat
willan in worulde.   Wæs se witedom
þurh fyrnwitan   beforan sungen
eall æfter orde,   swa hit eft gelamp
1155 ðinga gehwylces.   Þeodcwen ongan
þurh gastes gife   georne secan
nearwe geneahhe,   to hwan hio þa næglas selost
ond deorlicost   gedon meahte,
dugoðum to hroðer,   hwæt þæs wære dryhtnes willa.
1160 Heht ða ġefetigean   forðsnotterne
ricene to rune,   þone þe rædgeþeaht
þurh gleawe miht   georne cuðe,
frodne on ferhðe,   ond hine frignan ongan
hwæt him þæs on sefan   selost þuhte
1165 to gelæstenne,   ond his lare geceas
þurh þeodscipe.   He hire þriste oncwæð:
"Þæt is gedafenlic   þæt ðu dryhtnes word
on hyge healde,   halige rune,
cwen seleste,   ond þæs cininges bebod
1170 georne begange,   nu þe god sealde
sawle sigesped   ond snyttro cræft,
nerigend fira.   Þu ðas næglas hat
þam æðelestan   eorðcyninga
burgagendra   on his bridels don,
1175 meare to midlum.   Þæt manigum sceall
geond middangeard   mære weorðan,
þonne æt sæcce mid þy   oferswiðan mæge
feonda gehwylcne,   þonne fyrdhwate
on twa healfe   tohtan secaþ,
1180 sweordgeniðlan,   þær hie ymb sige winnað,
wrað wið wraðum.   He ah æt wigge sped,
sigor æt sæcce,   ond sybbe gehwær,

1149 weroda] weorda   1166 þriste] *Not in MS.*   1169 seleste] selest
1180 sige] *Not in MS.*   winnað] willað

æt gefeohte friðˌ se ðe foran lædeð
bridels on blancanˌ þonne beadurofe
1185 æt garþræceˌ guman gecosteˌ
beraðˌ bord ond ord. Þis bið beorna gehwam
wið æglæce unoferswiðed
wæpen æt wigge. Be ðam se witga sangˌ
snottor searuþancumˌ (sefa deop gewodˌ
1190 wisdomes gewitt)ˌ he þæt word gecwæð:
‘Cuþ þæt gewyrðeð þæt þæs cyninges sceal
mearh under modegum midlum geweorðodˌ
bridelshringum. Bið þæt beacen gode
halig nemnedˌ ond se hwæteadigˌ
1195 wigge weorðodˌ se þæt wicg byrð.’ ”
      Þa þæt ofstlice eall gelæste
Elene for eorlum. Æðelinges hehtˌ
beorna beaggifanˌ bridels frætwanˌ
hire selfre suna sende to lace
1200 ofer geofenes stream gife unscynde.
Heht þa tosomne þa heo seleste
mid Iudeum gumena wisteˌ
hæleða cynnesˌ to þære halgan byrig
cuman in þa ceastre. Þa seo cwen ongan
1205 læran leofra heap þæt hie lufan dryhtnesˌ
ond sybbe swa same sylfra betweonumˌ
freondræddenneˌ fæste gelæston
leahtorlease in hira lifes tidˌ
ond þæs latteowes larum hyrdonˌ
1210 cristenum þeawumˌ þe him Cyriacus
budeˌ boca gleaw. Wæs se bissceophad
fægere befæsted. Oft him feorran to
lamanˌ limseoceˌ lefe cwomonˌ
healteˌ heorudreorigeˌ hreofe ond blindeˌ
1215 heaneˌ hygegeomreˌ symle hælo þær
æt þam bisceopeˌ bote fundon
ece to aldre. Ða gen him Elene forgeaf
sincweorðungaˌ þa hio wæs siðes fus
eft to eðleˌ ond þa eallum bebead

1183 foran] fonan   1189 deop] *A letter erased after this word*

1220 on þam gumrice   god hergendum,
     werum ond wifum,   þæt hie weorðeden
     mode ond mægene   þone mæran dæg,
     heortan gehigdum,   in ðam sio halige rod
     gemeted wæs,   mærost beama
1225 þara þe of eorðan   up aweoxe,
     geloden under leafum.   Wæs þa lencten agan
     butan VI nihtum   ær sumeres cyme
     on Maias kalend.   Sie þara manna gehwam
     behliden helle duru,   heofones ontyned,
1230 ece geopenad   engla rice,
     dream unhwilen,   ond hira dæl scired
     mid Marian,   þe on gemynd nime
     þære deorestan   dægweorðunga
     rode under roderum,   þa se ricesta
1235 ealles oferwealdend   earme beþeahte.   Finit.
       Þus ic frod ond fus   þurh þæt fæcne hus
     wordcræftum wæf   ond wundrum læs,
     þragum þreodude   ond geþanc reodode
     nihtes nearwe.   Nysse ic gearwe
1240 be ðære rode riht   ær me rumran geþeaht
     þurh ða mæran miht   on modes þeaht
     wisdom onwreah.   Ic wæs weorcum fah,
     synnum asæled,   sorgum gewæled,
     bitrum gebunden,   bisgum beþrungen,
1245 ær me lare onlag   þurh leohtne had
     gamelum to geoce,   gife unscynde
     mægencyning amæt   ond on gemynd begeat,
     torht ontynde,   tidum gerymde,
     bancofan onband,   breostlocan onwand,
1250 leoðucræft onleac.   Þæs ic lustum breac,
     willum in worlde.   Ic þæs wuldres treowes
     oft, nales æne,   hæfde ingemynd
     ær ic þæt wundor   onwrigen hæfde
     ymb þone beorhtan beam,   swa ic on bocum fand,
1255 wyrda gangum,   on gewritum cyðan

1228 kalend] .kl.   1234 ricesta] ricesða   1237 wordcræftum] word cræft
1240 rode] *Not in MS.*   1241 þeaht] eaht *with* þ *added before* e   1244
bisgum] bˡesgum

be ðam sigebeacne. A wæs secg oð ðæt
cnyssed cearwelmum, �windrusende,
þeah he in medohealle   maðmas þege,
æplede gold. ᚱ gnornode
1260 ᚾ gefera, nearusorge dreah,
enge rune, þær him ᛗ fore
milpaðas mæt, modig þrægde
wirum gewlenced. ᚹ is geswiðrad,
gomen æfter gearum, geogoð is gecyrred,
1265 ald onmedla. ᚢ wæs geara
geogoðhades glæm. Nu synt geardagas
æfter fyrstmearce forð gewitene,
lifwynne geliden, swa ᛚ toglideð,
flodas gefysde. ᚠ æghwam bið
1270 læne under lyfte; landes frætwe
gewitaþ under wolcnum winde geliccost,
þonne he for hæleðum hlud astigeð,
wæðeð be wolcnum, wedende færeð
ond eft semninga swige gewyrðeð,
1275 in nedcleofan nearwe geheaðrod,
þream forþrycced.
      Swa a þeos world eall gewiteð,
ond eac swa some þe hire on wurdon
atydrede, tionleg nimeð,
1280 ðonne dryhten sylf dom geseceð
engla weorude. Sceall æghwylc ðær
reordberendra riht gehyran
dæda gehwylcra þurh þæs deman muð,
ond worda swa same wed gesyllan,
1285 eallra unsnyttro ær gesprecenra,
þristra geþonca. Þonne on þreo dæleð
in fyres feng folc anra gehwylc,
þara þe gewurdon on widan feore
ofer sidne grund. Soðfæste bioð
1290 yfemest in þam ade, eadigra gedryht,
duguð domgeorne, swa hie adreogan magon

1256 secg] sæcc   1263 ᚹ] *Another* ᚹ *erased before this one*
1268 ᛚ] *Preceded by another* ᛚ *erased*   1277 a] *Not in MS.*

ond butan earfeðum   eaðe geþolian,
modigra mægen.   Him gemetgaþ eall
ældes leoma,   swa him eðost bið,
1295 sylfum geseftost.   Synfulle beoð,
mane gemengde,   in ðam midle þread,
hæleð higegeomre,   in hatne wylm,
þrosme beþehte.   Bið se þridda dæl,
awyrgede womsceaðan,   in þæs wylmes grund,
1300 lease leodhatan,   lige befæsted
þurh ærgewyrht,   arleasra sceolu,
in gleda gripe.   Gode no syððan
of ðam morðorhofe   in gemynd cumað,
wuldorcyninge,   ac hie worpene beoð
1305 of ðam heaðuwylme   in hellegrund,
torngeniðlan.   Bið þam twam dælum
ungelice.   Moton engla frean
geseon, sigora god.   Hie asodene beoð,
asundrod fram synnum,   swa smæte gold
1310 þæt in wylme bið   womma gehwylces
þurh ofnes fyr   eall geclænsod,
amered ond gemylted.   Swa bið þara manna ælc
ascyred ond asceaden   scylda gehwylcre,
deopra firena,   þurh þæs domes fyr.
1315 Moton þonne siðþan   sybbe brucan,
eces eadwelan.   Him bið engla weard
milde ond bliðe,   þæs ðe hie mana gehwylc
forsawon, synna weorc,   ond to suna metudes
wordum cleopodon.   Forðan hie nu on wlite scinaþ
1320 englum gelice,   yrfes brucaþ
wuldorcyninges   to widan feore.   Amen.

1294 ældes] eðles

NOTES

ABBREVIATIONS IN THE NOTES

An. Andreas   Ap. Fates of the Apostles   Beow. Beowulf   Brun.
Battle of Brunanburh   Dan. Daniel   El. Elene   Ex. Exodus   Gen.
Genesis   Guth. Guthlac   Jud. Judith   Jul. Juliana   Rid. Riddles
Soul and Body II. Soul and Body (Exeter Book)

For Grein, Kemble, Thorpe, Wülker, see Bibliography, Part II. For
Baskervill, Cook, Grimm, Holthausen, Kluge, Krapp, Stephens, Zupitza,
see Bibliography, Part III. For Craigie, Ettmüller, Körner, Sweet, see
Bibliography, Part IV.

Anglia Beibl.   Beiblatt zur Anglia.
Anz.fdA.   Anzeiger für deutsches Altertum.
Archiv.   Archiv für das Studium der neueren Sprachen und Literaturen.
Beitr.   Beiträge zur Geschichte der deutschen Sprache und Literatur.
Bonner Beitr.   Bonner Beiträge zur Anglistik.
Bonnet.   Acta Andreae et Matthiae, in Part 2, Vol. I, of Acta Apostolorum
    Apocrypha, ed. Lipsius et Bonnet.
Bos.-Tol.   Bosworth-Toller, Anglo-Saxon Dictionary.
Eng. Stud.   Englische Studien.
Grein, Dicht.   Dichtungen der Angelsachsen, Vol. II.
Grein, Spr.   Sprachschatz der angelsächsischen Dichter.
Grein-Köhler.   Sprachschatz der angelsächsischen Dichter, revised ed. by
    Köhler.
JEGPh.   Journal of English and Germanic Philology.
Kock, JJJ.   Jubilee Jaunts and Jottings.
Kock, PPP.   Plain Points and Puzzles.
Leo.   Quæ de se ipso Cynevulfus poeta Anglosaxonicus tradiderit.
MLN.   Modern Language Notes.
Records.   The Anglo-Saxon Poetic Records, ed. Krapp.
Sievers, Angels. Gram.   Angelsächsische Grammatik, 3d ed., 1898.
Tijdschrift.   Tijdschrift voor Nederlandsche Taal- en Letterkunde.
Trautmann, BEV.   Berichtigungen, Erklärungen und Vermutungen zu
    Cynewulfs Werken, in Bonner Beitr. XXIII, 85–146.
Von der Warth.   Metrisch-sprachliches und Textkritisches zu Cynewulfs
    Werken.
ZfdA.   Zeitschrift für deutsches Altertum.
ZfdPh.   Zeitschrift für deutsche Philologie.

NOTES ON ANDREAS

1–100

Andreas] For the title, see Introd., p. xviii.   1 gefrunan] Preterite plurals in *-an* are very frequent in the Vercelli Book and have not been altered. 18 gesceode] Grimm and Kemble alter to *gesceod*, but the meter requires *gesceode*. On *gesceode* as a weak variant of the more regular *gesceod*, see Bright, MLN. XVII, 426.   23 ah] The spelling *ah* occurs eight times in Andreas, the spelling *ac* five times, and *ach* only in l. 1592.   31 heafodgimmas] Cosijn, Beitr. XXI, 8, proposed this emendation, the word being a masculine noun. The spelling *-gimme* was obviously an echo of *-grimme* in the first half-line.   32 agetton] See l. 1143, and Brun. 18, *garum ageted*. 36 heortan on hreðre] The edd. retain the MS. reading *heortan hreðre*, except Krapp and Craigie, who supply *on* before *hreðre*. So also Kock, Anglia XLIII, 298. The preposition evidently was omitted by the scribe because of its similarity to the ending of *heortan*.   38–39] Trautmann, BEV., p. 108, would change *meðe*, l. 40, to *muðe*, and *gedrehte* to *geræhten*, "with their mouth they sought hay and grass." But *meðe* is an adj., agreeing with *hie*, "but hay and grass afflicted them, weary for lack of food." See l. 1157.   43 gedræg] The dictionaries assume one word of two forms, *gedræg* and *gedreag*, but Kock, Anglia XLVI, 64, would distinguish these, deriving *gedræg*, "bustle," from *dragan*, and *gedreag* from *dreogan*.   51 abreoton] Grimm and Kemble change to *abruton*, but the form *abreoton* seems to be by attraction to the reduplicating verbs, see Sievers, Angels. Gram., § 384, 2, and Bright, MLN. II, 160.   54 onmod] "Resolute," as in l. 1638, and not the same as *ānmōd*, "of one mind," as in ll. 1565, 1601. 64 seowað] Grimm reads *seowað*, "sew, weave," for the MS. *seoðað*, followed by Kemble, Grein, Cosijn, Beitr. XXI, 8, and Krapp. But Grimm also suggested the possibility of retaining the MS. reading in the sense "coquunt" = "weld, fashion." Kock, Anglia XLVI, 64, would retain *seoðað* in the sense "torment," with *elþeodige inwitwrasne* as subject, translating, "foreign chains torment me." Kock does not translate *searonet*. The parallel of Beow. 406, *searonet seowed*, strongly supports the reading *seowað*, with *inwitwrasne* and *searonet* as objects.   66 geohða] Cosijn, Beitr. XXI, 8, would read *geahða*, "foolishness," "mockery," anticipating *dumban*, l. 67, instead of *geohða*, "sorrow."   85 scyldhetum] See *niðhetum*, l. 834. 82–83] Kock, Anglia XLV, 105, would have no punctuation after *stapolige* and a comma after *fæste*, taking *fæste* as an adverb modifying *stapolige*. But if one insists on taking *fæste* as adverb, "to confirm firmly," it is better to take it so only with the second of the two parallel objects *mod* and *fyrhð-lufan*.   89 segl] The spelling *segl* occurs in l. 50, the spelling *sægl* in l. 1456. Perhaps the MS. form *sęgl* was intended to indicate this second spelling.

101–200

106 willan] A genitive, parallel to *tyres*, as Kock, JJJ., p. 1, points out.
109 synnige] The MS. reading *synne* might be retained, as it is by all edd.
except Krapp, as an instrumental noun, but one expects a parallel to *wær-logan*, l. 108, and see ll. 565, 710, 964. Trautmann, BEV., p. 109, reads
synge.   **115** of nede most] Von der Warth, p. 12, would alter to *of nedum eft*, retaining *hweorfest*, l. 117.   **117** hweorfan] All edd. retain *hweorfest*
except Krapp, who reads *hweorfan*, following Cosijn, Beitr. XXI, 8. So
also Trautmann, BEV., p. 109.   **120** on riht] All edd. read *on riht*, except
Grein, who reads *onriht* as adj., and so also Trautmann, BEV., p. 109.
See ll. 324, 700.   **127–128**] Monroe, MLN. XXXI, 374, would place l. 128
before l. 127. But Grein's arrangement of the lines is satisfactory with l.
127 in parentheses, and *hrysedon* as intransitive.   **134** on rimcræfte]
Cosijn, Beitr. XXI, 8, would omit *on.*   **140** hira mod] Equivalent to
"they"; see l. 454, *ure mod* = "we," l. 1242, *þæt æðele mod* = "he," and
other examples in El. 597, Jul. 26, 209, Guth. 711.   **142** eafeðum] The
late MS. spelling *eaueðum* may well have been a customary spelling of the
scribe's day, but that it was accidental here is sufficiently proved by the
fact that among the innumerable opportunities the scribe had of writing
u for voiced *f*, this is the only example that occurs in the whole text of
Andreas. See El. 89, note.   **145** þæs] The edd. read *hwæs* for the MS.
wæs, except Krapp, who reads *þæs*, following Bright, MLN. II, 160, and so
Craigie. The first letter of *þæs* was probably miswritten by the scribe as the
usual runic symbol for *w*, the opposite to what apparently happened in
seoðað, l. 64. But Lohmann, Anglia III, 126, Zupitza, Anglia III, 369,
Klaeber, Archiv CXX, 153, defend *hwæs*, and Trautmann, BEV., p. 142,
approves Bright's *þæs*.   **157** symble] An adverb, "ever," as in ll. 659,
1384, 1581. But Trautmann, BEV., p. 109, thinks that *symble* violates
sense and meter. He supposes an omission in the MS. and would print:

> Swa hie symble ... .
> ... ymb þritig   þing gehedon
> nihtgerimes.

164 oft] The edd. retain *of*, except Krapp, *oft*, following Cosijn, Beitr. XXI,
9, and so also Trautmann, BEV., p. 109.   **167** sio] Equivalent to "his,"
i.e. Andrew's. See Sievers, Beitr. XII, 192.   **171** cirebaldum] The only
occurrence of this compound. Müller (see Wülker, Bibliothek II, 9),
suggested *cynebaldum.*   **174** frið] For *frihð*, a variant of *ferhð*, see Gen.
107, 1142, notes, in Records I, and also An. 282, 337, 430. Cosijn, Beitr.
XXI, 9, Simons, Cynewulfs Wortschatz, p. 39, Trautmann, BEV., p. 109,
change *frið* to *ferð*, but Kock, JJJ., p. 2, would retain *frið*. Trautmann
also thinks l. 174*a* is too short metrically and would read *þu feran scealt* or *þu
scealt geferan.*   **185** fore] Cosijn, Beitr. XXI, 9, Simons, Cynewulfs Wortschatz, p. 107, would read *ofer* for *fore*. But take *fore* as adverb, "it is now
three days before." Kock, Anglia XLVI, 66, confirms this reading.
þære] Von der Warth, p. 13, would omit *þære* for metrical reasons.

195 halig of heofenum] The emendation was made by Von der Warth, p. 14, and Kock, Anglia XLVI, 66. Trautmann, Kynewulf, p. 117, had previously suggested *heah* before *of.* 198 wegas ofer widland] All edd., except Krapp, read *wid land,* "ways over the wide land," but Grein, Germania X, 423, changes to *widland* = the earth. Whether one should read *wegas,* "ways, paths," or *wēgas,* "waves," is debatable, see Krapp, Andreas, l. 198, note, and Klaeber, Archiv CXX, 154. winas] Cosijn, Beitr. XXI, 9, would change to *weras,* but Kock, Anglia XLII, 111, would retain *winas* as meaning "people," not "friends." But the meaning "friends" is better, "These stranger earls are not my familiar friends."

201–300

216*a*] Trautmann, BEV., p. 110, suggests omitting *þa fore* to shorten the line metrically. 224 mine] For similar word-order, see l. 479*b*. 234 gearo, guðe fram] Wülker has a comma after *guðe* and no punctuation after *fram.* The punctuation in the text was suggested by Cosijn, Beitr. XXI, 9, and approved by Trautmann, BEV., p. 110. 236 faruðe] For the confusion between *faroð* and *waroð,* see Krapp, Modern Philology II, 405–406. 243 blac] Kock, Anglia XLVI, 67, would take *blac* as adj., "resplendent," and therefore would place only a comma after *heolstre.* 245 gemette] Kemble supplied *gesceawode* for the obvious omission here, and Grimm, followed by Grein, Wülker and Baskervill, supplied *geseah.* Since neither of these words is adequate metrically, the reading *gemētte* by Sievers, Beitr. X, 517, is to be preferred. Trautmann, BEV., p. 110, suggests *funde* or *mētte,* or *gemētte,* with Sievers. 255 fægn] The MS. reading *frægn* is retained by all edd. except Krapp, who reads *fægn* with Cosijn, Beitr. XXI, 9. The juxtaposition of two verbs would be doubtful in any case, but the reading *fægn* here is placed beyond question by the corresponding passage in the Greek text, see Bonnet, p. 70, ἐχάρη χαρὰν μεγάλην σφόδρα. The Anglo-Saxon prose Legend of St. Andrew, Bright, Reader, p. 116, has: *and he wæs gefeonde mid mycle gefean and him to cwæð.* 257 macræftige] See l. 472. These are the only two occurrences of this compound, the first element of which seems to be *ma-,* comparative of *micel.* Grimm, note, suggests, however, that *ma-* may be a substantive, synonym of *mere,* "sea." Sweet, Student's Dictionary, p. 111, suggests *mægen-* for *ma-.* 258 ane ægflotan] The phrase may be taken as appositive to *macræftige men,* in which case *ane* is best translated as "solitary," or as appositive to *ceolum,* with *ane* in the sense "admirable," see Beow. 1885, *þæt wæs an cyning.* 261 swa þæt ne wiste] "As though he (God) did not know," and see l. 501 for this sense of *swa.* Kock, Anglia XLVI, 68, explains the passage as meaning "without Andrew knowing," but this does not accord with l. 262. 267 snude] Cosijn, Beitr. XXI, 9, followed by Simons, Cynewulfs Wortschatz, p. 130, Trautmann, BEV., p. 110, would change to *sunde.* 298 aras] All edd. retain *aras* here, but Grein, Germania X, 423, suggests *ara,* and Cook, First Book, p. 214, reads *ara* in his text, "honors," "respects," as gen. pl. object of *unnan*, and with a semicolon after *gescrifene*. But this emended reading does not give a very appropriate meaning. Klaeber, Archiv CXX, 154, would take *swa*, l. 297, in the sense "then" (if you pay your fare, etc.), would place a comma after *aras* but none after *ȳðbord*, translating, "they [*scipweardas, aras*] will grant you [to go] up to the ship." Among the various difficulties of the passage, the least seems to be to take *unnan* in the sense "grant" = appoint, "as the ship-guardians, the attendants on the vessel shall appoint to you."

301–400

303 landes ne locenra beaga] Apparently taken over bodily from Beow. 2995, *landes ond locenra beaga*, and perhaps never completely assimilated to the context in Andreas. In Beowulf the genitives are dependent on *þusendra*, in the preceding line, but there is no word in Andreas governing the genitives. Monroe, MLN. XXXI, 375, takes the genitives as dependent on an implied noun, and cites Jud. 158, 330. Sievers, Beitr. XII, 461, gives this as a regular expanded line, but Trautmann, BEV., p. 110, regards *landes ne* as not by the poet. Omitting *landes ne*, the genitive *locenra beaga* would be coördinate with *wira*, l. 302. Schröer, Eng. Stud. X, 121, would also omit *landes ne.*   **308** woldes] For other examples of this ending, see *hæfdes*, l. 530, *feredes*, l. 1363, *forhogedes*, l. 1381.   **320** sarcwide] Object of *sece* and parallel to *ondsware*.   **323** his] See l. 1664 for the opposite scribal error.   **328** hefon] Grimm, Kemble and Grein alter to *heofon*, and as this is the only occurrence of the spelling *hefon* in Andreas among many examples of *heofon*, the spelling may be due to a scribal accident.   **329** selost] Cook, First Book, p. 216, note, suggests *sellend* for *selost*, as in Jul. 668, 705 and Panther 64.   The phrase *sigora selost*, "best" or "most eminent in victories," does not occur elsewhere.   **334** stedewangas] Cosijn, Beitr. XXI, 9, reads *stedewanga*, a genitive plural.   The use of *gelicgaþ* as a transitive is unusual. **339** est ahwette] Trautmann, BEV., p. 110, takes *on eowerne | agenne dom* as one line, and *est ahwette* as half of a following line with the other half lost. So also Holthausen, Anglia Beibl. XXXI, 27.   **359** helmwearde] The edd. all retain *holmwearde*, except Krapp, who reads *helmwearde*, following Cosijn, Beitr. XXI, 9.   The change is not necessary for meaning, but the parallel passages in the Greek text and the AS. prose legend make it extremely probable.   The passage in the prose is as follows, Bright, Reader, p. 117, l. 2: *and he gesæt beforan þam steorreþran þæs scipes, þæt wæs Drihten Hælend Crist.* See l. 396 and note.   **367** feasceafte] All edd. except Grein, Krapp and Craigie retain *-sceaftne*. Cosijn, Beitr. XXI, 9, and Trautmann, BEV., p. 111, also prefer *-sceafte*.   The corresponding passage in the Greek text, Bonnet, p. 72, l. 14, adds a detail not contained in the poem, that the angel gave three loaves, one for each of the strangers.   The plurals in l. 368 also favor *-sceafte*.   In favor of *-sceaftne*, it should be noted, however, that in l. 386 ff., the poem speaks only of Andrew as having eaten. Perhaps we are to infer from ll. 391–395 that his attendants were too seasick to eat. **375** wædo gewætte] Cosijn, Beitr. XXI, 9, would emend to read *wada gewealce*, which fits the context but requires too great an alteration of the text. Kock, Anglia XLIV, 245, would read *wædo geweddon*, "the waves raged." Holthausen, Anglia Beibl. XXXII, 137, prefers *wædo gewæðdon*, citing Ex. 481, or as alternative, *wæde gewætte*, "wet with the wave," referring to *strengas*, l. 374. But it is better to take *wædo* as nom. pl., in the sense "sails, cordage," with Baskervill, Bos.-Tol., under *wæd*, Simons, Cynewulfs Wortschatz, p. 148, Trautmann, BEV., p. 111, parallel therefore to *strengas*. **382** holmwege] The word may be *holmweg*, "sea-way," or *holmwēg*, "sea-wave," but probably the former, see the frequent Anglo-Saxon metaphors *bæð-, flōd-, flotweg* and *brimrād*. **383** argeblond] The first element is for *ear-*, "sea," as in El. 239, *earhgeblond*, and elsewhere. So also in *aryð*, l. 532, *arwela*, l. 853. **393** geofon] The MS. reading *heofon* is retained by Thorpe, Grimm and Wülker, but if it is retained, see also ll. 1508, 1585, it can be only as a variant spelling for *geofon*. Such a variant spelling is highly improbable, and the form is best explained as a scribal inadvertence. It is to be sure somewhat remarkable that the word *geofon* in the eight times it occurs in this poem should be spelled *heofon* three times. A triple repetition of the same mischance in spelling would be very doubtful in most cases, but *heofon* occurs so much more commonly, thirty-two times in Andreas, than *geofon*, that three misspellings seem quite credible. It should be noted also that the word *geofon* occurs an unusually large number of times in Andreas, eight times as against four times in Beowulf, a poem almost twice as long, and that consequently the chances of error would be increased. Finally one may note that other words with initial *g* are not written indifferently with *h*. **396** helman] See l. 359, note. The edd. all retain *holme* here, except Krapp. Grein, note, suggested *helme*, but the word is recorded only as a weak noun *helma*. Cook, First Book, p. 221, note, suggested *helman*, repeated by Trautmann, BEV., p. 111.

401–500

406 gode orfeorme] The phrase occurs again in l. 1617, and several times in other poems. Whether one should interpret as "destitute of God" or "destitute of good" cannot be determined from the text; Cosijn, Beitr. XXI, 9, defends *gŏde*, Trautmann, BEV., p. 112, defends *gŏde*. The prose version, Bright, Reader, p. 117, ll. 11–13, reads: *þonne beo we fremde fram eallum þam godum þe þu us gearwodest*, and thus supports *gōde*. **408** bioð laðe] Trautmann, BEV., p. 112, would read *laðe bioð*. **412** hlaforde] Trautmann, BEV., p. 112, would read *hlaford* for metrical reasons. The half-line is discussed by Sievers, Altgermanische Metrik, § 85, Anm. 2. It may well be that the *e* of *hlaforde* was added inadvertently, as the *e* of *fore-* in l. 413 certainly was. **414** nearu] The form of this word as an accusative feminine is discussed by Sievers, Beitr. I, 493, and by Klaeber, Archiv CXX, 155. **424** sund] All edd. retain *sand*, except Grein, Krapp. Cosijn, Beitr. XXI,

10, and Trautmann, BEV., p. 112, also prefer *sund*.   The word is obviously parallel to *grund*, "abyss," "ocean," in l. 425.   See El. 251.   **425** grund] Grein, note, suggests *grand* for *grund*, preterite of *grindan*, a reading which might justify *sand* in l. 424.   But the change of *sand* to *sund* is more plausible.   **432** Ælmyrcna] The first element of this compound is an intensive, *æl-* = *eal-*, and the second is the adj. *myrce*, "dark, black," the whole apparently meaning Africa or Ethiopia.   For the probable situation of Mermedonia, see Krapp, p. lxvi.   **442** bordstæðu] "The rigging of the ship." For *stæð*, see Ælfric's glossary, Wright-Wülker, Anglo-Saxon and Old English Vocabularies, I, 288, 26, where the word is glossed *safon* (= *funis in prora*, Du Cange).   brim] Grein, Germania X, 423, and Simons, Cynewulfs Wortschatz, p. 18, would read *brūn* for *brim*.   oft] Kemble alters to *eft*.   **452** Windas þreade] Thorpe and Grimm read *windes*, and Grimm, note, suggests *windes þreate*, but note to l. 453, *windas þreade*, as an emendation on the supposition that the MS. reading is *windes*.   **458** to] Grimm, Kemble and Grein omit *to*.   **483** este] The meter requires *este* as in Gen. 1509, Beow. 945.   **485** nu þe tir, etc.] Cosijn, Beitr. XXI, 10, would reconstruct to read *nu þe tircyning | þa miht forgef*.   **487** bestemdon] A past participle.   Grimm and Kemble alter to *bestemdan*, but see *bruconne*, l. 23, for *brucanne*.   **489** gifeðe] Grein, note, suggests *geofon*, "ocean," for this word, repeated by Kock, Anglia XLIII, 298, who would read *gifene*. So also Grein-Köhler, p. 261, Trautmann, BEV., p. 113.   This suits the context better, but *on gifeðe*, "by chance," "as it happened," is also permissible and requires no change.   The Greek text, however, supports *gifene*, see Bonnet, p. 75, l. 17, ἐζκαιδέκατον γὰρ ἔπλευσα τὴν θάλασσαν.   þa] Without *þa* the line is too short metrically.   Holthausen, Anglia XIII, 357, reads *iu ond nuþa*, Bright, MLN. II, 161, reads *þa iu and nu*.   Kock, Anglia XLIII, 298, would read *iu ond nuna*, "of yore and recently."   Trautmann, BEV., p. 113, would read *iu ond nyhst*, "vor langer zeit und unlängst," citing Christ 535 for similar metrical structure.   Von der Warth, p. 17, proposes *gifene | ginnum nuþa* for the MS. *gifeðe iu ond nu*.   **491** mundum freorig] "Cold as to my hands," modifying *Ic*, l. 489.   Trautmann, BEV., p. 113, would alter *freorig* to *drefde*, a verb.   **494** hæleða] All edd. retain *hæleð*, which would juxtapose two appositive nouns, except Krapp, following Cosijn, Beitr. XXI, 10.   The reading *hæleða* improves both sense and meter.   **495** steoran ofer stæfnan] Cosijn, Beitr. XXI, 10, takes *steoran* as infinitive, and suggests omitting *ofer* to make *stæfnan* object of *steoran*. But *steoran* is better taken as noun, *steora*, "steersman," as in the comment of Sievers on Cosijn's note.   **496** beateþ] The subject is *Streamwelm*, and *brimstæðo* is a plural object.   scrid] "Swift," from *scriðan*.   Trautmann, BEV., p. 114, would change to *snūd*.   **499** yðlade] The MS. *yðlafe* would mean "shore," and so all edd. read except Krapp, who has *yðlade*, following Grein in his Nachträge, Cosijn, Beitr. XXI, 11, and Cook, First Book, p. 226.   Trautmann, BEV., p. 114, would alter to *yðhofe*, making *ofer yðhofe* parallel to *ofer stæfnan*, l. 495.   Trautmann also reads *seah* in l. 499a for metrical reasons, and likewise in l. 493a.   **500** on sæleodan] Grimm and Kemble read *on sæ lædan*.

501–600

501 landsceare] See l. 1229 and *folcsceare*, l. 684. Thorpe misreported the MS. as reading *lansceape*, and Grimm, Kemble, Grein, Wülker, Baskervill and Cook, First Book, p. 226, all read *landsceape*. **504** brondstæfne] Grein reads *brontstæfne*, but Grein, Germania X, 423, and Spr. I, 136, have *brondstæfne*, an acc. sg. masc. adjective. Cosijn, Beitr. XXI, 11, would read *brontstæfnne*. **515** sið nesan] See El. 1003, *gif hie brim nesen*. In l. 516 *geferan* is a verb in the same syntax. But Grein, Spr. II, 446, and Cosijn, Beitr. XXI, 11, would read *siðnesan* as a noun, object of *geferan*. **523** wuldras] A genitive in -*as*, as in l. 1501. **552** wis on gewitte] See ll. 316, 470. The MS. has *wis ongewitte*, though the spacing of words is not always of significance. Grein reads *wisan gewitte*, Wülker has *wison gewitte*, and so Trautmann, BEV., p. 115. This makes *wison gewitte* parallel to *geofum*, a possible but improbable interpretation. That the Lord should be described as wise in wit and in words is not strange. **556** fruma ond ende] Kemble and Baskervill read *fruman*, as object of the verb, and Kock, JJJ., p. 2, repeats. Taking *fruma ond ende*, the Alpha and the Omega, the words are appositive to *cyninga wuldor*. **561** ahof] Trautmann, BEV., p. 115, would read *ahofon*, because *arleasan* is plural and *cynn* is collective. But the singular verb can agree formally with the singular *cynn*. Cosijn, Beitr. XXI, 12, would change ða *arleasan* to ðæt *arlease*, to modify *cynn*, again a mechanical grammatical emendation. **569** ah] Grein reads *and* for *ah*. **570** dæl nænigne] The edd. retain *ænigne*, except Krapp. That a negative is needed here is shown by the Greek text, Bonnet, p. 76, ll. 17–18, and also by Andrew's answer, ll. 573 ff. Kock, JJJ., p. 3, proposes to read *ne* for *he* in l. 569, or *ne he*, retaining *ænigne*. Holthausen, Anglia Beibl. XXI, 27, would read *na* for *a*, l. 569, and retain *ænigne*. **575** gif] Grein alters to *gife*, but in Germania X, 423, and in Spr. I, 505, he returns to *gif*, as an exceptional neuter singular noun. See Cosijn, Beitr. XXI, 252. **579** ða] As Trautmann, BEV., p. 116, points out, one expects ðam, but ða, nom. pl., may stand as a new grammatical start. **582** grundwægle] For *grundwege*, "ocean way." On æ = e, see -*ræced*, l. 709, *sægl*, l. 1456. The opposite, e for æ, appears in *meðlan*, l. 1440. **584** Swylce he eac] Trautmann, BEV., p. 116, would omit either *Swylce* or *eac*. **587** win of wætere] Trautmann, BEV., p. 116, would alter to *wæter to wine*. Cosijn, Beitr. XXI, 12, would take *ond* as equivalent to ðæt, a relative with *wæter* as antecedent, "which he commanded to change." But neither proposal is necessary: "He consecrated wine out of water and commanded [the water] to change." The Greek text, Bonnet, p. 77, l. 2, reads: ὕδωρ εἰς οἶνον μετέβαλεν. **592** reonigmode] Sievers, Beitr. X, 506, Krapp read *reonig*-, but the earlier edd. retain *reomig*-. Grimm has *reomig*- in his text, but discusses *reonig*-, p. 112. The word *reonigmod* occurs twice elsewhere in Anglo-Saxon poetry, but there are no examples of *reomigmod*.

601–700

601 weges weard] "The ruler of the wave," i.e. *wēges*, not *wĕges*. So also in l. 632.   **630** þe] Bright, MLN. II, 163, would read *þeh = þeah*, and so Krapp in his text. But the change is not necessary, since *þe* can be taken as a dative of reference, "for thyself."   gehwære] Sievers, Beitr. X, 485, would change to *gehwæm*, Cosijn, Beitr. XXI, 12, to *gehwæs*. See also Sievers, Angels. Gram. § 341, Anm. 4.   **633** ne] Grein and Baskervill retain the MS. reading *nu*, but the sense requires *ne*.   **636** ðæt] Trautmann, BEV., p. 117, would change ðæt to *glæd*.   **640** hweorfon] See *hweorfan*, l. 1050, and l. 51, note.   **658–667**] A rectangular blot on the right hand side of fol. 38a of the MS. obscures some words of this passage. Most of the passage is legible in the reproductions, but in a few instances the readings of Napier's collation in ZfdA. XXXIII, 66–73, and of Wülker are followed. For *getimbred*, l. 667, Wülker gives *getimbred*, with the first *e* illegible in the MS. Napier gives it as legibly but not clearly *atrimbred* (misprint for *atimbred*?).   **659** Symble] The adverb, as in l. 651.   **669** Huscworde] Grein, Spr. II, 112, suggests *us worde* for *huscworde*, and Simons, Cynewulfs Wortschatz, p. 82, citing Trautmann, suggests *usic worde*. Kock, JJJ., p. 3, would read *Wordhusce*, thus regularizing the alliteration. But *Huscworde* fits the context too well to permit changing it, even for metrical regularity.   **682** dæghwæmlice] Trautmann, BEV., p. 117, would read *dæghwæm*, citing Guth. 357, *dæghwæm dreogeð*.

701–800

712 wundor agræfene] An accusative plural, parallel in syntax to *anlicnesse*, l. 713. All edd. take the two words together as an adjective compound, except Krapp. Cosijn, Beitr. XXI, 12, would change *wundor* to *wundrum*. Kock, JJJ., p. 3, repeats Krapp's reading.   **717–719**] The addition of *þe*, l. 718, was suggested by Holthausen, Beitr. XVI, 550. With this addition, translate, "This is a representation of the most illustrious of the tribes of angels which is in that city [i.e. Heaven] among the dwellers there." Kock, Anglia XLVI, 68, would change *is*, l. 719, to *his*, and would take *þæs bremestan* as meaning "God's."   The meaning of *in þære ceastre* [*h*]*is*, he takes to be that the images were placed in the temple of Jerusalem, the city of the Lord. Kock translates, "This is, amongst the people of His city, a representing of angelic orders of the most Glorious one." For the unusual word-order and syntax of his emendation [*h*]*is*, he cites Gen. 1738, *On þam wicum his*, but the passages are not parallel, since *his* in Gen. 1738 modifies *feorh* in l. 1739. In the Greek text the two images are two sphinxes, Bonnet, p. 79, ll. 11–12, which are, however, said to be like the Cherubim and Seraphim. The phrase ἐν οὐρανῷ (Bonnet, p. 79, l. 15) apparently corresponds to the words *in þære ceastre*, l. 719. The corresponding passage does not appear in the Anglo-Saxon prose legend. The Greek text says nothing about the Cherubim and Seraphim as the highest of the orders of angels, and it may be that this elaboration, of a kind not frequent in *Andreas*, is the work of some hand other than that of the poet.   **726** þegnas] Holt-hausen, Beitr. XVI, 550, alters to *þegna*.   **733–734** secge soðcwidum, etc.] Grein supposes a loss in the MS. here and to avoid the alliteration of *s* and *sc*, he supplies *þæt ic eom sunu godes* as l. 733*b*, taking *þy sceolon gelyfan* as l. 734*a* and supplying *leoda ræswan* as l. 734*b*.   Trautmann, BEV., p. 117, and Holthausen, Anglia Beibl. XXXI, 27, also think that a full line has disappeared from the MS. after l. 733*a*.   On the alliteration of *s* and *sc*, see Sievers, Altgermanische Metrik, § 18, 3.   Von der Warth, p. 20, supplies *þæt ic eom sunu meotudes* as completing l. 733*a*, taking l. 733*b* as the first half of a following line and adding *sceolu arleasra* as completing this line. The MS. shows no indication of loss.   **736** ahleop] The number changes from the plural, see *syndon*, l. 720 and the following lines, to the singular in this passage, reflecting the Greek text, in which only one of the sphinxes comes down and speaks.   **743** werede] Cosijn, Beitr. XXI, 12, changes to *wenede*, as in l. 1682, but *wordum werede*, l. 1053, is a stronger argument in favor of the MS. reading.   **746** Ge mon cigað] The emendation was pro-posed by Cosijn, Beitr. XXI, 12, and it is supported by the Greek text, Bonnet, p. 80, l. 8, λέγοντες τὸν θεὸν εἶναι ἄνθρωπον. Kock, Anglia XLVI, 68, suggests *ge mon e[h]tigað*, "you take to be a man."   **770** ælfæle] "Baleful," and see Rid. xxiv, 9, *ealfelo attor*. On *æl-* = *eal-*, an intensive, see l. 432, note. For the second element, Kern, Taalkundige Bijdragen I, 206, Cosijn, Beitr. XXI, 13, and Trautmann, BEV., p. 117, would read *-fe(a)lo*.   þær orcnawe wearð] Von der Warth, p. 20, would read *þær wæs orcnawe*.   **774** on] Needed both metrically and syntactically, and supplied by Kemble, Sievers, Beitr. X, 517, Cosijn, Beitr. XXI, 13, Trautmann, BEV., p. 117.   **780** ærest] Kemble and Grein read *ærist*, the more usual form of the word meaning "resurrection."   **782** gaste onfon] Trautmann, Kynewulf, p. 29, would supply *ond* before *gaste*, and Sievers, Beitr. X, 476, would gain a metrical syllable by using the uncon-tracted form of *onfon*.   **787** scyppend wera] Trautmann, BEV., p. 117, would read *scyppend weroda* to gain a metrical syllable.   **794** to godes geþinge] Trautmann, BEV., p. 117, would read *to godes þinge* as a metrical improvement.   **799** hwær se, etc.] Trautmann, BEV., p. 118, suggests adding *ðē* before *se* in l. 799*a* and *sē* before *þē* in l. 799*b*.

801–900

801 ða ða] Trautmann, BEV., p. 118, would omit one *ða* or both for metrical reasons.   **808** to eadwelan] Monroe, MLN. XXXI, 375, suggests placing a comma after *eadwelan* and supplying a verb of motion with *het*, with *secan* as parallel to the verb supplied. Kock, Anglia XLIII, 300, assumes that *secan* goes both with *to eadwelan* and with *dreamas*. But *to* in *to eadwelan* may merely indicate the direction or limit of action, "seek in blessedness."   **810** þæs] The edd. read *þær*, except Krapp, although the MS. plainly has *þæs*. The word is a genitive object of *neotan*. Kock, Anglia XLVI, 69, takes its antecedent to be *eadwelan*, but it may as well be found in *swegles*, "of heaven." 816 aræfnan] Trautmann, BEV., p. 118, proposes *areccan*, "explain," for *aræfnan*, "endure." But there is apparently here a recollection of John xvi. 12. 819 herede] See ll. 873, 998. The MS. has *herede*, the first letter being a small capital *h*. The MS. was misread by the earlier edd. as *berede*, and so Baskervill and Wülker in their texts. The other edd. emend to *herede*. But Napier, ZfdA. XXXIII, 68, read *herede* correctly. 826 sæwerige] This seems to refer to the attendants of the apostle, but they were already asleep, see l. 464. Trautmann, BEV., p. 118, suggests that some words have dropped out here which referred to the apostles again. Or should one read *sæwerigne*, appositive to *leofne*? Note that l. 826 is almost a repetition of l. 820. Kock, Anglia XLVI, 69, says that the words *sæwerige slæp ofereode* crept into the text by mistake and he proposes to read *oððæt þurh lyftgelac*, etc., thus shortening the poem by one line. Von der Warth, p. 22, had previously maintained that l. 826 had got into the text by error and should be deleted. See l. 862. 828 engla] There is no interruption in the MS. following *engla*, but the break in the sense indicates that something has been lost. The corresponding passage of the Greek version indicates that nothing of importance has been lost. Grein supplies a full line after *engla*, reading *in Achaia ær getacnode*. For the following line he reads *Gewiton þa þa aras eft siðigean*. Trautmann, BEV., p. 118, approves, except that he would read *getæhte* instead of *getacnode* for metrical reasons. For the line following *engla*, Kock, Anglia XLIII, 300, reads *ær ætywde. Gewiton ða þa aras siðigean*, which Holthausen, Anglia XLIV, 352, rejects as an "unmöglicher Schwellvers." Baskervill adds nothing but places *ða þa* after *engla* in l. 828, but in American Journal of Philology VIII, 95–97, he revises, reading *þa þær* for the MS. *ða þa*, and he takes *engla ða þær* as a first half-line following his l. 828b, *þe him cining*, the second half-line being *aras siðigean*. 843 wisa] All edd. follow the MS. reading *wis*, except Krapp, but Grimm, note, suggests *wisa*. 846 þa] Grein replaces the MS. *þā* by *and*. Monroe, MLN. XXXI, 375, suggests that the mark over *a* in *þā* may not have been intended as the mark of abbreviation. Grimm, Kemble, Baskervill and Wülker read *þam him* for *þa he him*. Cook, First Book, p. 229, reads *þa him*. fore] Cosijn, Beitr. XXI, 13, supplies the article *þa* before *fore*. 853 arwelan] See l. 383, note. Trautmann, BEV., p. 119, suggests that the second element of this compound may be corrupted from *wēlas* = *wǣlas*, the plural of *wǣl*, "pool, gulf." 855 werðeode] Grimm, Kemble and Baskervill retain the MS. reading as a verb. Thorpe suggested *wer-ðeode*, and Grein reads *werþeoda*. Bright, MLN. II, 163, proposed *weoroda*. 864 faran] Supplied by Grein, Cook, First Book, p. 231, Krapp and Craigie. 869 ond swegles gong] Cook, First Book, p. 231, suggests that the scribe mis-wrote *ond* for *geond*. But the MS. has the customary abbreviation for *ond*. Simons, Cynewulfs Wortschatz, p. 131, suggests *sweges* for *swegles*. For *swegles gong*, see ll. 208, 455. The phrase does not fit the context very well, but it may have been taken bodily from stock phraseology for the sake of the rime with *sang.* **874** on hyhte] *Dream on hyhte* is pleonastic, and Simons, Cynewulfs Wortschatz, p. 85, suggests *hyhðe,* from *heah.* But see l. 873*a.* Trautmann, BEV., p. 119, would read *tyhte,* "die freude war im zuge (gange)." But see ll. 239, 637. Von der Warth, p. 23, would change *hyhte* to *lyfte.* If any change is made it should be in *dream*—perhaps *duguð?* **890** gefeana] Grimm, Kemble, Grein, Wülker, Krapp and Craigie supply *gefeana.* Bright, MLN. II, 163, would supply *frean,* and *Trautmann,* BEV., p. 119, prefers *fremena.* **894** gehyrdon] Kemble changes to *gehyrde,* and Kock, Anglia XLIII, 301, repeats this suggestion, taking *gingran* as equivalent to *gingrena,* a genitive plural. But the reference may be to the disciples and the song they heard, see ll. 877 ff. **900** ðeh ic on yðfare] *ðeh ic þe on yðfare,* to supply an object for *ongitan?*

901–1000

914 Wes ðu, etc.] Holthausen, Anglia Beibl. XXXI, 27, regards the alliteration in this line as defective and supposes two half-lines have disappeared between *hal* and *mid,* or as alternative, would read *eorlgedryht* for *willgedryht.* Kock, Anglia XLIV, 245, puts a metrical stress on *Wes,* as in Beow. 1224, and places the caesura after *Andreas.* Holthausen, Anglia Beibl. XXXII, 137, objects to this awkward caesura, and Kock, Anglia XLVI, 183, defends it by citing l. 1689, but l. 1689 is scarcely a parallel to the set phrase in l. 914. **915** ferðgefeonde] See l. 1584, and El. 174, 990, where the same elements are not compounded. **938** to widan aldre] Von der Warth, p. 23, would change *aldre* here and in l. 1721 to *feore,* in order to satisy an extraordinary confidence in his metrical theories. **942** hrinen] The edd. all read *hrinan* with the MS., except Krapp (1906). The same emendation is made by Trautmann, BEV., p. 119 (1907), and by Kock, Anglia XLIII, 301 (1919). heafodmagan] Thorpe and Grimm read *-magum,* Baskervill and Wülker have *-magu,* and Trautmann, BEV., p. 119, defends *-magu* as a Northumbrian form surviving in the text. But the MS. has *magū = magum.* The ending in *magū* is probably an echo of the ending in *heorudolgun ,* l. 942*a,* or in anticipation of *searonettum,* for which the MS. has *searo mettū.* The reading *heafodmagan,* of Grimm, note, Kemble, Grein and Krapp gives an appropriate accusative singular form appositive to *Matheus.* **952** dæled] The edd. retain the MS. reading *dælan,* except Krapp, following Grein, Germania X, 423, and Cosijn, Beitr. XXI, 13, who read *dæled.* **954** faran flode blod] "Thy blood shall go in flood likest to water." The syntax is awkward and the statement extravagant. Should one read *faran on foldan blod?* See Bonnet, p. 88, *ita sanguis tuis fluent in terra sicut aqua.* **960** læt] Trautmann, BEV., p. 120, suggests *lær* for this word, citing Beow. 1722. **986** him] Grein, note, suggests *hine* for *him,* as a direct object. Retaining *him,* one must take the word as a kind of dative of interest. **996** hæleð heorodreorige] *Hæleð* is a plural and the adjective must agree with it. The edd. read *-dreorig,* except Krapp, who has *-dreorige.* **998–999**] The MS. reads here *heofoncyninges gód* dryhten dom with no indication of omission. Grein, in his Nachträge and in Germania X, 423, suggested making a genitive godes of god, parallel to heofoncyninges. Cosijn, Beitr. XXI, 13, reads heofoncyninges þrym, dryhtendom godes, or heofonrices god, dryhtnes ecne dom. Craigie follows Cosijn, except that he has Godes dryhten-dom. Trautmann, BEV., p. 120, proposes herede on hēhðo | heofon-þrymmes god, || dryhten dōm-fæstne. Von der Warth, p. 24, reads heofoncyninges god for l. 998b, and dryhtendōm ēcne, or dryhtnes dryhtendōm for l. 999a. Kock JJJ., p. 4, reads herede on hehðo | heofoncyninges || dugoð, dryhtendom, taking dugoð (from god + du) and dryhtendom as juxtaposed nouns in the same syntax. Cosijn's first suggestion seems the most plausible. It should be noted that the accent over gód is frequent in the MS. to indicate gŏd as distinguished from gōd.

1001–1100

1003 dreore druncne] Cosijn, Beitr. XXI, 13, compares with beore druncne, Beow. 480, and see Jul. 486. But the context here favors dreore. See also ll. 21–25.   deaðwang rudon] "They stained [with blood] the death-place." Trautmann, BEV., p. 120, would change to deaðwoman budon, "boten ein bild des todes, d.i. schliefen einen wahren totenschlaf."   **1013** geseon] An intransitive, see Krapp, p. 128.   **1024**] The matter on the folio lost after fol. 42 recounts in further detail the meeting of Matthew and Andrew, see Bright, Reader, p. 120, ll. 14 ff.   **1036** feowertig] There is no indication of loss in the MS. after feowertig, nor after fiftig in l. 1040. It is extremely probable that these half-lines were never filled in by the poet. Grein adds eac feorcundra for l. 1036b, and Cosijn, Beitr. XXI, 13, adds eac feorran cumene. Wülker reads seofontig for feowertig, making the number of men 270, and thus agreeing with the number in some of the MSS. of the Greek text, see Bonnet, p. 94. Von der Warth, p. 25, would supply feorrcunde men as completing l. 1036a. Trautmann, BEV., p. 121, thinks that more than a half-line has fallen out after feowertig. Holthausen, Anglia Beibl. XXXI, 28, supplies fira togædre for l. 1036b. For this defective half-line Kock, Anglia XLVI, 71, would read ond fif ond feower eac, his whole number being 249. The numbers given in the prose legend, Bright, Reader, p. 121, are 248 men and 49 women. In the Greek version some of the MSS., see Bonnet, p. 94, give 270 men and others give 249 men, though all of the Greek MSS. give 49 women. As the number stands in the present text, tu ond hundteontig swylce feowertig would mean 142, and probably ond is to be omitted, giving 242. Kock, Anglia XLV, 105, suggests that the MS. tu 7 is an error for tuwa or twa.   **1037** nænigne] Either nænige of the MS. must be changed to nænigne, or fæstne, l. 1038, to fæste. Reading nænigne, translate, "not a single man." For this acc. sg. form, Holthausen, Anglia Beibl. XXXI, 28, would read nænne. Trautmann, BEV., p. 121, prefers to change fæstne to fæste. See ll. 1081–1082.   **1040** fiftig] Grein omits þe in l. 1040 and completes the line by reading anes wana ealra fiftig, and so

Cosijn, Beitr. XXI, 14, except *efne* instead of *ealra*.   Von der Warth, p. 26, rewrites elaborately as follows:

> [el]þēodigra   efne] ānes wana
> þe fīftig [on rīme   for feorhlege]
> forhte gefreoðode.

Holthausen, Anglia Beibl. XXXI, 28, reads *anes wana þe | idesa fiftig*. Kock, Anglia XLVI, 71, places *anes wana þe fiftig* in the second half-line and supplies *earmra idesa* as a first half-line. Wülker indicates an omission between *wana* and *þe*, but supplies nothing.   **1074** gelah] For *geleah*, see Cosijn, Beitr. XXI, 14.   **1082** cwicne ne gemetton] The MS. reading *cwicne gemette* does not fit the context. Trautmann, BEV., p. 121, suggests that *gemette* may be for *gemetten;* he would also change *ænigne* to *ænige*, l. 1081, and read *cwic nē* for *cwicne*. The addition of *ne* in l. 1082 might be avoided by reading *nænigne* for *ænigne*, l. 1081. See l. 1037. Von der Warth, p. 26, would read *ænne tō lāfe*, and *cwicne nē mētte*, taking *mētte* as for a plural *mētten*. Wülker reads *ænig ne to lafe*, taking *ænig* as subject of *gemette*, but as Sievers points out, Beitr. XVI, 551, note, *gemette* or *gemetton* requires an object.   **1090** deade gefeormedon] The word *deade* is supplied by Ettmüller, Grein, Wülker and Krapp, for alliteration. Sievers, Beitr. X, 517, criticizes this emended line as metrically irregular, but metrical parallels can be found, see Krapp, p. 131.   Holthausen, Anglia XIII, 357, reads *dryht gefeormedon*. Cosijn, Beitr. XXI, 14, reads *hra gefeormedon* and changes *duruþegnum* to *huru þegnum*. But *duruþegnum* is too necessary to be given up. Von der Warth, p. 27, reconstructs to read *gefeormedon | [nū fromlīce || ac dēaðrēowum] | duruþegnum wearð*.   **1092** hildbedd styred] "A battle-bed [i.e. death-bed] prepared," *styred* from *styran, stieran*, see Grein, Spr. II, 491, Grein-Köhler, p. 643. Cosijn, Beitr. XXI, 15, would derive the verb from *strewian*, citing Beow. 2436 as parallel. Trautmann, BEV., p. 122, suggests *hild-bealu* for *hild-bedd*, or, p. 142, *hrif-bedd*, "das bauch- oder magenbett," translating, "ward ... auf ein mal das bauchbett (das grab im magen der menschenfresser) abgewehrt"— but see ll. 1089–1090. Holthausen, Anglia Beibl. XXXI, 28, thinks that meter requires *hilde-*, and *strēd* for *styred*.   **1099 ff.**] The motivation is not clear here, but the Greek version, Bonnet, pp. 94–95, relates that as the hands of the Mermedonians were lifted in the act of mutilating the bodies of the dead watchmen, at the prayer of Andrew the knives fell from their hands and their hands were turned to stone. It thus became necessary to cast lots to determine which of their number should be offered as food for the rest. In the poem the one chosen offers, *lifes to lisse*, to save his own life, his young son instead, and the offer is gratefully accepted. See Krapp, p. 132, Kock, Anglia XLIII, 301, Holthausen, Anglia XLIV, 353.

1101–1200

1114 hordgestreonum] Trautmann, BEV., p. 123, suggests omitting *hord-* to shorten the line metrically.   **1116** reow] All the edd. retain *hreow*, except

Grein and Krapp, see Sievers, Beitr. IX, 257.   For the opposite accident in spelling, see the MS. *reðre* for *hreðre*, Soul and Body I, 162.   **1130** wolde] Ettmüller suggests *nolde* for *wolde*, and so Trautmann, BEV., p. 123.   But the clause beginning with *þe* is explanatory of what precedes.   See Pogatscher, Anglia XXIII, 272.   **1139** þrist ond] See l. 1264 for the words supplied.   **1147** sceððan] The edd. retain *sceaðan*, except Krapp, who reads *sceððan*, with Schubert, De Anglosaxonum arte metrica, p. 33, Sievers, Beitr. X, 517, and Cosijn, Beitr. XXI, 15.   So also Trautmann, BEV., p. 123, and Craigie.   The scribe apparently mis-wrote *sceaðan* as an appositive to *scyldhatan*.   Perhaps one should emend to *scyððan*, see ll. 1047, 1561.   **1160** brucanne] Sievers, Beitr. X, 482, reads *brucan* as a metrical improvement, and so also in ll. 1481, 1659, 1689.   **1171** hellehinca] "Hell-limper," i.e. the devil, though etymological parallels to *hinca*, "limper," are not available in Anglo-Saxon.   Trautmann, BEV., p. 123, suggests that *hinca* is an error for *hyra* (*hira*), "hireling," or for *hyra* (*hiera*, *hera*), "the obedient one," "servant."   But it is easier to accept "hell-limper" than these explanations.   **1180** gewyrhtum] All edd. read *gewyrhtum*, but Holthausen, Beitr. XVI, 551, Simons, Cynewulfs Wortschatz, p. 66, Trautmann, BEV., p. 143, prefer *gewyrhtan*, a singular.   But see Cosijn, Beitr. XXI, 16. wæpnes] Grein supplies *wæpna*, Wülker has *wæpnes*.   **1181** ealdorgeard] All the edd. retain the MS. *eadorgeard*, except Kemble, who has *ealdorgeard*, and so Krapp and Craigie.   Napier, Anglia IV, 411, made the same suggestion independently of Kemble, and Trautmann, BEV., p. 143, approves. The first element of *ealdorgeard* is appositive to the first element of *feorhhord*, l. 1182.   **1191** ond on heolstor] The preposition *on* is supplied, with Grein, Germania X, 423, and Cosijn, Beitr. XXI, 16.   Kock, Anglia XLIII, 302, takes *7 = ond* in the MS. to be for *on*, therefore reads merely *on heolstor besceaf*.   **1194** a] For *æ*, as in l. 1403, Ap. 10.   Kemble changes to *æ*, and perhaps *a* here is only an echo of *a* in l. 1193.

1201–1300

1218 manslaga] If *manslaga* is the object of *þolige*, it is an unusual form, and Cosijn, Beitr. XXI, 16, would read *mánslægas*. Simons, Cynewulfs Wortschatz, p. 97, would read *mánslæge*. Bos.-Tol., p. 670, suggests *mánslagan*, appositive to the plural subject of *magon* and *moton*, l. 1215.   Trautmann, BEV., p. 124, reads *măn-slagan*, the first element for *monn*, "man," instead of *mān*, "evil."   if the text is not altered, *mánslaga* must be taken as an acc. pl. fem., though *slæge*, *slege* is otherwise masculine in its occurrences. **1219–1227**] For the punctuation, see Kock, Anglia XLIII, 302.   See ll. 1212–1214.   **1224** hie] Grein, Spr. I, 6, reads *hi hine andweardne*.   **1229** Heton þa lædan] Cosijn, Beitr. XXI, 16, supplies *hine* before *þa*.   **1230** ðragmælum] Grein, Germania X, 423, reads *tragmælum* for the sake of the alliteration, and so also Spr. II, 550, Trautmann, BEV., p. 143.   Kock, Anglia XLIV, 97, would transpose, reading *teon ðragmælum*.   But *teon* is strong enough to carry the alliteration here, see Bright, MLN. II, 163.

1232 deormodne] Cosijn, Beitr. XXI, 16, made the emendation *-modne*, and also *-ferhþne* for *-ferþþe* in l. 1233. Von der Warth, p. 29, would retain *deormode* as referring to the Mermedonians. **1235** enta ærgeweorc] Baskervill has no punctuation after *lagon*, l. 1234, therefore takes *enta ærgeweorc* as object. So also Klaeber, Archiv CXX, 155. **1241** hatan heolfre] Grein altered the MS. *hat of heolfre* to *hatan heolfre*, see l. 1277, but in Germania X, 423, he returned to the MS. reading. Cosijn, Beitr. XXI, 16, reads *hat of hreþre*, and Trautmann, BEV., p. 124, proposes *hat of heolstre*, hot from its hiding-place, i.e. from the veins, the body. Trautmann makes the same change in l. 1277. **1242** untweonde] So Grein, Cosijn, Beitr. XXI, 16, Krapp, Trautmann, BEV., p. 125, and Craigie, but Grein, Germania X, 423, returns to the MS. reading. **1246** sigetorht] Ettmüller, Grein, Cosijn, Beitr. XX, 16, Krapp, Trautmann, BEV., p. 125, and Craigie read *sigetorht*. **1258** hildstapan] "Battle-stalkers," an epic figure, see Cosijn, Beitr. XXI, 16. Grimm, p. xxxv, suggested changing to *hlid-* or *hæðstapan*, and Grein, note, suggests *hlið-* or *hæðstapan*. **1276** þurh] Trautmann, BEV., p. 125, would alter to *of* or *from*, and see l. 1241, note. **1277** sann] "Cease from," and see Sievers, Beitr. XI, 352–353 on the meaning of the word. Trautmann, BEV., p. 125, translates, "verlangte," had desire of. **1278** hring] Trautmann, Anglia XXXIII, 276 ff., would read *brim*, and BEV., p. 87, *bring*, and so also in El. 1131. But for *hring*, "sound," see Klaeber, Archiv CXX, 155. Kock, JJJ., p. 5, takes *wopes hring* as parallel to *waðuman stream*, l. 1280, defining as " 'globe of wailing,' the 'round, clear pearl from man's or woman's eye,' " i.e. tear. **1279** blat] A noun, "moan," but Klaeber, Archiv CXX, 155, suggests that *blat* is an adjective, "pale, livid," transferred in meaning to sound, "a low or hoarse quality of sound." Trautmann, BEV., p. 127, suggests *blāc*, "shining," as descriptive of tears, for *blat*.

1301–1400

1305 niflan] Trautmann, BEV., p. 128, would alter to *niwlan* (*neowlan*). **1309** sceal] Trautmann, BEV., p. 128, thinks that *sceal þōn* of the MS. is a mis-writing for *sceolde*. Grein alters *sceal* to *sceolde* to agree with the tense of the verbs in ll. 1305–1308. **1313** gescyrded] "Shrouded or enveloped." Grein, Spr. I, 449, proposes *gescryded* or *gescyrted*, but Cosijn, Beitr. XXI, 17, defends *gescyrded*, apparently in the sense "shrouded." **1316** Andreas] Sievers, Beitr. XII, 478, would omit, to normalize the scansion. þinne] Trautmann, BEV., p. 128, suggests *þine* as instrumental for *þinne*, translating, "Was beabsichtigtest du mit deinem hierherkommen?" But take *Hwæt* in the sense "why," as in ll. 629, 1413, and *hogodest* in the sense "contemplate, strive for," see l. 622, with *hidercyme þinne* as object. **1317** Hwæt] Grein, note, suggests *hwær* for *hwæt*. The Greek text favors the change to *hwær*, see Bonnet, p. 104, l. 10: ποῦ ἐστιν ἡ δύναμίς σου, etc. **1319** gild] The context requires *gild*, as suggested by Grein, note; see also Bugge, Beitr. XII, 95, and the Greek text, Bonnet, p. 104, l. 13.

1330 gingran] May go either with *hie* or *ðe*, l. 1329, see Kock, Anglia XLIII, 302.   **1345** Him þa earmsceapen] This reading was suggested by Sievers, Beitr. X, 517, and so also Cosijn, Beitr. XXI, 17, Trautmann, BEV., p. 128. See l. 1375.   Kock, Anglia XLIII, 303, proposes an alternative *Edre him earmsceapen*, see ll. 401, 643.   **1353** gelæran] Kock, Anglia XLIII, 303, places a colon after *gelæran*. A full stop seems advisable here, and *weald*, l. 1355, is best taken as an imperative, "determine," not as conjunction, see Cosijn,, Beitr. XXI, 17.   **1376–1377**] As the text stands, it supposes a rhetorical anacoluthon of the verb. After *eaðe* Grein supplies *gescildeð*. Root, Andreas, p. 58, supplies *mæg* after *eaðe*, and reads *generian* for *neregend*, l. 1377.   Kock, JJJ., p. 6, reads *neregeð* for *neregend*.   **1380** wræc] Ettmüller suggested *wræce*, Grein *wræce*, and Trautmann, BEV., p. 129, reads *wræce*, see l. 1383.   The change is necessary only if one refuses to take *wræc*, "exile, suffering," as a neuter accusative.

1401–1500

1404 leoðu] "Limbs," see Holthausen, Beitr. XVI, 551. All edd. except Krapp retain the MS. reading *leoð*, but this is not a proper plural form. **1406** swatige] Trautmann, BEV., p. 129, reads *swate*, "with blood."   **1425** toslopen, adropen] All edd. except Krapp misread the MS. as *toslowen* and *aðrowen*, but Wülker, Nachträge, p. 565, reads as in the MS., and Grein, note, suggested *toslopen* and *aðropen*. Sievers, Beitr. X, 517, and Cosijn, Beitr. XXI, 18, read *toslopen, adropen*.   **1434** ofer eall] Ettmüller fills out the line by reading *ofer eallne middangeard*, Grein supplies *geond middangeard* after *eall*.   **1443** lices lælan] Take *lælan*, "bruise, wound," as object of *þurh* and parallel to *bangebrec*. The edd. retain the MS. reading as *liclælan*, except Krapp, who reads *lices lælan*, with Sievers, Beitr. X, 517, Bright, MLN. II, 164. Cosijn, Beitr. XXI, 18, reads *lices læla*, taking *læla* as a genitive plural. See Guth. 670–671. Kock, JJJ., p. 6, would take *bangebrec, stige* and *lælan* as parallel objects of *þurh*. But the subject *swat* calls for an object for *aget*. See l. 1449.   **1461** magorædendes] Trautmann, BEV., p. 130, suggests *mægen-rædend(e)* for this word.   **1464** synne] For the spelling *y* for *i*, see *scyna*, l. 766, *tyres*, l. 105.   **1467** Ne scealt ðu] Trautmann, BEV., p. 130, would remove *ðu* and *a* as a metrical improvement.   **1474** lice gelenge] Grein, Wülker read *lice lenge* for the MS. *lic ge lenge*, and Grimm, note, Grein, Spr. I, 421, and Cosijn, Beitr. XXI, 18, propose *lice gelenge*. Perhaps a complete transposition of parts has taken place and one should read *laðe gelenge ne lices dæl*, see Krapp, Modern Philology II, 408.   **1477** lof lædende] Trautmann, BEV., p. 130, suggests a form of *lið* or *lim* for *lof*, and he regards *lædende* also as doubtful.   **1478–1480**] Kock, JJJ., p. 6, translates:

> "Well, for a while I've now put forth in words
> the tale about the holy man, the praise,
> in songs, of what he did, unhidden facts."

Kock places a period after *undyrne*, l. 1480, and takes *ofer min gemet* |

mycel, "beyond my power great (to tell)," as synonymous with *langsum leornung,* l. 1482, see Anglia XLVI, 72.   **1485** þæt] Not "who," but the subject of *cunne* is to be supplied, "that he knows from the beginning," etc., see Pogatscher, Anglia XXIII, 266, and also Cosijn, Beitr. XXI, 14. **1487** grimra guða] A genitive plural phrase, dependent on *earfeðo,* or Kock, Anglia XLVI, 73, would take *guða* as accusative parallel to *earfeðo* and *grimra* as a noun, translating, "(a man) that knows from the beginning all the woes and the attacks of cruel foes which bravely he endured."   **1493** under sælwage] "In the hall," the MS. reading *under sælwange* meaning "under the earth." The edd. read *sælwange,* except Grein, Krapp and Craigie, and Cosijn, Beitr. XXI, 18, also follows Grein.   Kock, Anglia XLVI, 73, objects that pillars in the prison could not be *storme bedrifene,* but this phrase is obviously a bit of emotional, not realistic, description.   See also the Greek text, Bonnet, p. 109, l. 8, and the prose in Bright, Reader, p. 125, ll. 14–15.

1501–1600

1503 staþole] Trautmann, BEV., p. 130, alters to *stapole.*   **1508** geofon] See l. 393, note.   **1516** Tobias] Neither Joshua nor Tobias is mentioned in the Greek text or in the Anglo-Saxon prose legend.   Perhaps Tobias is for Caleb, see Numbers xiv. 6, xxxii. 12.   **1526** Meoduscerwen] The second element of this word was misread as *scerpen* by some of the earlier edd., but the MS. plainly reads *scerwen.*   The general meaning of the word is "terror," but the precise figure involved is still debateable, see Krapp, pp. 151–152, and Kock, Anglia XLV, 105.   See Beow. 767–769.   **1532** sealtne weg] The MS. *scealtes sweg* gives no meaning.   The *c* of *scealtes* apparently was an inadvertence, see l. 196.   Grimm, note, suggests *sealtes,* or *scealces,* "of terror," Ettmüller, note, suggests *swealhes,* "abyssi."   Grein, Baskervill, Wülker and Craigie read *sealtes sweg,* "tumult of the salt (ocean)." Cosijn, Beitr. XXI, 19, reads *sealtne sweg,* "salt tumult."   Krapp reads *sealtne wēg,* "salt wave," and it seems probable that in the scribe's general confusion, an unnecessary *s* was prefixed to *weg.*   See ll. 748–749, and for the spelling *weg,* see ll. 198, 601, 932.   See also Dan. 322.   Trautmann, BEV., p. 131, approves *sealtne wēg.*   **1540** ondwist] The MS. has 7 *wist.* Ettmüller, note, reads *onwist,* and so Kock, Anglia XLIII, 302.   The spelling *onwist* occurs in Ex. 18, but these are the only two appearances of the word.   **1541** oferbrægd] Trautmann, BEV., p. 131, changes to *ymbbrægd.*   **1548–1549** mændan, golon] The edd. retain the MS. *mænan* and *galen,* except Krapp, who reads as in the text.   Grimm, note, suggested *mæned,* and Ettmüller, note, proposed *wrecan* for *wrecen* and *galan* for *galen.*   Trautmann, BEV., p. 131, thinks one or two lines may have dropped out between ll. 1548 and 1549.   **1562** her] Supplied for alliteration, following Grein.   Grimm, note, supplies *hæleðum,* and Ettmüller reads *swa here-cuð.*   Von der Warth, p. 30, supplies *huru* before þæt.   Trautmann, BEV., p. 132, approves Grimm's reading *hæleðum* but would omit *swa.*

1571 mægen] Thorpe, note, and edd., except Baskervill, supply *mægen*. **1577** ymbe] All edd. read *ymb*, except Wülker and Krapp, who give the correct MS. reading *ymbe*.   **1585** geofon] See l. 393, note.   **1597** wifa] Supplied with Ettmüller, Grein and Wülker.

1601–1700

1604] The alliteration is defective. Ettmüller supplies *us*, Grein *este* before *onsende*. Grein, note, suggests *on sende*, which would make *on* adverbial and capable of bearing a metrical accent. Holthausen, Anglia Beibl. XXXI, 28, supplies *halgan* before *ar*. Perhaps one should read *þider* for *hider*.   **1606** gumcystum] Monroe, MLN. XXXI, 376, proposes *gumcystgum*, "that we earnestly listen to (heed) the excellent man." Otherwise *gumcystum* seems best taken as adverbial.   **1617** ðæt] Trautmann, BEV., p. 132, reads *ðætte* to lengthen the line metrically.   **1622** ræswan] The context requires a singular.   **1631** wedde] An instrumental singular aspedde] Trautmann, BEV., p. 133, would change to *ahredde*.   **1635** fulwiht] Grein, Germania X, 423, suggests *fultum* for *fulwiht*, and Trautmann, BEV., p. 133, proposes *fullēst* (*-læst*), "aid."   **1650** gehalgode] Perhaps *hine* should be supplied before this word.   **1651** nemned] Trautmann, BEV., p. 133, would change to *nemde*, "appointed," with no punctuation following.   **1659** weorc] The edd. follow the MS. *weor*, except Wülker, *weorce*, and Krapp, *weorc*. Kluge, Anglia IV, 106, Cosijn, Beitr. XXI, 20, Trautmann, BEV., p. 134, read *weorc*. The word is object of *geþoligenne*.   **1663**] Comparison with the Greek text and with the prose legend, Bright, Reader, p. 127, ll. 19–27, shows that little has been lost here.   **1667**] As a second half-line after *mod*, Grein supplied *nu þu on merebate*, and for the following line he reads *wilt ofer flodas fore sneowan*. Cosijn, Beitr. XXI, 20, supplies only *me* before *fore*, and Holthausen, Anglia Beibl. XXXI, 28, also supplies *me* but before *sneowan*, but neither reading makes a satisfactory alliterative pattern, and it is probable that more than a single word has dropped out. For the corresponding passage in the prose, see Bright, Reader, p. 127, l. 24.   **1700** Achaie] Bright, MLN. II, 164, supplies *eft* before *Achaie* (*Achaia* by error?) to gain a metrical syllable.

1701–1722

1704 syððan] The form *syððan* occurs frequently in this text but *syð* only in the MS. reading of this passage.   **1713** wunn] For *wynn*, and see Ap. 42, *wurd* for *wyrd*.   **1714** seolhpaðu] The edd. except Krapp read *seolhwaðu*, but the MS. has plainly *seolh paðu*. Grein, note, suggests *paðu*, and Sievers, Beitr. I, 492, reads *seolhpaðu*. Cosijn, Beitr. XXI, 21, proposes *seolhbaðu*.   **1719** breme] Kock, Anglia XLVI, 73, would take *breme* as an adjective and would therefore place a comma after it.

NOTES ON FATES OF THE APOSTLES

1–100

Fates of the Apostles] For the title, see Introd., p. xviii.   **1** þysne sang]
Holthausen, Anglia Beibl. XXI, 175, reads *sang þysne*.   **4** wæron] Grein,
note, suggests *foron*.   **30** Effessia] For the spelling with doubled *s*,
see *Asseum*, l. 38, and *Essaias*, El. 350.   Brown, Eng. Stud. XL, 7 ff.,
attributes these spellings to the influence of Irish-Latin texts.   **32** swegle]
Holthausen, Anglia Beibl. XXXI, 28, reads *swegles*, but *swegle* may be
an adj., see Beow. 2749, *swegle searogimmas*.   **36** ealdre] Kock, Anglia
XLIII, 303, reads *ealdor* as an object parallel to *feorh*, l. 37.   Note a
similar spelling *aldre*, l. 43, which Kock, JJJ., p. 7, would change to
aldor.   The word is accusative in both passages, but a double accident
in spelling is scarcely probable.   **43** gelædde] Grein, Germania X, 423,
proposes *geneðde* for *gelædde*.   See An. 1351.   **47** he ða] Trautmann,
BEV., p. 136, would omit one or both of these words for metrical reasons.
hyran] A more appropriate word would be *herian*, "praise," parallel to
weorðian, l. 48, as suggested by Klaeber, Modern Philology II, 146.   **57 b**
ond him] The MS. has the abbreviation for *ond*, which Trautmann, BEV.,
p. 136, thinks was miswritten for þ = *þe*.   He would therefore read *þe him*,
"to whom." But þ for anything but *þæt* is of extremely rare occurrence,
see Records I, p. xxii.   **62** sawle] A nominative, as in Christ 1326, Soul and
Body I, 10.   **84** ealle] Kock, Anglia XLVI, 74, retains the MS. *ealne*
by taking *æhtwelan* as a singular and changing *idle* to *idelne*.   **88** þonne]
Trautmann, BEV., p. 136, would change to *þone*, "him, that one."   **91**
Hu] Kemble and Grein change to *nu*, and so Sievers, Anglia XIII, 22.   **92**
sceal] Wülker omits in order to retain the MS. reading *gesece*, l. 93.   **94**
lætaı] Thorpe, Kemble, Grein and Wülker read *læt* with the MS., Sievers,
Anglia XIII, 22, reads *læte*.   The reading *gesecan* in l. 93 carries with it the
reading *lætan* here, though less plausibly one might read *læte* as resuming
the first person of *sceal*.   **96** foreþances] The MS. has *for þances*, a form
that does not occur elsewhere, but for *foreþanc*, see El. 356, Jul. 227, Beow.
1060.   **96–122**] This passage in the MS. has been much obscured by a
large blot or stain.   The readings given in the text, when they are not decipherable in the reproductions, are those of Napier, ZfdA. XXXIII, 70–72,
unless otherwise specified.   See also Wülker, Bibliothek II, 566–567, and
Codex Vercellensis, p. viii.   A copy is given below of all that Napier found
visible in the MS.   Italics indicate letters somewhat faded but still legible;
italicized letters in parentheses are very much faded or only partly legible,
therefore somewhat uncertain.   Letters entirely illegible are represented
by colons, the colons standing for the greatest number of letters that could
have stood in the passages if the passages had been occupied by single
words.   If the passages were occupied by several words with the usual
spacing between them, the number of letters would be less.   Napier's
transcript is as follows:

Her mæg findan for þances gleaw. seðe *h*ine lysteð leoð gid
dunga. Hwa þas fitte f*egde* .ᚱ. þær on ende standaþ
eorlas þæs oneorðan *b*(*r*)*:ca*þ. Nemoton hie awa æt
somne woruld wu*nigende* . (ᚠ). sceal gedreosan .ᚻ.
on eðle æfter to (*h*) :::::::: (*l*)*:æn*e lices frætewa efne
swa .ᚱ. to glideð.: (*swa*). (ᚻ) (ᚱ?). cræftes neotað. nihtes
nearowe on him. ::::::::::::ninges þeo dóm. Nv ðu
cunnon miht .(*h*)::::::::::(*r*)*d*um wæs werū on cyðig Sie
þæs ge myndig::::::::::::(*lu*)fige þisses gal dres begang
þæt he geoce:::::::::re fricle ic sceall feor heo
nan án elles (*f?*):::::::*rd*es neosan . sið asettan. Nat
ic sylfa hwær .*o::*(*i*)*sse* worulde wíc sindon un cuð
eard 7 eðel . Swa (*b*):ð ælcū menn. nemþe he god cundes
gastes bruce . (*A*)h(*u*)*t*u we þe geornor togode cleopigan
sendan usse be*ne* on þa beorhtan gesceaft. þæt we
þæs botles brucan motan hames in hehðo þær is hihta
mæst þær cyning engla . clænum glideð. lean un hwilen
nu ahis lof standeð mycel 7 mære 7 his miht
seomaþ ece 7 ed giong . ofer ealle gesceaft. fiᴎit.

The chief commentators on this passage are Sievers, Anglia XIII, 1–25;
Cosijn, Cynewulfs Runenverzen, pp. 54–64; Gollancz, Cynewulf's Christ,
pp. 173–184; and Trautmann, Kynewulf, pp. 50–54. In the remainder of
these notes on the Fates of the Apostles, these articles will be referred to only
by the names of their authors.   98 ᚠ] The rune for the letter F and also
for its name, *feoh*, "money, wealth." Translate: "F stands there at the end,
earls enjoy it [wealth] on earth."   standeþ] The MS. has *standaþ*, but
with the rune as subject, the verb must be singular. Napier ends l. 98 with
ende, his l. 99 extending from *standeþ* to *bruca* ð. This is followed by a line
from *Ne* to *ætsomne*, which is made a full line by the addition of *eardian*
between *awa* and *ætsomne*. The arrangement in the text is by Sievers, p. 1.
99 brucaþ] One letter of this word is illegible and one only faintly visible,
but there can be little doubt that the word is *brucaþ*, as Napier reads.   100
ᚹ] Napier and later commentators agree in supplying this rune, which is
only faintly visible in the MS. It stands for the letter W, and for the word
wyn, "joy," according to Sievers, p. 3, Cosijn, p. 59, and Gollancz, p. 178,
or *wela*, "riches," according to Trautmann, p. 52.

101–122

101 ᚢ] Interpreted by Cosijn and Gollancz as standing for the letter U and
for the word *ur*, "our," referring to *wyn* in the preceding line. Sievers, p. 7,
takes the word as a noun *ur* = *feoh*, but no example of *ur*, "wealth," is
known. Trautmann, p. 52, interprets the word as *unne*, a noun meaning
"what is granted, grant," extending this to the sense "possessions, property."
But this is also a doubtful and unrecorded meaning.   tohreosan] Only
the first three letters in the MS. are decipherable, followed by a blotted

space sufficient for seven more letters, or if space between this and a following word is allowed, for six more letters. Napier completes as *tohreosaþ*, Sievers, p. 7, and Trautmann, p. 50, as *tohreosan*. Sievers remarks that the rime with *gedreosan*, l. 100, favors the reading *tohreosan*, but since rime is not characteristic of this passage, the argument could be turned the other way. **102 ᚱ]** The rune for the letter L, and for its name, *lagu*, "water, sea." **103 Þonne h ond ᚱ]** For the first word of this half-line, Napier read very dubiously *swa*, but Sievers, p. 9, thinks that the word was more probably *poñ* = *ponne*, as in Christ 797 and Jul. 705. Gollancz, p. 176, and Trautmann, p. 50, also read *ponne*. After this first word Napier believed that he could distinguish the rune h, and after this, faintly visible remains of another rune. All commentators agree in restoring h and ᚱ, standing for the letters C and Y. But it is uncertain what words these letters stand for. Sievers, p. 10. thinks the runes here may stand only for letters and not for words. Gollancz, p. 178, interprets the runes as standing for *cēne* and *yfel*, "the bold warrior and the afflicted wretch." Trautmann, p. 53, takes the runes ·as standing for *cearu*, "sorge," and *ȳst*, "leidenschaft," but, BEV., p. 137, takes the second rune as standing for *yfel*, "krankheit." Kock, PPP., p. 25, would take the first rune as meaning *cēn*, "torch," and the second as meaning *ȳr*, something belonging to military equipment, not further defined. He would also take the rune in l. 104*b* as standing for *nyd*. "servitude." Retaining the MS. reading *neotaᵹ* in l. 103*b*, he translates:

"Then torch and *yr* exert their craft
at night with anxious care:
incumbent is on them the king's
restraint and servitude!"

The most plausible suggestion is that which takes the runes as standing for *cene* and *yfel*, "the resolute and the wretched," but this is by no means certain. **neosaᵹ]** The MS. reads plainly *neotaᵹ* and Trautmann, p. 53, retains *neotaᵹ*, with doubtful justification, extending the meaning of *neotan*, "enjoy," to the sense "devour," "verzehren." Sievers, pp. 8–9, Gollancz, p. 176, alter to *neosaᵹ*, "seek for," and if the runes indicate a subject "the resolute and the wretched," the change is necessary. But it is perhaps a little perilous to make any change in consideration of the uncertainty of the first half-line. **104 on him ᚾ ligeᵹ]** After *him*, the MS. is illegible for a space sufficient for ten letters. The commentators agree in the insertion of the rune ᚾ, "N," which is needed for alliteration. Sievers, p. 8, proposed *ligeᵹ* as the word following the rune, the rune word being the subject and appositive to *þeodom*, l. 105. Trautmann, p. 54, reads *legeᵹ*, with the rune word, *nyd*, "distress," as subject and *þeodom*, "service," as object, translating, "auf sie [die menschen] legt die not den dienst des herren, d.i. die not führt die menschen zu gott." Napier, p. 72, suggests that possibly two runes are to be supplied in l. 104*b*, ᚾ = N, and ᛗ = E, but there seems scarcely space for two runes. For the two forms of the name, *Cynwulf* and *Cynewulf*, see Sievers, p. 11. **105 cyninges]** The final six letters of this word are legible and there can be little doubt that the whole word was *cyninges*.   cunnon] Napier, Sievers, and Trautmann, p. 51, change to *cunnan*.   **106** hwa on þam wordum] So restored by Napier, and so also Sievers and Trautmann, except that Sievers reads þæm for þam.   **107** mann se ðe lufige] Obscure in the MS. but thus restored by Napier.   **108–109** me ond frof-] Restored by Napier.   **112** of þisse] So restored by Napier. Wülker reads *on þisse*.   **115** Ah utu] So restored by Napier, who suggests *utun*. But see Sievers, Angels. Gram. § 360, 2 for the contracted form, and see Christ and Satan 216, note.   **119** gildeð] The MS. has *glideð*, but the sense requires *gildeð*, and so all commentators.

NOTES ON SOUL AND BODY I

1–100

Soul and Body I] For the title, see Introd., p. xxxviii.   **5** lang] "For a long time," i.e. through eternity, not "long afterward," see Klaeber, Archiv CXIII, 148.   **10** sawle] See Ap. 62 for this form as a nominative.   **11** hie] Soul and Body II has *heo*, and Grein changes *hie* to *heo*, but see Sievers, Angels. Gram. § 334, 1, on *hie* as a nom. sg. fem.   **17** druh ðu] Grein suggests *hwæt druge þu?*, taking *druge* as a verb from *drēogan*. Though not otherwise recorded, it is best to take *druh* as a noun, "Lo! thou gory dust!", Bos.-Tol., p. 215, and so Grein, Dicht., p. 145, "Du kümmerlicher Staub!"   **23** lustgryrum] Grein changes to *lustgrynum*, "snares of desire," and translates, Dicht., p. 145, "du willig folgtest allen Lockungen der Lüste." But this is no improvement over *lustgryrum* "desire-horrors," i.e. horrible desires. A more natural compound would be *gryrelust*.   **24** ful geeodest] Grein places *eallum*, l. 23*b*, in l. 24, and reads *ful-eodest* for the MS. *ful geodest*.   hu] Grein alters to *nu*, but Germania X, 421, returns to the MS.   **27** þe la engel] Grein reads *þurh engel*, for *la engel*, following the reading of Soul and Body II. So also Wülker. As the text stands, *engel* is appositive to *meotod*, l. 29, which implies an unusual use of *engel*. But see Clubb, Christ and Satan, p. 124, Cook, Christ, p. 91, for *engel* meaning Christ.   **40** þunedest] The MS. has þune at the end of a line, followed by dest at the beginning of the following line. Ettmüller, Grein read þu neðdest, but Grein, Germania X, 421, has þunedest, following Kemble.   ic] Supplied by Grein and Wülker from Soul and Body II.   **44** wære] Holthausen, Eng. Stud. XXXVII, 198, would place *wære* after *flæsc* as a metrical improvement.   **45** gestryned] Grein reads *gestyred*, from Soul and Body II.   **47** wið] Ettmüller alters the MS. *mid* to *wið*, and so Grein, Wülker.   heardum helle witum] Holthausen, Eng. Stud. XXXVII, 198, reads *heardra hellewita*, following Soul and Body II, and to govern this genitive, he reads *nearwe* for *ne*, l. 48, a noun, "hardship," from *nearo*. Corresponding to *ne generedest*, Soul and Body II has *ne gearwode*. In Anglia Beibl. XXXI, 28, Holthausen suggests that *næfre*, l. 47, be transferred to the beginning of l. 48*a* to lengthen the line metrically.   **49** minra gesynta] Soul and

Body II has *minra gescenta*. Grein in his text reads *minra gescenda*, but Spr. I, 446, has *gescenta*, gen. pl. of a noun, *gescentu*, otherwise not recorded, meaning "shame, overthrow." But *gesynta* may stand as a gen. pl. of *gesynto*, "health, welfare,"a plural with a singular meaning, as often with this word, "Shalt thou on the great day of my prosperity suffer in shame," etc. The alliteration with *sceame* favors *gescenta* of Soul and Body II as the poet's original reading, but the variation must be allowed to stand. **50** eall] Grein omits *eall*.   **57** magon] The context requires the plural, as it is in Soul and Body II. Grein and Wülker read *magon*.   þa] Also from Soul and Body II, to agree with the plural subject, and so in Grein, Wülker.   **59** boldwela] The alliteration requires *bold-*, and so Kemble, Ettmüller, Grein, Wülker. No corresponding line to l. 59 appears in Soul and Body II.   **62** synum] Soul and Body II has *seonwum*, both forms of *seonu*, "sinew."   **63** unwillum] Grein reads *unwillan*.   **74** æhta] Soul and Body II reads *geahþe*, and see l. 9.   This provides the proper alliteration, and Grein reads *geahðe awiht*. The scribe of Soul and Body I probably made a mistake, but his reading satisfies meaning if not meter.   **79** þær] Both Soul and Body I and II have *þær*, "if," see Grein-Köhler, p. 693.   **82** wildra] The form *wildra*, which is the reading of Soul and Body II, is required metrically. Grein reads *wildra deora*, but Wülker has *wilddeora*.   **83** þær swa god wolde] The repetition of this half-line in l. 85, and the lack of alliteration in l. 83, indicate a disturbance in the text here. Soul and Body II, for the lines corresponding to ll. 83–84, reads:

þæt grimmeste,   þær swa god wolde,
ge þeah þu wære wyrmcynna   þæt wyrreste.

The text of Soul and Body II is thus one line shorter than the text of Soul and Body I. Grein replaces the reading of Soul and Body I by that of Soul and Body II, but Wülker retains the MS. reading.   **84** wyrma] The genitive form is necessary to gain a metrical syllable. Soul and Body II also reads *wyrmcynna*, and this was probably the original form of the word, inadequately adapted by the scribe of Soul and Body I to his reconstruction of the passage.   **88** unc bæm] Grein reads *unc bu* from Soul and Body II. **95** wunde wiðerlean] See l. 90 for the sense of *wunde*. Both Soul and Body I and II have *wunde* in l. 95. Grein changes to *wunda*, a gen. pl. dependent on *wiðerlean*, taken as a noun. Thorpe, Codex Exoniensis, suggests *wiðer-leanian* with *wunde* as object. Ettmüller reads *wunda* and suggests that a verb *settan* or *gifan* is to be supplied as governing *wiðerlean*. Wülker takes *wiðerlean* as a verb, "condemn, pass sentence on," with *wunde* as object. See Grein-Köhler, p. 409, for the verb *lēan, belēan*. Wülker's interpretation is the most satisfactory, though it still leaves a metrically awkward half-line.   **97** nan na] Grein reads *nænig* for *nan na*, following the reading of Soul and Body II.   **98** þæt ðu, etc.] The corresponding line in Soul and Body II reads *þæt þu ne scyle for æghwylc anra onsundran*, and Grein replaces the reading of Soul and Body I by this line. It is undoubtedly a better line, and the lack of alliteration in Soul and Body I, 98, shows that the scribe has confused his text. An alliterative word in l. 98*b* might easily be supplied by changing *gehwylcum* to *æghwylcum*, but perhaps a modern reader need not be more exacting than was the scribe in this matter. 100] After this line, Grein supplies *þonne he unc hafað geedbyrded oðre siðe*, taken from Soul and Body II.

101–166

101 eft] Not in Soul and Body II and omitted by Grein. 103 Fyrnað] From *firnian, firenian*, "chide." Grein reads *Firenað*, following Soul and Body II. 106–107] Grein changes *gehatan* to *secgan* from Soul and Body II, and adds from the same source a line following, *ne þær edringe ænge gehatan*. Wülker indicates a loss of two half-lines between *ondsware* and *ænige*, and remarks that *gehatan*, if placed in l. 106, would disturb the alliteration. But the alliteration is vocalic, and though it is probable that the scribe of Soul and Body I has omitted something, his text as it stands is adequate, taking *gehatan* in the sense "assure, give assurance of." 110 asocene] Soul and Body II has *asogene*. Grein reads *asolcene*, but in Spr. I, 43, he glosses *asocene*, from *asucan*, "absorb." 111 fingras tohrorene] Soul and Body II contains nothing corresponding to this half-line. Grein completes the line by supplying *fet toclofene*. 112] After this line Grein supplies *druncað hloðum hra heolfres þurstge* from Soul and Body II, *druncað* being a misreading of the MS. *drincað*. 113 hira tungan] Soul and Body II reads *seo tunge*. Grein reads *seo tunge*, and to maintain the singular, alters *hie* to *heo* and *magon* to *mæg* in l. 114. Wülker reads *seo tunge* in l. 113, but retains the plurals in l. 114. Note *þa tungan*, l. 119. 116 eaglas] For *geaglas*, as in l. 109. 117 to] In the MS. *to* is followed by *me*, probably as an unreflecting impulse on the part of the scribe to provide *to* with an object. But *to* is adverbial, as in the corresponding line in Soul and Body II, *se geneþeð to*. The present tense of the verb is better than the preterite, but the Vercelli reading is permissible, "he hath brought it to this pass." Grein reads *se geneðeð to* from Soul and Body II, and Wülker reads *se genydeð to*, following Grein's suggestion in Spr. I, 439. 119 teð] Grein reads *toðas*, following Soul and Body II. 122 þonne þæt werie] Soul and Body II has *þonne biþ þæt werge*, and Grein reads *þonne þæt werge bið*, to the improvement of the alliteration, and for the first half of the following line he reads *lic acolod*. Perhaps *lic* should be transferred to the end of l. 122, though this change disturbs the alliteration in l. 123. For the form *werie*, see *cearie*, l. 160. 123 lic acolod bið] Soul and Body II has *acolad*, but Wülker suggests *lic bið alocen*, "when the body is separated (from the soul)." Ettmüller suggests *lic atol, lað* for *lic acolod*. But *acolod* seems to be the necessary word here. he] Supplied from Soul and Body II, to provide *werede* with a subject, and referring to "man" in general. 125 æt] Supplied by Kemble, Grein and Wülker from Soul and Body II. 126] Grein reads *men to gemyndum modsnottera*, from Soul and Body II, the last line of this poem. 127–166] This passage on the *halige sawl* is not con-

tained in Soul and Body II.   **133** soðlice] Grein, Germania X, 421, proposes *softlice* for *soðlice*.   **134** gretaþ] Grein gives *gretæþ* as the MS.
reading, but the letter is merely a slightly unusual form of *a*.   **135** þeah
ðe] So Kemble, Grein and Wülker. Klipstein, Analecta, p. 135, reads
agon for *ah*, "the worms possess thee yet."   **137** of] Grein alters to *on*,
but in Germania X, 421, returns to *of*.   **138** arum] The MS. spelling
earum was probably an unconscious anticipation of *eala*.   **139** þær]
Wülker suggests þæt here, and so Thorpe, Codex Exoniensis, previously,
and þær in l. 140. But see l. 79, note.   **152** a langaþ] Grein, Germania X,
421, proposes a compound verb *alangaþ*, but *a* as adverb, "ever," is better.
158-159] Grein thinks a line may have dropped out between l. 158 and l. 159,
and suggests *swylcra arna, swa þu unc her ær scrife*, see l. 102.   **159** unc]
Thorpe, Codex Exoniensis, proposes transferring *unc* to l. 158, after *ætsomne*.
This gives a smoother reading syntactically, but it leaves l. 159*a* metrically
too short.   **165** þysses] The last word at the end of fol. 103*b*. The con-
tinuation of the poem is lacking because of the loss of one or more folios
following fol. 103, see Introd., p. xiv.

NOTES ON HOMILETIC FRAGMENT I

1–47

Homiletic Fragment I] For the title, see Introd., p. xxxix.   **1** sorh cymeð]
These are the first words on fol. 104*a* of the MS. and are evidently from the
middle, not the beginning of a sentence. On the loss of one or more folios
in the MS., see Introd., p. xiv.   **7-8**] Grein supplies *sylfa* after *gewita*
and ends l. 7 with this word. His l. 8 consists then of l. 7*b* and l. 8*a*. Wülker's l. 8 is the same as Grein's, but he supplies nothing after *gewita* and his
l. 7 is consequently too short metrically. Thorpe thinks l. 7*b* is in the MS.
by mistake and notes l. 10. Kemble omits l. 7*b*. This omission improves
both the sense and the meter of the passage.   **12** spræce] Grein reads
sib-spræce, see l. 29.   **21** hafað] Grein and Wülker change to *habbað*,
and so also in l. 28, because the subject is plural.   **23** stinge] There is no
indication of loss in the MS., but something is needed to complete the sense.
Kemble translates, "sore with (their sting)," and Wülker, note, approves
mid stinge. Grein reads *mid swice*, "with treachery," see *beswicaþ*, l. 27.
But *swice* makes a short line metrically.   **28** hunigsmæccas] Holthausen,
Eng. Stud. XXXVII, 201, reads *huniges smæccas* as a metrical improvement.
32 weaxeð] Wülker, note, suggests *wealwað* as a possible substitute for
weaxeð.   **40** hyht] Holthausen, Anglia Beibl. XXXI, 28, would read *est*
for *hyht* to provide alliteration. But see l. 43, note.   **43** beteran] The
noun idea to be supplied is probably "life." Thorpe suggests *ham*, but that
is not an appropriate word here. bot] Grein supplied *bealu*, but *bot* suits the
context better. Holthausen, Eng. Stud. XXXVII, 201, supplies *bu*,
"both," before *cunnon*, "Let us think on the better, now that we know

both (the better and the worse)," but this reads too much in the text. The line might be allowed to stand without alliteration, see l. 40, except that *nu we cunnon* seems bald and incomplete in meaning.

NOTES ON DREAM OF THE ROOD

1–100

Dream of the Rood] For the title, see Introd., p. xviii.   **3** reste wunedon] The verb can be taken as an intransitive, with *reste* as a dative, but Klaeber, Anglia Beibl. XVII, 102, prefers *reste*, "resting-place," as acc. sg., citing An. 131, 1310, 1697.   **4** syllicre] Herzfeld, Archiv CXVII, 189, would supply *ne* before *syllicre*, following Dietrich, Disputatio, p. 12, note, but for the absolute use of the comparative, see Klaeber, Anglia Beibl. XVII, 102, and Modern Philology III, 251 f.   Craigie indicates an omission after l. 4.   **5** lyft] Grein alters to *lyfte*, but in Germania X, 425, he reads *on lyft*.   **8** fægere] Bouterwek reads *feowere*, and so Stephens and Wülker. Grein, Dicht., p. 140, translates, "vier," but in his text has *fægere*. But the presence of *fife* in the second half-line does not require a numeral in the first. **9** eaxlegespanne] A compound, and Sweet alters to *eaxlgespanne*. But for the spelling *eaxle-*, see Klaeber, Anglia Beibl. XVII, 102.   þær] Grein, Sweet alter to *þæt*, and so also in l. 10. Cook reads *ðæt* in l. 10, but *þær* in l. 9.   ealle] Omitted by Sievers, Beitr. XII, 478, with *englas* for *engel*. Retaining *ealle*, should one read *engla*? See Shipley, Genitive Case in Anglo-Saxon Poetry, pp. 91–92, for examples of *eall* with genitives. As a nom. pl., *engel* is highly improbable, though Grein, Dicht., p. 140, translates, "alle Engel Gottes." Cook alters *engel* to *englas*. But syntactically *ealle* may be subject and *engel* object, in the sense "Christ," see Soul and Body I, 27, note. In view of these conflicting possibilities, it seems best to let the text stand.   **10** fracodes] Stephens, Kluge, Sweet and Wülker retain the MS. reading *fracodes*, as a permissible variant spelling of *fracoð*, as in Beow. 1575.   **15** geweorðode] Sweet, Sievers, Beitr. X, 518, Cook and Craigie alter to *geweorðod*.   **17** bewrigene] Kemble, Sweet, Cook and Craigie alter to *bewrigen*.   wealdendes] Dietrich, Disputatio, p. 12, note, suggests *wealdendes*, and so Sievers, Beitr. X, 518, Kluge, note, Cook and Craigie. The MS. reading *wealdes*, followed by the other edd., leaves the half-line too short metrically.   **18** gold] Holthausen, Eng. Stud. XXXVII, 201, proposes *godweb* for *gold* as a metrical improvement.   **19** earmra ærgewin] Bouterwek, p. clxviii, alters to *ealdora ærgewinn*, and in his note, he proposes (*þurh*) *ylda* or *ealdora* or *enta ærgeweorc* or *ærgewinn*.   þæt] Grein, note, suggests *þær*.   **20** sorgum] The edd. read either *sorgum* or *sargum*.   **23** beswyled] "Washed," see Bos.-Tol., p. 956, *swilian, swillan*. Bouterwek, Sweet, Cook and Craigie alter to *besyled*, and Cook, note, cites El. 697 in support of *besyled*. But the MS. reading in El. 697 is *besylced*, and the change to *besyled* is not justifiable, see Klaeber, Anglia Beibl. XVII, 102.

Kluge alters to *besylwed*.   **24** Hwæðre] On this use of *hwæðre* as a loose connective, see Klaeber, Anglia Beibl. XVII, 102, who cites Sievers, Beitr. IX, 138. See l. 57.   **31** wergas] Sweet alters to *weargas*.   **41** heanne] Grein alters to *heahne*.   **47** ænigum] Thorpe, Kemble, Bouterwek and Wülker retain the MS. reading *nænigum*, but this leaves the line without alliteration.   **54** forðeode] The MS. has *forð eode*.   Thorpe, Bouterwek, Cook and Wülker take this as *forð-eode*, with *scirne sciman* therefore as object of *hæfdon bewrigen*.   Grein takes the verb as preterite of *forþywan*, "overcome," see Grein-Köhler, p. 734, with *scirne sciman* as its object, and so also Sweet, see his glossary, p. 254.   Cook, MLN. XXII, 207, suggests that *forð eode* in the MS. may be a scribal error for *sweðrode*.   But there seems nothing improbable in making *scirne sciman* an amplification of *wealdendes hræw*, though *hræw* and *sciman* may both be objects of *hæfdon bewrigen* without necessarily being appositives.   **58** to þam æðelinge] Sweet replaces this by *æðcle to anum* from the Ruthwell Cross, *æþþilæ til anum*.   **59** sorgum] The Ruthwell Cross has *miþ sorgum gidræfid*.   **63** ðær] Sweet replaces by *hine*, from Ruthwell Cross, *hinæ*.   **66** banan] Bouterwek, p. clxx, alters to a gen. pl. *banana*, and Cook and Craigie read *banena*.   **70** greotende] So far as meaning goes, the MS. reading *reotende* might stand, and Thorpe, Grein, Wülker and Craigie do not alter.   The lack of alliteration, however, favors a change. Kemble and Cook read *geotende*.   Grein, Germania X, 425, Sweet and Kluge read *greotende*, Herzfeld, Archiv CXVII, 189, reads *gretende*, mis-quoting the MS. as *restende*. Retaining *reotende*, Grein alters *gode* to *rode*, "wir Kreuze," thus securing alliteration at the expense of a very improbable meaning.   Stephens reads *Hwæðere we ðær reotende | [rode] gode hwile*, with *rode* appositive to *we*, as Grein had read.   **71** stefn] A word for alliteration and to account for the gen. pl. *hilderinca*, l. 72, is required in l. 71*b*.   Grein supplied *storm*, Kluge, Sweet, Cook and Craigie supply *stefn*, and Kluge, Sweet and Craigie omit *syððan*, or rather replace *syððan* by *stefn*.   Wülker indicates an omission between *syððan* and *up* but supplies nothing.   In the MS. *syððan* stands at the end of a line, and a word, *stefn* or some other, was probably dropped by the scribe in passing to the next line.   **72** hilderinca] Kemble supplied *sum*, Stephens *eored* after *hilderinca*.   **76** freondas gefrunon] Grein supplies *hie me þa of foldan ahofon* as a second half-line, and so also Cook and Craigie. Stephens supplies *fram me hofon*.   The sense is adequate without an addition, and on incomplete lines, see Gen. 703, note.   **77*a*** ond] Supplied by Grein and justified as an additional metrical syllable.   **79** bealuwara weorc] Grein, note, suggests *bealuwa weorn (worn)*, but Grein, Germania X, 425, returns to the MS. reading, taking *bealuwara* as a gen. pl. adj. in the same syntax as *sarra*, l. 80.   Cook and Craigie read *bealuwa weorc*, and Klaeber, Anglia Beibl. XVII, 102, approves *bealuwa*, a gen. pl. noun with *weorc*.   **91** holmwudu] Kemble, Sweet, Cook and Craigie read *holtwudu*, and Grein, note, suggests *holtwudu*. A compound *holtwudu* occurs several times, but *holmwudu* only in this passage.   But there seems no convincing reason for thinking that the scribe miswrote *holm-* for *holt-* here.   **100 ond Adomes**] Kemble, Bouterwek, p. clxxi, Grein, Cook and Craigie alter to *Adames,* and Grein supplies *for* after *ond.*

101–156

117 ðær] Grein omits *ðær.*   ænig anforht] Bouterwek, p. clxxi, alters to *ænigum fyrht.* Grein reads *onforht,* and Grein, Germania X, 425, Cook and Craigie read *anforht.*   **125 forðwege**] Klaeber, Anglia Beibl. XVII, 102, would read *forðweg.*   **138 on**] Grein, note, suggests *of,* and Stephens, Sweet, Cook and Craigie place *of* in the text. But *on* may stand, see Klaeber, Anglia Beibl. XVII, 102, "shall fetch me here in this transitory life."   **142 me**] Bouterwek, p. clxxii, Sweet, Cook and Craigie alter the MS. reading *he* to *me.* If this is not done, *me* must be understood as carried over from l. 139.   **146 guman**] Sweet, Cook and Craigie alter to *gumena.* But see *banan,* l. 66, and note.   **149 þær**] Grein, note, suggests *ær* for *þær,* or that two half-lines may have fallen out between l. 149*a* and l. 149*b* which referred to the descent into hell. Craigie places *ær* in his text.

NOTES ON ELENE

1–100

Elene] For the title, see Introd., p. xviii.   **6 heo**] Craigie alters to *heow.* **11 leodhwata lindgeborga**] Thorpe, Grimm, Ettmüller, Grein and Zupitza (1 ed.) follow the MS., and so also Kemble, except *leodhwate.* Grein, note, suggests *lindhwata leodgeborga,* and repeats this in Germania X, 424. Körner and Wülker follow Grein's suggestion, and ten Brink approves, Anz.fdA. V, 57, though he prefers *leodgebyrg(e)a.* Zupitza (2 and later ed.) reads *lindhwata leodgebyrga,* and so Holthausen (1 ed.) and Craigie, but Holthausen (2 ed.) changes to *lofhwata leodgebyrga,* and so Cook. In his 3 ed. Holthausen returns to the MS. reading, (except *-byrga* for *-borga*), citing Kock, Eng. Stud. XLIV, 393, who would retain the MS. reading. For *leodgebyrga,* see ll. 203, 556. The emendation of Grein and Zupitza is plausible but perhaps unnecessary in a poetic style that makes so much of verbal variation as Anglo-Saxon does. Retaining the MS. reading, Grein, Dicht., p. 104, translates, "Der lindenschildkühne Leuteschirmer." Kock takes the first element of *leodhwata* as merely intensive.   **16 hroðer**] Grimm, Ettmüller and Kemble change to *hroðre,* but for the dative without *-e,* see Sievers, Angels. Gram. § 289.   **17 wræce**] Ekwall, Anglia Beibl. XXXIII, 65, proposes *wræþe* or *wraþe* for *wræce,* (and Kock, Anglia XLVII, 264, and Holthausen, Anglia Beibl. XXXV, 276, approve), taking *wræþe* from *wraðu,* "support, aid," l. 17*a* being then parallel to l. 16*b.* But an antithesis between the two half-lines is just as plausible, see l. 18*a.*   **18 hetendum**] For *hettendum;* see l. 119, Beow. 1828 for the same spelling.   **21 Hugas**] The MS. *hunas* is apparently an echo from l. 20*a.* Zupitza reads

Hugas, and so Holthausen, Cook, Craigie. For the Hugas, see Klaeber, Beowulf, p. xl.   **22** Wæron hwate weras] These words stand at the beginning of a line in the MS., with no indication of loss. Ettmüller supplied *hildemecgas*, Grein, *on̄ herebyrnan*, Körner, *hereþreatas*, Holthausen (1 ed.), Craigie, *hilde gefysde*, following Sievers, Götting. gel. Anzeiger (Aug. 9, 1882). In his 2 ed. Holthausen reads as in his first, except *hearde* for *hwate*, but in his 3 ed. he reads *wæron wighwate weras ætsomne*. Klaeber, Anglia XXIX, 271, would supply *swylce Hetware* as a first half-line. Trautmann, BEV., p. 98, suggests *wæron hwate hæleþas, heaþu-rofe weras* for the line.   **25** herecombol] Zupitza, Holthausen (1 ed.), Craigie change to *herecumbol*, Cook to *heorucumbol*, see l. 107. Holthausen (2 and 3 ed.) reads *herewoman*. Trautmann, BEV., p. 98, thinks the passage is corrupt, but does not emend. A strict logical interpretation of *wordum*, l. 24, is not possible, but the intent seems clear.   **26** sib] Supplied by Sievers, Götting. gel. Anzeiger (Aug. 9, 1882), for alliteration, and so Holthausen, Cook (*syb*), see Ex. 214, Beow. 387, 729.   Grimm supplied *sweot*, followed by Ettmüller and Kemble. Grein has *siðmægen*, and Korner supplies *siðwerod* between *ond* and *eal*. **31** burgenta] Grimm reads *burgenta*, "over the mountains," in his text, but suggests *burg enta*, or *Burgendas, Burgendan* in his notes. Ettmüller suggests *būrgeatu* or *būrggeatu*, and Craigie has *burg-geatu* in his text. Kemble, Körner read *burg enta*, and so Kock, Anglia XLV, 125, translating, "over the fastness of the giants," i.e. over the mountains, and so also Kock, Eng. Stud. XLIV, 393.   Grein, Wülker read *Burgenta*, but in Spr. I, 148, Grein has *burgenta*, acc. pl. from *burgent*, "urbs?"   Holthausen (1, 2 ed.) alters to *burglocan*, followed by Cook; see Holthausen's note, Anglia XXV, 386.   In Grein-Köhler, p. 877, Holthausen reads *byrg enta*, "Burgen der Riesen," and so in his 3 ed., following Körner, p. 268. Zupitza retains *burgenta*, glossed "burg, stadt??"   A noun *burgent* seems highly improbable, and unless the MS. is emended, it seems best to take as two words, though written as one in the MS.   **32** hergum] "In troops," see Kock, Eng. Stud. XLIV, 394.   **34** burgwigendra] Grein, note, suggests *byrnwigendra*, and so Holthausen and Cook in their text.   **35** Feðan trymedon] Kern, Eng. Stud. LI, 10, would make a parenthesis of this half-line, and Cook adds l. 36*a* to the parenthesis.   Trautmann, BEV., p. 98, proposes taking *trymedon* as a weak participial adjective, "die verstärkten fussvölker." It is possible to take *trymedon* as a pret. pl. intrans. verb, as perhaps in Ex. 158, but not necessary.   An unexpressed personal subject may be understood, with *Feðan* as object.   In any case, l. 35*b* is merely an amplification of l. 35*a*. **36** þæt] A result clause, or perhaps limit of motion, "until," see Klaeber, Anglia XXVII, 401 f.   Holthausen (1 ed.) supplies *oþ*- before *þæt*, but cancels this in his notes.   **49–50** þonne Huna cining, etc.] Zupitza, Holthausen construe to mean *þonne ridon ymb rofne cining*, and so Cook, in his text, but in his glossary *cining* is given as a nominative. But see Körner's text, also Eng. Stud. II, 253, and Kock's comment, Anglia XLVII, 265, for the reading in the text.   **54** Hleopon] The MS. has *hleopon*, not *hleowon*, as in Wülker and some earlier edd. Ettmüller alters to *bleowon*, and so Trautmann, BEV., p. 98.   **58** sceawede] So ten Brink, Anz.fdA. V, 58, and Wülker, Holthausen, and Cook; but Ekwall, Anglia Beibl. XXXIII, 65, thinks *sceawedon* may be retained, citing Beow. 130 ff.   But if *sceawedon* is retained, a subject *hie*, referring to Constantine and his army, must be understood.   In the MS. *scea* stands at the end of a line, *wedon* at the beginning of the following line.   **59** ðæt he] Grein altered to *þæt þe*, and so Zupitza and Holthausen (1 ed.).   But Grein, Germania X, 424, returns to the MS. reading, and so Holthausen (2 and 3 ed.).   Ten Brink, Anz.fdA. V, 58, suggests that *he* is for *hie*, which would necessitate also a change to *samnodon* in l. 60.   In the MS. ðæt has a small capital ð; the word may introduce a result clause, or perhaps stand for *oððæt*.   See Records I, The Junius Manuscript, p. xx.   Or read ðæs for ðæt, "after, when"?   Kock, Eng. Stud. XLIV, 394, takes the antecedent of *he*, l. 59, to be *here*, l. 58. **65** hrora] Grimm, note, Grein, note, suggest *hrorra*, and Zupitza, Holthausen, Cook place *hrorra* in their text.   But *hrora* may stand as a mere spelling variation of *hrorra*.   See l. 379, note, l. 1058, note   **86** hreðerlocan onspeon] Ekwall, Anglia Beibl. XXXIII, 65, suggests placing these words in parentheses, "he, i.e. the angel, had spoken."   Otherwise the subject would be Constantine and the meaning more general.   **89** wliti] The MS. spelling *wliti* may stand as a late scribal variant, though it may also have been accidental and unintentional, the very frequent ending -*ig* being regularly thus spelled in the MS.   Thorpe, Zupitza, Körner and Wülker retain *wliti*, the other edd. emend to *wlitig*.   See An. 142, note.

101–200

106 wreccan] Grimm, note, suggests *weccan*, and so Kemble in his text. ond wæpenþræce] Perhaps one should read *on wæpenþræce*, as Holthausen (1 ed.) does, following Swaen, Anglia XVII, 123.   Reading *ond*, it is possible to take *wæpenþræce* as obj. of *hebban*, but it is better as an instrumental. Retaining *ond*, Holthausen (2 and 3 ed.) supplies *to* after *ond*, following Von der Warth, p. 45, and so Cook, Craigie.   **115** gring] For *cring*, and Ettmüller, Holthausen, Cook so emend, as they do *grungon*, l. 126.   **119** heorugrimme] See ll. 25, note, 107, 1214.   **122** in dufan] Trautmann, BEV., p. 99, would read *inne* or *ingedufan* for metrical reasons.   But scan ⏗|⏗◡, *bil in dùfan*.   **124** sweotum] So Thorpe, note, and all edd. **126** grungon] See l. 115, note.   **140** Daroðæsc] In the MS. *daroð* stands at the end of a line, *æsc* at the beginning of the following line.   A compound *daroðæsc* as subj. of *flugon* is questionable only because *æsc* is masc. and the pl. should be *æscas*.   Grein, Spr. I, 182, suggests taking the word as a neuter here, and so Grein-Köhler, p. 112.   Körner, p. 274, takes the word as singular, but with a plural verb as a collective or because of the following *hildenædran*, and so Klaeber, Archiv CXIII, 147.   Holthausen separates as two words, *daroð*, *æsc*, both subjects of the plural verb, and so in Anglia Beibl. XV, 73.   Swaen, Anglia XVII, 124, reads *daroð ond æsc*.   Zupitza (1 and 2 ed.), Cook emend to *daroðas*, but Zupitza (3 and 4 ed.) reads *daroð* *æsc* as two words, with indication that the passage is corrupt. It seems necessary to retain *daroðæsc* and to accept either Grein's or Körner's explanation of the plural.   **141** gescyrded] "Cut to pieces," from *sceard.* Grimm altered to *gescyrted,* from *sceort,* and Kemble, Ettmüller and Grein follow. Zupitza (1 ed.) reads *gescynded,* but *gescyrded* in later editions. **151** þryðbold secan] Retaining the MS. reading, Grein, Spr. II, 478, interprets, "to adorn the shield with stones, i.e. gems," and so Zupitza and Wülker. Grimm altered *stenan* to *scenan,* "to make to shine, to show," and so Kemble, Ettmüller. Körner, p. 274, suggested *stunan* or *stunian,* "resound, quake," and so also Eng. Stud. II, 254. Trautmann, BEV., p. 99, would change *stenan* to *stellan,* lay down the shield, their warfare over. The emendation in the text is that of Sarrazin, ZfdPh. XXXII, 548, and is followed also by Holthausen, Cook, and Grein-Köhler, pp. 631, 726. For *þryðbold,* see l. 162, *boldes brytta.*   **162** boldes brytta] Appositive to *sigerof cyning,* l. 158. Zupitza emends to *blædes brytta,* and so Holthausen (1 ed., *blædes,* 2 and 3 ed., *blēdes*) and Cook. Körner alters to *goldes brytta.* See l. 151, note.   **175** ðæt] The word begins with a capital *Đ* in the MS., perhaps for emphasis. See l. 181.   **181** Alysde] The word begins with a capital in the MS., and the syntax also favors a new sentence here.   **184** tacen] Appositive to *gesceaft,* l. 183. Zupitza emended the MS. *tacne* to *tacen,* and so Holthausen (1 ed.). Holthausen (2 ed.) reads *to tacne,* following Trautmann, BEV., p. 99, and so Cook. Wülker retains *tacne* as instrumental, and so Kock, Eng. Stud. XLIV, 394, who explains the word as an instrumental parallel to the prepositional phrase *þurh þa ilcan gesceaft,* as Körner, p. 275, had previously done. So also Holthausen (3 ed.).   **197** hyhta nihst] The earlier edd. retained the MS. reading *hyht nihst,* but this is short metrically and awkward syntactically. Körner, p. 275, suggests *hyhta nihst,* and so Wülker. Zupitza reads *hyhta hihst,* and so Holthausen, Cook.

201–300

205 beorhtme] See ll. 39, 864.   **207** swa] Holthausen, Cook supply *hie* after *swa,* following Sievers, Anglia I, 579.   **213** firhðsefan] The MS. has *firhð,* not *fyrhð,* as Wülker, note, records.   forð gemyndig] Zupitza (1 and 2 ed.) supposes a loss in the MS. before these words and suggests *fæste bewunden,* | *folces fruma* to be supplied, but in the 3 and 4 ed., *aldor* (or *hyrde, ræswe*) is suggested in place of *fruma.* Cook supplies *he wæs* before *forð,* citing Pogatscher, Anglia XXIII, 289. Pogatscher assumes that *wæs,* l. 212, is implied in l. 213*b,* and so previously Körner, Eng. Stud. II, 255. Kock, JJJ., p. 18, takes *gemyndig* as applying to *lof,* translating, "The praise of Christ then in the emperor's mind was ever bent on the illustrious tree."   **215** foldwege] Grein, Germania X, 424, proposed *flodwege,* and so Holthausen, Cook in their text.   **217** þreate] ten Brink, Anz.fdA. V, 59, suggests that *þreate* is an echo from l. 215 and that *werode* may have been the proper word. Holthausen replaces *þreate* by *heape.*   **230** helm]

Grimm, note, alters to *holm*, Zupitza to *welm*, and Holthausen, Cook follow Zupitza. This is an obvious but not for that reason a convincing emendation, see Grein-Köhler, p. 325.　　**243** meahte gesion] Cook reads *gesion meahte*, following Von der Warth, p. 45.　　**245** swellingum] "Swelling sails," but an otherwise unrecorded word. Kock, JJJ., p. 19, proposes *snellingum*, citing O. Icel. *snillingr*, and *snellic*, Beow. 690, and translating, "beneath the spirited men."　　**251** sæfearoðe] Cook reads *sæwaroðe*, following Krapp, Modern Philology II, 407. But the confusion between *faroð* and *waroð* was probably present in the Anglo-Saxon mind and consistent emendation seems unnecessary.　　sande] Grein, note, suggests *sunde*, and so Zupitza, Holthausen and Cook.　　**268** Iudeas] Wülker, Holthausen, Cook read *Iudea*, a gen. pl., following Zupitza (2 and later ed.). But *Iudeas* is parallel to *lindwigendra land*, l. 270, nouns like this meaning either people or country, see Kock, Anglia XLIV, 105. See l. 278.　　**273** Hierusalem] ten Brink, Anz.fdA. V, 59, would read *Gerusalem* or *Jerusalem*, on the ground that the alliterating word in l. 273*a* is *guðrofe*, not *hæleþ*. But see Dan. 2.　　**279** meðelhegende] Kock, JJJ., p. 19, would take this word as parallel to *gehwylcum*, therefore as an uninflected appositive, agreeing in number but not in case. But that *burgsittendum*, l. 276, *snoterestum*, l. 277, and *gehwylcum*, l. 278, should all be syntactical appositives and all have corresponding inflection, and that *meðelhegende* should be in the same syntax without ending, seems very improbable.　　**285** M] To be resolved as *þusendu*, Sievers, Beitr. X, 518.　　**293** ealle snyttro] The MS. reading *þære snyttro* provides no alliteration and no adequate syntax for a genitive or dative *þære snyttro*, unless the words are taken as a dative object of *wiðweorþon*. In his text Grimm indicates an omission after *unwislice*, and in his notes suggests *swicon* to be supplied. Sievers, Anglia I, 579, would supply *swicon* before *unwislice*. Kemble supplies *swicon* before *snyttro*. Grein supplies *soð* after *snyttro*, citing Dan. 28, but Grein, Germania X, 424, replaces *soð* by *swiðe*. Zupitza (1 ed.) reads *soð* with Grein, but in the second and later editions he removes *soð* and merely indicates an omission. Bos.-Tol., p. 1256, suggests *stan* after *snyttro*, citing Luke xx. 17. Cosijn, Tijdschrift I, 143, replaces *unwislice* by *samwislice*, and Kock, JJJ., p. 21, approves. ten Brink, Anz.fdA. V, 59, replaces *þære* by *ealre*. Holthausen (1 ed.) supplies *soðfæstne cwide* after *snyttro* as l. 293*b* and *ealne wisdom* as the first half of the next line. But Holthausen (2 and 3 ed.) merely replaces *þære* by *ealle*, and so Cook. This seems the simplest way out of the difficulty, though it is not apparent why *ealle* should have been miswritten as *þære*. The Latin text of the life of Helena reads *repellentes omnem sapientiam*, see Holthausen, p. 11.　　**300** spald] The Latin life has *per sputum oculos vestros illuminavit*, see Holthausen, p. 11.

301–400

302 to deaþe] Zupitza and later edd. supply *to*.　　**304** woruld] Zupitza alters to *worn*, and so Holthausen, Cook. But *woruld* may stand, and see

Christ 718, where *woruld* and *eorð̄buend* appear as appositives. **311** gedweolan] Sievers, Anglia I, 579, supplies *in* before *gedweolan*, and so Holthausen (1 ed.), Cook. But *gedweolan* may be instrumental, parallel to *geþancum*, 1. 312, as Klaeber, Anglia XXIX, 271, maintains. Holthausen (2 and 3 ed.) omits *in*, as supplied in his first edition. Kock, Anglia XLIII, 302, reads *on* for *ond*, see An. 1191, note. **313** Gangaþ] Holthausen (2 ed.) suggests *secaþ* for this word. geþencaþ] "Find out by thinking," like *geascian*, "find out by asking," Kock, JJJ., p. 21. Holthausen (1 and 2 ed.) supplies a full line after this word, *ond findaþ gen ferhð̄gleawe men*. Von der Warth, p. 45, would read *gesecaþ* for *geþencaþ*, and ten Brink, Anz.fdA. V, 60, suggested *geceosað, alesað* or some similar word. **314** cræftige] Cook reads *gleawe* to avoid the repetition in the next line. **315** æð̄elum cræftige] Zupitza, note, suggests that *cræftige* was an accidental repetition from 1. 314 for *gode*, and Holthausen places *gode* in his text. **318** eowic] Sievers, Beitr. X, 518, reads *eowic*, and so Zupitza (3 and 4 ed.), Holthausen, Cook. **320** geruman] Grein expanded the abbreviation as *gerun*, and this seems supported by l. 411, but in Germania X, 424, Grein reads *gerum*. Schwarz, Cynewulfs Anteil am Christ, p. 67, proposes *geryne, gerune*. Frucht, Metrisches und Sprachliches, p. 74, proposes *geruman*, and so Holthausen, Cook, Grein-Köhler, p. 558. Holthausen, Anglia Beibl. XVII, 177, Von der Warth, p. 46, would read *þa on gerum eodan*. The phrase *Eodan on geruman* merely means that they went out. **322** georne] The MS. *eorne* is a mere spelling variation, and perhaps accidental, see l. 399, *eare*, for *geare*. The edd. all emend to *georne*. **323** wordgeryno] Holthausen (1 ed.) reads *wordgeryna*, a gen. pl., following Shipley, The Genitive Case in Anglo-Saxon Poetry, p. 94, though in his 2 and 3 ed. Holthausen restores *wordgeryno*, still regarded as a genitive plural. But *wordgeryno* may be object of the verb and *þa wisestan* the subject. **326** M] To be resolved as *þusend*. **338** word] Supplied by Grein, Zupitza, Holthausen and Cook, and needed for alliteration. **348** wende] So Thorpe and all edd. **353** gingne] Zupitza alters to *ginge*, and so Wülker, Holthausen and Cook. See Isaiah i. 2, where the plural *filios* occurs. But *filios* would be adequately represented by *bearn*, and stylistically it is better to take *eaforan* as a singular, "a young son I raised up, children I begat," etc. **356** foreþances] Sievers, Anglia I, 580, suggests *foreþancas*, and so Zupitza (2 and later ed.), Holthausen and Cook. **357** ond] Coördinate with *ond*, l. 361, "although... nevertheless." **360** gifað] So Zupitza, Cook, Holthausen, but Wülker retains *gifeð* as in a relative clause beginning with *þe* even when the context is plural. **369**] For this line Holthausen (1 ed.) reads *ond ge þam soð̄e ond ryhte* | *wið̄secen hæfdon*, but in his later editions he returns to the MS. reading. **370b–371a**] Grein supplied *dryhtna* and placed *eallra* in l. 370 instead of l. 371, as earlier edd. had done. Later edd. follow Grein, except Zupitza (1 ed.), who supplies *eowerne* after *scippend* in l. 370, but Zupitza (2 and later ed.) follows Grein. **375** þæt me] Cook, note, would supply *hie* between these words, following Holthausen, note, and so also in l. 409. **377** modcwanige] Trautmann, Kynewulf, p. 82, proposes *modes cwange* or *mode cwange*, and Holthausen, Anglia XXIII, 516, would read *modcwange guman*, but in his text Holthausen has *mode cwanige*, i.e. *cwange*, though he also suggests *mod-cwange men* in his notes to his first edition. Cook reads *mode cwanige*. A compound *modecwanige* is not impossible, see *modewæga*, Ex. 500. These changes are made to provide a metrical syllable, but see l. 379*b* for a similar metrical half-line. **378** bead] Sievers, Beitr. X, 518, changes to *bebead* to gain a metrical syllable, and so Holthausen, Cook. A change in the order of words to read *swa sio cwen him bead* would be another way of gaining the same result. **379** Fundon] Grimm and later edd. read *fundon*. Though pret. plurals in *-an* are frequent, the ending *-en* is not so and the form *funden* of the MS. was probably accidental. See l. 432 for the opposite error. D] To be resolved as *fif hund*. forþsnottera] Grimm and later edd. read *-snotterra*, except Wülker, who retains the MS. spelling. See l. 65, note. **380** alesen] Cook alters to *alesenra*. But *alesen* modifies *fif hund*, and *forðsnottera* modifies *leodmæga*. See ll. 285–286. **399** geare] See *georne*, l. 322, and note. Thorpe and later edd. read *geare*.

401–500

403 þeodenbealwa] The MS. reads *þeoden bealwa*, but Thorpe has *þeodon*, which the edd. before Wülker try to explain as a verb. Wülker reads correctly *þeodenbealwa* and takes this to be an accusative plural form. Holthausen (1 ed.) reads *þeodbealwa ænig* and supposes that a line between l. 402 and l. 403 has been lost. Von der Warth, p. 46, proposes *þeodenbealwa sum* (or *ān*), and so Cook, Holthausen (2 ed.). Holthausen (3 ed.) follows the MS. and supplies nothing. Kern, Eng. Stud. LI, 11, takes *þeodenbealwa* as a gen. pl., but supplies nothing, taking the word as a genitive modifier of *æbylgð* and citing parallel constructions in Anglo-Saxon prose. Kern's explanation is adequate and nothing need be supplied. Kock, Eng. Stud. XLIV, 395, supposes a shift of construction, *æbylgð* an accusative object and *þeondenbealwa* a genitive object of *nyton*. **422** gnyrna] So Bouterwek, Angelsächsisches Glossar, p. 136, and all later edd. **423** orscyldne] Thorpe suggested *unscyldigne* for the MS. *scyldū*, and so Grimm, Kemble, Grein, Zupitza (1 and 2 ed.) and Wülker. Zupitza (3 and 4 ed.) reads *scyldum*, and otherwise as the MS., but with indication that the passage is corrupt. Holthausen (1 ed.) reads *scyldum* with the MS. and supplies after this word *asceredne | sceaðan be ræde, || ealles orhlytne* Trautmann, BEV., p. 99, proposes *orscyldne* for the MS. *scyldū*, and so Cook, Holthausen (2 and 3 ed.) and Craigie. Kern, Eng. Stud. LI, 11, approves Trautmann's emendation, but suggests *escyldne = æscyldne*, citing *æfelle*, *æmenne*, etc., as also possible. **432** forleten] Kemble and later edd. change the MS. *forleton* to a past participle. See l. 379, note. **438** fæder] Cook, Holthausen change to *fædere*, following Sievers, Beitr. X, 483. So also in l. 454. minum] There is no indication of loss in the MS. after *minum*, and Thorpe and Grimm assume none, nor does Kemble, though he changes *minum* to *sinum*. But the speech that follows, ll. 441 ff., cannot have been addressed to Zachaeus, as this alteration would make it be, see ll. 418, 454–455, 530. Grein supplies *þe hit siððan cyðde sylfa his* before *eaferan* and as completing that line. Zupitza indicates an omission but supplies nothing. Holthausen (1 and 2 ed.) supplies *þe wæs Symon haten,* | *swæsum* before *eaferan,* and so Cook. Holthausen (3 ed.) supplies *Symon wæs haten,* | *swæsum* before *eaferan.* Craigie supplies *þam wæs Simon nama,* | *swæsum.* This satisfies the sense, if we assume that the subject of *wende,* l. 440, is Simon, the words that follow being then addressed to Judas. The Latin text, Holthausen (3 ed.), p. 16, reads, *Zacheus autem, avus meus, praenuntiavit patri meo et pater meus, cum moreretur, adnuntiavit mihi dicens.* **451**] For l. 451*b* Grimm, note, supplied *mid yldrum deah*; Grein has *bið gedyrsod æfre,* but Germania X, 424, he changes to *dreames bruceð.* Brenner, Eng. Stud. XIII, 481, would supply *dreosan ne sceal* or *na dreosan sceal.* Holthausen supplies *deorlice bið.* Zupitza and Cook indicate an omission but supply nothing. The sense is complete without assuming an omission. **454** fæder] See l. 438, note.   **476** bearna] Grimm changes to *beorna,* and so also Grein, Germania X, 424, and ten Brink, Anz.fdA. V, 60.   **477** hie] Zupitza, Holthausen, Cook alter to *him.*   **479** sarum] Trautmann, BEV., p. 99, suggests *searwum* for *sarum.*   **487** hine] Grein, Zupitza, Holthausen, Cook supply *hine.*   **494** þrohtherd] Grimm and later edd. alter to -*heard,* except Zupitza and Wülker, and -*herd* may well stand as a spelling variation of -*heard.*   **495** sette] Trautmann, BEV., p. 100, would change to *dyde* for metrical reasons.   **496** hie] Kemble and later edd. read *hie,* except Holthausen (2 and 3 ed.), *hine.*   **497** Sawles] Grein, Cook alter to *Saules.*

501–600

501 wearð] Supplied by Kemble and later edd., except Wülker, who assumes, however, that the word must be supplied in sense. **518**] There is no indication of loss in the MS. Thorpe, Grimm and Kemble assume the loss of a half-line before *syðþan,* Zupitza after *gelyfdon,* but supply nothing. Grein supplies *in lifes fruman* after *gelyfdon,* Holthausen (1 ed.) supplies *leohtum geþoncum.* Holthausen (2 and 3 ed.) supplies *þissum leofspelle,* following Von der Warth, p. 46, see l. 1016, and so Cook, Craigie. **522** leoðorune] The MS. reads clearly *leoðo* at the end of a line, followed by *rune* in the next line, not *leoða* as given by Cook. Sievers, Beitr. X, 504, emends to *lēoðrūne* (or *lĕoðurūne*), and so Zupitza (3 and 4 ed.), Cook, Holthausen and Craigie read *lēoðrūne.* In his 1 and 2 ed. Zupitza had read as in the MS. Grein-Köhler, p. 415, also emends to *lēoðrūne.* Sweet, Student's Dictionary, p. 107, glosses as *leoþo-rūn,* [or **leoþr-*], "advice(?)." In form *lēoðrūne,* "advice in song," "secret advice," would be beyond question, but the evidence of the MS. does not permit lightly setting aside the form *leoðorune,* nor is the meaning *lēoð-,* "song," particularly appropriate here. What one expects as the first element of the compound is some meaning like "kindly," "friendly," "gentle," as in *leofspell,* l. 1016. See Grein-Köhler, under *leoðu,* and Bos.-Tol., under *leoðu, geliðewæcan, geliðian* for possible cognates. Trautmann, BEV., p. 100, proposes *leornunge* for the MS. *leoðorune.* See l. 1250, note.   **530** septe] See An. 742.   Thorpe and other edd. before Zupitza (2 ed.) misread as *sewde.*   **531** gehðum] Thorpe corrected the obvious error of the MS. to *gehðum,* and so the earlier edd. and Wülker, who cites *geomorfrod,* Gen. 2226.   Zupitza alters to *giddum,* and so Cook.   Holthausen (1 ed.) reads *gidda,* but in his 2 and 3 ed., he returns to the MS.   Trautmann, BEV., p. 100, proposes *gearum* for *gehðum.*   cunnon] Cook changes to *cunniað,* glossed, "think out, decide."   Holthausen (1 ed.) indicates the loss of a line after *cunnon.*   In Anglia Beibl. XVIII, 77, Holthausen reconstructs this passage to read:

> Nu ge eal geare cunnon!
> Hwæt eow þæs on sefan   selest þinceð
> to gecyðanne,   gif ðeos cwen usic
> frigneð ymb ðæt foldgræf,   nu ge fyrhðsefan
> ond modgeþanc   minne cunnon?

In Anglia Beibl. XVIII, 204, Holthausen proposes for l. 532, as a metrical improvement, *hwæt eow þæs selest | on sefan þinceð,* and he doctors l. 1164 in the same way, and so also in 2 ed.   Trautmann, BEV., p. 100, proposes other metrical variations.   But Holthausen (3 ed.) reads as in the text, except *fregnum,* "questions," for *treo,* l. 534.   Kock, Eng. Stud. XLIV, 395, would read as in the text.   **534** frigneð ymb ðæt treo] Zupitza (3 and 4 ed.) proposes *ða rodl* for *ðæt treo.*   Holthausen (1 ed.) has *foldgræf* for *treo,* but changes in his 2 ed. to *freotreo* and in his third to *fregnum.*   In Anglia XXIII, 516, he proposes *fyrntreo,* "altes Holz," and in Eng. Stud. LI, 183, he reads *beacen* or *becen* for *treo* and *breostsefan* for *fyrhðsefan* in l. 534b. Trautmann, BEV., p. 100, proposes *ymb ðæt forctreow,* or simply *ymb forcan,* "gallows," for *ymb ðæt treo.*   Cook reads *freotreo* with Holthausen's 2 ed. These changes are all made to satisfy theories of metrical propriety.   **547** Weoxan] Zupitza (2 ed.) reads *Wrixledan,* following Cosijn, Tijdschrift I, 144, but in the 3 and 4 ed. he returns to *weoxan,* as in his first edition.   **548** gehwær] Zupitza, Holthausen, Cook alter to *gehwæne.*   **558** cyðdon] Zupitza, Holthausen, Cook change to *cyðan.*   **561** witgan] So Thorpe and later edd.   **571a**] Trautmann, BEV., p. 100, would omit *þæt* or *hio* for metrical reasons.   **578** bæl fornimeð] Frucht, Metrisches und Sprach-liches, p. 30, proposed *bælfyr* for *bæl for-,* Trautmann, BEV., p. 101, approves, and Holthausen places this in his text.   **580b**] Grimm and Kemble read incorrectly *þæs leas* for *þæt leas.*   Grein reads *þæt leas-spell,* but Grein, Germania X, 424, reads *þæt eow þæt leas sceal,* a reading which is rejected by Sievers, Anglia I, 580, on metrical grounds.   Zupitza (2 ed.) follow's Grein's second reading; in his 3 and 4 ed. Zupitza reads *þæt eow seo leasung sceal,* and so Cook.   Holthausen (1 ed.) reads *þæt eow sceal þæt lease spel;* in his 2 and 3 ed. Holthausen reads as in the MS., but places *apundrad,* l. 581, at the end of l. 580.   The alliteration might be regularized by reading *þæt þæt leas eow sceal.*   **581** apundrad] Although the distinction between *W,* written with the runic symbol, and *P* is not always clear in the MS., in this instance there can be no question that the scribe wrote *a þundrad,* which may of course have been intended for a compound *apundrad*. The reading is so clear that it should be retained if at all possible. Thorpe prints *awund-rad*, and all edd. before Zupitza (2 ed.) take this as the MS. reading. Grimm has *awundrad* (see Bos.-Tol., p. 63, "the falsehood shall be made a wonder of for you"), but in his notes he suggests *awended*. Grein reads *awundrad*, and so Wülker as an emendation. Zupitza, Holthausen (1 ed.), Cook read *awended*. Strunk, MLN. XVII, 372, emends to *asundrad*, "falsehood shall be separated from you," a meaning which does not fit the context. Retaining *apundrad*, the word must be taken as from *pund*, "a weight," in the sense "weigh out, apportion," see Bos.-Tol., Supplement, p. 45, *apyndrian*, "to weigh," p. 682, *pundar*, "a balance or weight," *pundern*, "a plumb line," and possibly a verb *pundernian*, "to weigh." Trautmann, BEV., p. 101, Grein-Köhler, p. 539, and Holthausen (2 and 3 ed.) accept the word in this way. Placing *apundrad* at the end of l. 580, Holthausen (2 and 3 ed.) takes the remainder of l. 581 as his l. 581*a* and l. 582*a* as his l. 581*b*, followed by indications for a first half-line lost, the second half-line as in the text. So also Trautmann, BEV., p. 101, except that he takes *þe ge hwile nu* of l. 582*b* as a first half-line, and for the second half-line reads *hyddon on unriht*, with no omissions and nothing supplied except *hyddon*. In his notes (3 ed.), p. 91, Holthausen suggests *hydan þa halgan geryno* for his missing half-line. In his first edition Holthausen, following Zupitza (1 ed.), had taken l. 582*a* as in the text, with a second half-line and the first half of the following line lost, followed by *þe ge hwile nu on unriht hyddon* for the second half-line. 590 orde] So Thorpe and all later edd. except Wülker.

601–700

608 þæs to þinge] Holthausen (1 ed.) alters to *þissa þinga*, but Anglia Beibl. XXI, 174, reads *þæs to þance*, and so in his 2 and 3 ed. Cook reads *þæra þinga*. Trautmann, BEV., p. 102, would read *þæs to þinum*, "zu dem deinen, als das deine," i.e. as your fate. But *þæs* may stand as a genitive of specification, and *þinge* in the sense "consideration, deliberation," see *þingode*, l. 609, "what you about this on deliberation." 610 rex] This Latin word appears again in l. 1041, where it fits into the context more easily. As it seems scarcely credible that the word is a scribal innovation, it seems best to let it stand as perhaps a bit of learned pleasantry on the part of the poet. The simplest explanation of the word is that which takes it for *cyning*, as part of an intensive compound *cyninggeniðlan*, appositive to *gehðu*. This is Holthausen's reading in his 2 and 3 ed., and so also Craigie. In his 1 ed. Holthausen had taken the word as for *cræfte*, an instrumental. Sievers, Anglia I, 580, proposed *cyninges*, and Wülker approves, though he retains *rex* in his text. Cosijn, Tijdschrift I, 144, proposes *cyningan*, "reginae." Trautmann, BEV., p. 102, suggests *carena*, from *cearu*, which he thinks was misread as *cyning* and the misreading then turned into Latin *rex*. Cook reads *cwealmgeniðlan*, taking *rex* as a scribal mistake for Latin *nex*, and translating *nex* as *cwealm*. The earlier edd. retained *rex* in their text without

adequate explanation.   **614** samod] The addition of *samod* was made by
Zupitza, and so Holthausen, Cook.   Grimm, note, supplied *beorne*, a dative
singular, after *gesihðe*, Grein supplied *gebroht* before *on*, and ten Brink,
Anz. fdA. V, 60, suggested *gesette weorðað* or *geweorðað* after *bu*.   Wülker
indicates an omission after *gesihðe*, but though he approves ten Brink's
reading, he supplies nothing in his text.   **615** streac] Holthausen, Cook
alter to *stearc*.   **624** radorcyninges] Holthausen (2 and 3 ed.), Cook,
Craigie supply *beam* after this word, following Von der Warth, p. 47.   **629**
hyht swa mode] The MS. has *heofon rices swamode* with no indication of
omission.   The lack of alliteration and of a word to account for the genitive
heofonrices indicates a loss here.   Grimm reads *heofonrices...swa mode*,
but in a foot-note, he suggests *hwurfe* to be supplied, retracted on p. 153 in
favor of *hygde*, "cogitaret."   Kemble supposes a loss after *heofonrices*.
Grein reads *heofonrices hyhte swa mode*, but in Germania X, 424, he proposes
niode for *mode*, and so Spr. II, 289.   Zupitza (1 ed.), note, suggests *ge him
heofonrices hyht swamode*, but in later editions he reads *ge he heofonrices
hyht swa mode*.   Wülker indicates an omission after *heofonrices*, but supplies
nothing, though he approves Grimm's *hygde*, or better *hogde*, and he reads
swa mode.   For Zupitza's *hyht*, Klaeber, Anglia XXIX, 272, suggests *hyht-
wynne* to fill out the line, for the MS. *swamode* or *swa mode*, reading *samod*,
with Cosijn, Tijdschrift I, 145.   Holthausen (2 and 3 ed.) follows Klaeber.
In his 1 ed. Holthausen had read *hyht swa meðe*.   Cook reads *hyht swa
mærne*.   Trautmann, BEV., p. 102, thinks the MS. reading should be
retained as a verb, "verlustig ginge," as Zupitza (1 ed.) had done, and so
Craigie.   Kock, JJJ., p. 21, would also retain *swamode*, with *hyhtes* for
Zupitza's *hyht* to be supplied, meaning "moved or strayed from the joy
of heaven."   Kock renders the passage as follows: "he regretted that he
should both forego the joy of heaven and leave this present realm beneath
the skies, if he did not reveal the Holy Rood."   But a verb *swamode* at this
place is very doubtful.   If the scribe miswrote *niode* as *mode* (see Grein-
Köhler, p. 500, for other examples), and supplying *hyht*, the sense of the
passage would be, "to him was a sad spirit, hot at heart, and sorrow for
both, that (or if) he should thus of necessity (i.e. that he should thus be
compelled) give up the joy of heaven and this present kingdom under the
skies (i.e. life on earth), if he should not reveal the cross."   Retaining *mode*,
on would replace "of necessity" by "in his mind or heart."   See ll. 963–966.
630 ond] Trautmann, BEV., p. 102, replaces *ond* by *ge*, and in l. 631 reads
gif for *ge*.   Cook follows Trautmann's reading in l. 631, but not in l. 630.
631 ða rode ne tæhte] Zupitza omits *ne*, thus taking the thought expressed
in l. 631*b* as the second half of a dilemma indicated by *gehwæðres wa*.   Holthausen (1 and 2 ed.) follows Zupitza, but in his 3 ed. Holthausen reads
ðæt reht for *ða rode ne*, citing l. 601.   Klaeber, Anglia XXIX, 272, also
omits *ne*, translating, "dass er sowohl das irdische als das himmlische leben
preisgäbe, oder dass er das kreuz zeigte."   But *gehwæðres wa* more probably
refers to the heavenly and the earthly life.   **634** CC] Resolved as *twa hund*
by Grimm, Kemble and Grein, as *tu hund* by Cook.   **636** feala] The edd.

retain the MS. reading *feale*, except Grein and Cook, who have *feala*, and Holthausen, who reads *fealo*.　**639** siðdagum] Cook has *siddagum*, a misprint.　**645** Troiana] Holthausen (2 and 3 ed.), Cook alter to *Troianas*. **646** fyr mycle] For the MS. *fær mycel*, Grimm, note, suggested *fyr mycle*, "much more remote," and so Kemble, Cook, Craigie.　Holthausen (2 and 3 ed.) has *fior mycle*.　Klaeber, Anglia XXIX, 272, Trautmann, BEV., p. 103, Kock, PPP., p. 5, accept Grimm's *fyr mycle*.　Imelmann, Anglia Beibl. XVII, 226, endeavors to retain the *fær mycel* by taking *þonne*, l. 647, in the sense "then," i.e. this *æðele gewyrd* took place after the Trojan war. Retaining *fær mycel*, Holthausen (1 ed.) supplies *ær geworden* || *Israhela folce*, after *ealdgewin*. Von der Warth, p. 48, supplies *þæt þe ær cuð wearð* || *eowrum ægleawum*.　Klaeber, l.c., points out, as Grein had previously done, that a positive might stand before *þonne*, i.e. that one might take *fær micel* ...*þonne* in the sense "a great conflict, greater than," but this meaning obviously does not fit the context.　**647** open] Holthausen (2 and 3 ed.) reads *opene*, and in Anglia Beibl. XXI, 174, he proposes also to add *þæt* before *opene*.　For *open ealdgewin*, Trautmann, BEV., p. 103, proposes *ofer eall gemynd*, "beyond all recollection." Kock, PPP., p. 5, takes *þæt*, l. 646, and *open ealdgewin* as parallel, translating, "yet that, the open ancient conflict, was much older than this notable event."　**657** nean] Kemble altered to *near*, Zupitza to *neah*.　**658** ond þa] A kind of loose parataxis, Klaeber, Anglia XXIX, 271, i.e. "because we have set those conflicts in writing."　**668** on tweon] For the MS. *ond tweon*, Grimm, note, suggests *ond on tweon* or *ond tweonde*.　Sievers, Anglia I, 580, would read *ond on tweon*, and so Holthausen, Cook.　Without *on*, *tweon* would be taken as instrumental.　Kock, JJJ., p. 22, reads *on tweon*, omitting *ond* as written in the MS. with the abbreviation for *ond* by mistake for *on*.　wende him trage hnagre] Literally, "had expectation to himself of a worse evil." Kemble altered *trage* to *þrage*, "humbled himself for a while."　**676** Caluarie] All edd. read *Caluarie* for the MS. *caluare*, and Cook, Holthausen (2 and 3 ed.) also add *on* before this word, following Von der Warth, p. 49. The Latin text has here, Holthausen (3 ed.), p. 25, *tantum ostende mihi, qui vocatur Calvariae locus*.　**683** can] Holthausen (1 ed.) alters to *wat*, but in 2 and 3 ed. returns to the MS. reading.　**691** swa] Grein omits without comment.　**697** besylced] Thorpe misreports the MS. as *besyleed*, which he emends to *besyled*, and so the earlier edd. before Zupitza (2 ed.).　**699** healsie] Thorpe misreports the MS. as *halsie*, and so later edd. before Zupitza (2 ed.).　Holthausen reads *halsie* as an emendation.

701–800

704 þreanyd] Cook supplies *to* after this word.　**709** scead] See l. 149. Grimm, Kemble, Grein alter to *sceod*.　Zupitza (1 ed.) merely indicates some disturbance in the text between *hæleðum* and *scead*, though he makes no change.　In later editions he accepts the MS. reading.　ten Brink, Anz.fdA. V, 60, would change to *scraf*, Trautmann, BEV., p. 104, would read *weold*, and so Holthausen (1 ed.). In his later editions Holthausen returns to the MS. reading. **720** halige] Zupitza and later edd. read *halige*, except Wülker, who retains *halig*. **721** feondes] The earlier edd. assume an extensive omission here, and Grein supplies to read *þurh searucræft besenced læg* || *on fyrndagum foldan*, etc. But Grein, Germania X, 424, thinks only *feonda* is to be supplied before *searu*. Zupitza supplies *feondes*, and so later edd. Wülker indicates an omission in his text and in his note approves Grein's *feonda* as the word to be supplied. **724** elnes oncyðig] Trautmann, BEV., p. 104, would alter to *eþles uncyðig*, "der des ortes unkundige." See ll. 828, note, 960, note. Grimm, note, had discussed *uncyðig* but rejected it. **755** He sceal] Grein alters the MS. *he* to *þe*, taking *sigorcynn* as the antecedent of *þe*. Zupitza reads *hie sceolon*, and so Holthausen (1 ed.), *hie sculon*, (2 and 3 ed.), *hie sceolon*. The change to the singular may have been occasioned by the fact that in Genesis iii. 24 only one sword is mentioned, *Cherubim, et flammeum gladium*. The poet does not make the hierarchical values of the Cherubim and Seraphim quite clear. **768** ful] Sievers, Anglia I, 580, takes *ful* as a noun object of *þrowian*. The simpler interpretation takes *ful* as adj., parallel to *fah*, "the foulest of the foul," Kock, PPP., p. 5, with *þeowned* object of both *þrowian* and *þolian*. **779** no] Zupitza suggests *ne* for *no*, with only a comma before, and so Holthausen in his text. **781** þin] Grimm, Kemble alter to *þinum*. **782** þurh ða beorhtan] "Through the glorious one." Trautmann, BEV., p. 104, supplies *bryd* after *beorhtan*, Cook supplies *mægð*. **787** geywdest] The spelling *gehywdest* of the MS. was apparently accidental, the alliteration being vocalic. The earlier edd. and Wülker retain the spelling *gehywdest*, but Grein and other later edd. read *geywdest*. **788** wyn] The MS. has here merely the usual runic symbol for *w*, with a dot before and after. Thorpe, Grimm, Kemble, Grein and Zupitza (1 and 2 ed.) resolve this as *waldend, wealdend*. Zupitza (3 and 4 ed.) resolves as *weard*. Sievers, Beitr. X, 518, resolves as *wen*, but Anglia XIII, 3, as *wyn* (though here not in reference to this passage but to the runic passages giving Cyn(e)wulf's name). Holthausen and Cook have *wyn*. See l. 1089. **790** þæt me] Cook supplies *ðu* between these words. **800** walde] "that he rules."

801–900

803 swylce rec] Schwarz, Cynewulfs Anteil am Christ, p. 59, would omit *swylce*, and so Trautmann, BEV., p. 104. Holthausen (2 and 3 ed.) and Cook omit *swylce* from their texts. **812** inwrige] Thorpe suggests *onwrige*, and so Holthausen, Cook. **821** broðor] Judas could be the brother of Stephen only in spiritual sense. The Latin life, Holthausen (3 ed.), p. 31, reads *et adnumera me [in caelo] cum fratre meo Stephano, qui scriptus est in Actibus...apostolorum.* **823** stangreopum] Grimm, Kemble alter to *stangreotum*. **827** þam] Trautmann, BEV., p. 104, omits for metrical reasons. **828** elnes anhydig] Trautmann, BEV., p. 104, would change to *eðles ancyðig*, see l. 724, note, "zuerst also *eþles uncyðig*, so lange er den

ort nicht kennt; dann aber, nachdem er ihn erfahren hat, *ēþles ancȳðig.*"
But Trautmann also thinks that perhaps *anhydig* may be retained, and only
elnes changed to *ēþles.*   **829 XX**] To be resolved as *tweontigum, twentigum.*
Holthausen (2 and 3 ed.) reverses the order of the two half-lines, but Kock,
Anglia XLVII, 265, points out that other examples are found of similar
alliteration as in the text.   **833** reonian] Zupitza (3 and 4 ed.), Holthausen
change to *reongan*, Cook to *reonigan.*   **836** cynn] Supplied by Grein and
later edd., except Zupitza in his first edition.   **838** leahtra fruman] "the
devil," see Kock, Anglia XLVII, 265, Grein-Köhler, p. 229.   **851** hangen]
Cook alters to *ahangen.*   **859** gere] For *geare*, and so Grein, Holthausen
and Cook in their texts.   .   **861** hwylcne] So Grein and later edd.   **862** ær]
Zupitza suggests *ac* for *ær*, and Holthausen (1 and 2 ed.) and *Cook* place *ac*
in the text. But Holthausen (3 ed.) returns to the MS.   **876** sawlleasne]
Cook alters to *sawolleasne.*   **884** on anbide] Holthausen, Cook read
on bide, following Frucht, Metrisches und Sprachliches, p. 30.   **889** sawl]
Cook alters to *sawol.*   hafen] Trautmann, BEV., p. 105, would read
ahafen to gain a metrical syllable.   **895** ingemynde] Regarded by Grein
and most commentators as an adj. modifying *wundor*, subj. of *wæs.* But
Kock, Anglia XLIV, 105, takes the word as a noun, parallel to *ferhðsefan*,
citing Gen. 2340–2341 for a similar instance. Kock's interpretation seems
the more probable, but in that case, there is nothing to prevent separating
into *in gemynde*, which would be parallel in form as well as meaning to *on
ferhðsefan*, except that *in*, prep., would be an unusually light syllable to bear
a metrical stress.

901–1000

920 oft] Altered to *eft* by Grein, Zupitza, Wülker, and Holthausen.   **923**
geasne] Grimm, Kemble alter to *gæsen*, Holthausen to *gæsne.*   **924** findan
can] Grein, Germania X, 424, and later edd. omit *ne*, except Zupitza in his
first edition.   **925** siððan] The earlier edd. retain the MS. *wiððan*, but
Grein changes to *siððan*, and so Zupitza, Holthausen and Cook. Kemble,
Grein, Germania X, 424, read *wið ðan*, and Wülker retains *wiððan*, taking
wiðercyr in the sense "opposition, apostacy," instead of "return," the sense
of the word if one reads *siððan.* Wülker's interpretation would therefore be
"an opposition or apostacy thereagainst," an implied reference to Julian the
apostate—ingenious but remote. Brown, Eng. Stud. XL, 20, would read
wið ðe, as in l. 926. But the probability that *wiððan* is a mere scribal echo
after *wiðer-* is so great that other explanations are scarcely needed.   **937**
witgan] Grein alters to *witan*, see l. 544, but in Germania X, 424, to *witgan*,
and so later edd. except Zupitza, Wülker, who retain *wigan.*   **941** þæt þe]
Zupitza supplies *þe* to provide *bescufeð* with an object, and so Holthausen
(1 ed.). Cosijn, Aanteekeningen, p. 32, would replace *þæt* by *þec*, and so
Trautmann, BEV., p. 105, Holthausen (2 and 3 ed.), Cook.   **943** syn-
wyrcende] Trautmann, BEV., p. 105, would alter to *synwyrcende.*   **957**
oferswiðedne] So Zupitza and later edd.   **960** uncyðig] Grein retains

uncyðig in his text, and translates, "ignorus?", Spr. II, 617, "er der zuvor so unwissend war?" But in a note he suggests *oncyðig*, and so Holthausen, Trautmann, BEV., p. 105, and Cook. But Holthausen glosses the word as "erfahren," p. 93, and Cook as "ignorant." Grein-Köhler, p. 533, glosses as "bewusst." The meaning of *uncyðig* here is undoubtedly "wise," "how he in so short time ever became so full of faith and so wise, he filled with discretion." See Kock, Anglia XLVII, 266. Grein, Dicht., p. 130, translated, "wie er in so kurzer Frist so glaubensvoll und so einsichtsvoll und mutig irgend wurde durchgossen mit Klugheit." See l. 724. **971** boden] So Grimm, note, and later edd. fæðmeð] Grimm, note, suggests *fæðmiað*, and Zupitza, Holthausen, Cook read *fæðmað*. **972** gehwære] Zupitza (3 and 4 ed.), Holthausen, Cook alter to *gehwæm*, following Sievers, Beitr. X, 485. rod] Thorpe and later edd. supply *rod*. **978** þær] Grein, note, suggests *þæt*, and with this change would also supply *ne* before *meahton*. So also Zupitza (2 and later ed.). ten Brink, Anz.fdA. V, 60, accepts Grein's suggestion, and so also Trautmann, BEV., p. 105, but Cosijn, Aanteekeningen, p. 32, rejects it. Kemble had supplied *ne* before *meahton* previous to Grein's suggestion. Klaeber, Anglia XXIX, 271, discusses the construction with *þær*. **984** þæt] Sievers, Anglia I, 580, suggests *þæt* for the MS. *þe*, and so Holthausen, Cook. **992** geferede] Sievers, Anglia I, 580, suggests *geferedra*, and so Holthausen, Trautmann, BEV., p. 106, and Cook. Undoubtedly the word goes as an appositive with *fricgendra*, but it may stand as an uninflected appositive, see Kock, JJJ., p. 20, and l. 279, note. **996** swonrade] So Thorpe and later edd. **997** aseted] So Dietrich, Kynewulfi poetae aetas, p. 2, followed by Grein, Spr. I, 41, Germania X, 424, and later edd. **999** gearwian] ten Brink, Anz.fdA. V, 60, would read *gegearwian*.

1001–1100

1003 brim nesen] Thorpe, Grimm, Kemble, Grein combine as a noun compound, and so Wülker. Zupitza (1 ed.) reads *brim nesan*, and so Cook, taking *nesan* as infinitive, and in the same syntax as *settan*, l. 1004. This is gramatically possible, but as Sievers points out, Anglia I, 580, "sprachwidrig." In his later editions, Zupitza restores *nesen*, but indicates a corruption in the MS. It is better to take *nesen* as optative pret. pl., with Cosijn, Tijdschrift I, 146, Trautmann, BEV., p. 106, Holthausen (2 and 3 ed.), and Craigie. In his first edition, Holthausen had read *hæfden brim nesen*. **1004** gesundne] Trautmann, BEV., p. 106, suggests *gesunde*. **1025** besettan] So Grimm, Grein, Cook, the other edd. retaining *besetton* as infinitive. **1028** æðelum anbræce] The earlier edd. retain *æðelu* as an adj., taking the following word as a noun, and so Wülker. Zupitza (2 ed.) alters to *æðelum*, and so Holthausen, Cook. Kock, JJJ., p. 23, would change to *æðele, unbræce*, "noble and unbreakable," as asyndetic adjectives. Thorpe, Grimm, Kemble, Grein, Zupitza (1 ed.) read *anbroce*, "material, wood." Körner, Eng. Stud. II, 261, proposes *onbræce = unbræce*, and

Zupitza (2 and later ed.), Cook read *unbræce*. Holthausen reads *unbrẹce*, but glosses under *unbrǣce*, and so in Grein-Köhler, p. 874. The word is undoubtedly an adj., and the meaning is "imperishable," but it is unnecessary to normalize the scribal variations of *un-*, *on-*, *an-*, see ll. 724, 828, 960, and notes. **1041** rex] See l. 610, note. **1042** meotud milde, god] The word *god* may be taken as adj. *gōd* or as the noun *gŏd*. As the text stands it is best to take it as adj., with Kock, Anglia XLVII, 266, but it is possible that the text was disturbed here by the strange word *rex*, and *meotud* or *gŏd* may have crept in as a gloss on *rex*. **1043** leoht gearu] The imperfect syntax and alliteration indicate a loss here. Grein supplies *lange forhogode*. Holthausen reads *gearolice leahtre forhogode*. **1046** gescreaf] Grimm, Zupitza (1 and 2 ed.), Holthausen, Cook alter to *gescraf*. **1050** Eusebium] Eusebius, the pope, is confused with Eusebius, bishop of Nicomedia, who baptized Constantine, see Cook, p. 95. **1058** gecorene] For *gecorenne*, and so Grimm and later edd., except Kemble and Wülker, normalize the spelling. See l. 65, note. **1062** æ hælendes] Cook, p. 95, takes these words to be a translation or gloss on the name *Cyriacus*, Gr. Κυριακός, but if this is so, Ekwall, Anglia Beibl. XXXIII, 65, suggests that it would be better to enclose *Nama...forð* within parentheses. **1074** rode rodera cininges] Grein suggested *cininges* for the MS. *cining*, and so later edd. Sievers, Beitr. X, 518, would omit *rode*, and so Zupitza (3 and 4 ed.), Holthausen, Cook. Kock, JJJ., p. 23, would retain *rode*, citing ll. 624, 886, etc., reading *rode rodercininges*. Similar verbal echoes are found in ll. 294–295, 648, 953, and see Gen. 23, note. **1075** þa] Zupitza (3 and 4 ed.), Holthausen, Cook change to *þam*, following Kemble. This change was made necessary by their omission of *rode*, in order to make the word agree with *beam*. **1089** wyn] See l. 788, note.

1101–1200

1106 eðigean] Sievers, Anglia I, 578, would change to *sìðigean*, and so Holthausen. Cosijn, Tijdschrift I, 147, suggests *ēwigean*, as a form of *ȳwan*. But there is a figure here—the fire comes forth like an exhalation. **1113** goldgimmas] Zupitza, Holthausen (3 ed.), Cook alter to *goldgimmas*. Holthausen (1 and 2 ed.) had *gold ond gimmas*. Grein, Spr. I, 518, reading *godgimmas*, explains the first element as like *god-* in *godweb*. This might be possible, and one would hesitate to change, except that the Latin life reads, Holthausen (3 ed.), p. 41, *clarior solis lumine...tamquam aurum*. **1127** þam næglum] The MS. *þan næglan* represents the English of the time at which the MS. was copied, not the English of the poet. But such late forms are not characteristic of this text, and a stray instance like this should be corrected as a scribal inadvertence. Thorpe suggested *þam næglum*, and so later edd. except Kemble, Wülker. **1131 ff.**] Kock, Anglia XLIV, 106, translates:

> "the globe of weeping then,
> the head's hot stream,   was shed upon the cheek,

but not from grief— the tears did fall
upon the wire's joints— with praise was filled
the empress' mind."

Cosijn, Aanteekeningen, p. 32, also places only l. 1133*b* and l. 1134*a* within parentheses. Zupitza has a full stop after *gespon*, and for l. 1134*b* he reads *wuldre wæs gefylled*, and so also Holthausen (1 ed.). In his 2 and 3 ed. Holthausen reads *wuldre gefylled*, and so Cook. Cosijn, l.c., also prefers *wuldre*. Trautmann, BEV., p. 106, proposes *wyrd wæs gefylled*. It may be that *wuldres* is not the right word here, and perhaps the original word was *wifes*, parallel to *cwene*, l. 1135*a*, see ll. 1130*a*, 1131*a*. But *wuldres gefylled*, with *wæs* to be supplied as with *goten*, is also permissible, see An. 523.   **1136** Heo on cneow sette] Zupitza, Holthausen (1 ed.), and Cook supply *hie* after *Heo* as reflexive object of *sette*. Holthausen (2 and 3 ed.) removes *hie*, taking *Heo* as acc. sing. fem., "sie kniete nieder." Unless *hie* is supplied, *Heo* must be taken as object, with *leohte geleafan* as an instrumental phrase. But Trautmann, BEV., p. 106, would take *Heo* as subject and *leohte geleafan* as containing in an obscured form a noun object of *sette*, referring to the nails, she set them on her knee, "wol in einem kästchen," though just what the noun in *geleafan* should be, he is unable to discover. **1164**] See l. 531, note.   **1166** þriste] Supplied by Grein, Zupitza (2 ed.), and later edd. except Wülker.   **1169** seleste] So Sievers, Beitr. X, 518, and later edd. except Wülker.   **1180** ymb sige winnað] Lack of alliteration and logical continuity indicate a disturbance in the text here. Grein reads *ymbsacan willað*, (also *ymb sige (segen?) wigað(?)*, see Wülker, El. 1180, note). Zupitza (1 and 2 ed.) emends to *ymb sige winnað*. In his 3 and 4 ed. Zupitza reads *ymb sigor winnað*, and so Holthausen, Cook.   **1194** hwæteadig] Holthausen, Cook alter to *hreðeadig*, but as Kock, JJJ., p. 24, points out, *hwæteadig* is a legitimate compound.   **1195** wigge weorðod] Cosijn, Beitr. VIII, 571, alters to *wigge geweorðod*, and so Cook. Holthausen reads *wige geweorðod*.   byrð] Zupitza (3 and 4 ed.), Holthausen, Cook alter to *byreð*. Metrically the word is a dissyllable, but the spelling *byrð* does not prevent taking it so. The object of the verb is not expressed, "he whom that steed beareth."

1201–1321

1228 on Maias kalend] "In the month of May," see Grein, Germania X, 424. Imelmann, Anglia Beibl. XVII, 226, giving the same interpretation of *kalend*, suggests *maius* for the MS. *maias*.   **1236** fæcne] Cook alters to *fæge*, following Rieger, ZfdPh. I, 315.   **1237** wordcræftum] To gain a metrical syllable, Sievers, Beitr. X, 518, reads -*cræftum* for the MS. *cræft*, and so Zupitza (3 and 4 ed.), Holthausen. Trautmann, Kynewulf, p. 97, proposed *wordcræft gewæf*, but later, BEV., p. 140, returned to the MS. reading. Cook reads *wordcræfte*, and so Kock, Anglia XLIV, 106. Sedgefield, Verse Book, has *wordcræftig wæs*.   **1238** reodode] Grimm, notes, alters to *reordode*, "mentem cibo refeci, i.e. abunde cogitavi." Kemble also has *reordode,* "spoke out my thought." Leo reads *hreodode,* "der gedanke erzitterte." Cook also has *hreodode,* "sifted," following a suggestion of Grein, Spr. II, 374, although Grein reads *reodode* in his text and in the Sprachschatz. But see Grein-Köhler, p. 550, for Cook's reading. Holthausen, citing l. 1146, reads *freoðode,* "cherished," suggested also in Grein-Köhler, l.c. Holthausen, Eng. Stud. LI (1917), 183, thinks *reodode* may be the same verb as appears in the compound *aredian,* see Gen. 1498, note, but that the meaning here is doubtful, "ausführen" or "finden?" In Anglia Beibl. XXXII (1921), 136, Holthausen regards this explanation as "vollkommen genügend," and Kock previously, Anglia XLIV (1920), 106, had cited parallels from O.N. in support of *reodode,* translating, "my thought was wandering anxiously at night." But Kock, PPP. (1922), p. 18, later changes the MS. *ond geþanc,* with the usual abbreviation for *ond,* to *on geþanc,* in which case the subject of the verb would be *ic,* l. 1236. This is plausible, but in the uncertainty which attaches to the meaning of *reodode,* the change seems inadvisable. Translate, "I arranged or pursued my thought," and see *aredian,* Grein-Köhler, p. 548. Sedgefield, Verse Book, alters to *neodode.* **1239** nihtes nearwe] A noun, according to Grein, Spr. II, 287, "in the anxiety of the night," or both words may be adverbs, "anxiously by night," Trautmann, BEV., p. 140. See Ap. 104. **1240** be ðære rode riht] The MS. reads *be ðære riht ærme,* etc., with no indication of loss, and no metrical pointing at this place in the MS. Grimm reads *be þære riht earme,* but with insuperable difficulties of interpretation. Ettmüller, note, reads *be þære rihtæ areaht,* "per rectam fidem explanatam." Leo reads merely *be ðære riht,* taking *ðære* to refer to the art of song, l. 1237, and *riht* as obj. of *Nysse,* "ich wusste gar nicht in ihr das rechte," followed by *ær me* as two words. Grein supplies *rode* after *ðære,* with *ær me* as two words. So also Rieger, ZfdPh. I, 316, Zupitza, Holthausen, Cook, though Holthausen reads *reht* for the MS. *riht,* following Sievers, Beitr. IX, 236, note, and also *geþæht,* l. 1240*b,* following Sievers. Wülker, note, would read *be ðære rihtan æ, ær me,* etc., which is close to Ettmüller's reading. Wülker objects to Grein's *rode* that there is no reason why the cross should be mentioned just at this point. It is true that there is not necessity for mentioning the cross just here, but certainly if *rode* had stood in the MS., no one would have thought it strange. Kock, Anglia XLIV, 107, would read *be ðære rehtan ræhð,* taking *ræhð,* unrecorded in Anglo-Saxon, in the sense "exposition." Holthausen, Anglia Beibl. XXXII, 136, suggests *rune,* "Geheimnis," for Grein's *rode.* Sedgefield, Verse Book, reads *be ðære rihtan eaht,* with *eaht* as a noun, "deliberating." **1241** miht] Holthausen reads *mæht,* following Sievers, Beitr. IX, 236, note, and also *æht,* l. 1241*b.* Sedgefield, Verse Book, reads *meaht.* **1242** onwreah] Grimm altered to *onwrah,* and so Ettmüller, Leo, Zupitza, Holthausen, Cook and Sedgefield. **1244** bitrum] Sievers, Anglia I, 578, emended to *bitre,* and so Holthausen, Cook. Kock, Anglia XLIV, 108, takes *bitrum* as an adj. qualifying *sorgum.* Ekwall, Anglia Beibl. XXXIII, 65, would retain *bitrum* as a plural noun, implying a substantive *bitru.* **1246** unscynde] Ettmüller proposes *unseoce* for this word, and Holthausen places *unseoce* (2 and 3 ed., *unsēce*) in his text.   **1247** begeat] Holthausen, *begæt*, following Sievers, Beitr. IX, 236, note.   Trautmann, BEV., p. 140, would alter to *begæf* = *begeaf*.   **1250** leoðucræft] Holthausen (2 and 3 ed.) suggests *lēoðcræft*, and so Cook in his text.   But in his text Holthausen retains *leoðucræft*, "Gliederkraft." The context requires this meaning, and the first element of the word is therefore probably not the same as in *leoðorune*, l. 522.   **1251** willum] Rieger, ZfdPh. I, 317, would alter to *hwilum*.   **1256** sigebeacne] Ettmüller alters to *sigebeame*.   secg] Leo altered the MS. *sæcc* to *secg*, "the man, i.e. I," and so Zupitza and later edd., except Wülker, who retains *sæcc* as for *secg*.   Grein reads *sæc*, "conflict," and so Brown, Eng. Stud. XXXVIII, 203 ff.   **1257 ff. h etc.**] The runes in this passage are all perfectly clear in the MS., though there is considerable variation among scholars in the interpretation of them.   Each rune is preceded and followed by a dot in the MS., except the first, which has a dot following and a comma preceding.   The edd. for the most part reproduce the runes, but Ettmüller and Grein replace them by the ordinary Roman capitals for the name CYNEWULF.   Zupitza replaces the runes by what he takes to be their corresponding words, i.e. *cēn*, "kien," *ȳr*, "nach der gewöhnlichen erklärung 'bogen,' nach Rieger 'geld,' " *nyd*(*gefera*), "notgefahrte," *eh*, "pferd," *wēn*, "hoffnung," *ūr*, "auerochse," *lago*, "see, meer," *feoh*, "vieh, habe." Sedgefield also replaces the runes by words, as follows: *C*(*ēn*), translating *cen drusende*, notes, "(like) a drooping pine torch," *Y*(*r*), "may stand for yrming, 'poor wretch,' " or may be only a letter, *N*(*ȳd*)*gefera*, "companion in distress or distressed companion," *E*(*oh*), "horse," *W*(*yn*), "joy, delight," *Ū*(*r*), possibly inserted "merely to preserve the alliteration," *L*(*agu*), "sea, waters," *F*(*eoh*), "possessions, money." The passage is translated as follows by Gollancz, Cynewulf's Christ, p. 183:

> Till then was nought but discontent,—
>
> C.   a *bold* warrior, drooping with age, buffeted by waves of care,—
>   yea, though in the mead-hall he received precious gifts,
>
> Y. N. apple-shaped gold. *In his affliction, sorrow's* comrade
>   murmured;   grief, the narrowing rune,
>
> E.   constrained him, when he beheld *the horse*
>   measuring the mile-paths,   rushing proudly on,
>
> W.   decked with ornaments. *Joy* is now lessened,
>   and delight, after many a year;   youth is gone,
>
> U.   the pride of old. *Ours* was once
>   youth's glorious radiance;   now, at appointed time,
>   those days of yore have passed away,
>
> L.   life's joy hath departed, as *the waters* ebb,
>   the rushing floods.   Transitory 'neath heaven
>
> F.   is *the wealth* of every man.

Holt, The Elene of Cynewulf, pp. 40–41, translates the passage as follows: "Ever until that time was the man buffeted in the surge of sorrow, was he a weakly flaring torch (C), although he had received treasures and appled gold in the mead-hall; wroth in heart (Y), he mourned; a companion to need (N), he suffered crushing grief and anxious care, although before him his horse (E) measured the miles and proudly ran, decked with gold. Hope (W) is waned, and joy through the course of years; youth is fled, and the pride of old. Once (U) was the splendor of youth (?); now after that alloted time are the days departed, are the pleasures of life dwindled away, as water (L) glideth, or the rushing floods. Wealth (F) is but a loan to each beneath the heavens," etc. For other translations and interpretative comment, see Ap. 96 ff., notes, and the titles listed in the Bibliography. **1259** æplede] The phrase *æpplede gold* occurs in Phoenix 506, Jul. 688, "embossed" or "apple-shaped"? See Cook, pp. 99–100. Grimm, notes, suggested changing to *æflede*, from *æflian*, "comparare." ᛞ] Trautmann, BEV., p. 138, takes ᛞ as standing for *ȳfel*, "der üble, untaugliche," and ✝*gefera* as for *nēod-gefēra*, the first element meaning "desire," and he translates, "Der üble genosse der lust war traurig, litt bange sorge, beklemmendes geheimnis." gnornode] Ettmüller reads *geornode*, probably an oversight. **1261** fore] An adverb, "before," see Klaeber, JEGPh. VI, 197, "the horse which bears the rider (cf. El. 1195) may be considered as taking the lead and, in running *onward*, making the man, as it were, follow him." But it may mean simply "in the van." Trautmann, BEV., p. 139, takes the word as *fōre* = *fōr*, "wo ihm das ross die meilenpfade der fahrt mass." Or *fore* may be a preposition governing *him*, see Gollancz, Cynewulf's Christ, p. 180, "the poet, I take it, was filled with grief when he watched the hunt, but could not join in it." **1276** þream forþrycced] The edd. all take l. 1277 as the second half-line of l. 1276, except Holthausen, though Grein, Germania X, 425, regards such a line as dubious, and Sievers, Beitr. X, 518, says it is impossible. Holthausen, Anglia XIII, 358, proposed to remove *swa* and *world* in l. 1277, and to replace *þeos* by *þeod*, thus reading *þeod eall gewiteð*, as completing l. 1276. In his l ed. he reads *þream forþrycced* | [*in þeosterlocan.*] for l. 1276, and *Swa þeos wor[u]ld[gesceaft]* | *gewiteð eall* for l. 1277. In Anglia Beibl. XVIII, 205, he reads for l. 1277, *swa þeos* [*æðele*] *world* | *eall gewiteð*, and so in his 2 and 3 ed., retaining l. 1276 as in his 1 ed. For l. 1277b Von der Warth, p. 50, reads *swa* (*þeos*) *world eall* [*þonan*] *gewiteð* as a long line. It is quite probable that *þream forþrycced* should stand as an incompleted line. Note that the logical continuity of the narrative is interrupted here. In l. 1277 *world* may of course be metrically dissyllabic, and the addition of *a* after *Swa* regularizes the alliteration. **1294** ældes] Leo proposed changing *eðles* of the MS. to *æledes* or *eledes*, from *æled*, "fire," and Zupitza reads *eldes*, Holthausen, Cook, *ældes*. Wülker, note, approves *eldes leoma*, or with metathesis, *edles leoma*. The phrase *ældes leoma* occurs in Christ 1005, and it is possible that *eðost* in l. 1294b may have influenced the scribe in writing *eðles*. Retaining *eðles*, Grein, Dicht., p. 139, translates, "die Leuchtglut des Aufenthaltes," but such an interpretation seems remote. **1296** þread] From *þreagan*, *þrean*, and for the meaning, see An. 1687, where *þreade* is used parallel to *todraf*. Grimm, note, suggested changing *þread* to *dreogað*, and Trautmann,

BEV., p. 107, would read *þryd* or *þyd*, "gedrückt, gedrängt." This is undoubtedly the meaning, but there is no necessity for changing the word. **1297** in hatne wylm] "Into the hot flame." Parallel to, or rather in amplification of *in ðam midle*. Ettmüller proposed *in hatum wylme*, and so Cook. Holthausen (1 ed.) reads *in hatne wylm* and supposes the loss of a full line after l. 1297. In his 2 and 3 ed. Holthausen emends to *hate wylme*, parallel to *þrosme*, with no loss indicated. **1308** Hie] Cook alters to *þe*, thus making l. 1308*b* and the following a relative clause, in support of which he cites l. 1278*b*.